JULIANA HORATIA EWING

AND HER BOOKS.

Juliana Horatia Ewing

JULIANA HORATIA EWING

AND HER BOOKS.

BY

HORATIA K. F. EDEN

(*née* GATTY).

SOCIETY FOR PROMOTING CHRISTIAN KNOWLEDGE,

LONDON : NORTHUMBERLAND AVENUE, W.C.

43, QUEEN VICTORIA STREET, E.C.

BRIGHTON : 129, NORTH STREET.

NEW YORK : E. & J. B. YOUNG & CO.

REPUBLISHED BY GALE RESEARCH COMPANY, BOOK TOWER, DETROIT, 1969

[Published under the direction of the General Literature
Committee.]

Library of Congress Catalog Card Number 71-77001

PREFACE.

In making a Selection from Mrs. Ewing's Letters to accompany her Memoir, I have chosen such passages as touch most closely on her Life and Books. I found it was not possible in all cases to give references in foot-notes between the Memoir and Letters; but as both are arranged chronologically there will be no difficulty in turning from one to the other when desirable.

The first Letter, relating Julie's method of teaching a Liturgical Class, should be read with the remembrance that it was written thirty-two years ago, long before the development of our present Educational System; but it is valuable for the zeal and energy it records, combined with the common incident of the writer being too ill to appear at the critical moment of the Inspector's visit.

In a later letter, dated May 28, 1866, there are certain remarks about class singing in schools, which are also out of date; but this is retained as a proof of the keen sense of musical rhythm and accent which my sister had, and which gave her power to write words for music although she could play no instrument.

It is needless to add that none of the letters were intended for publication; they were written to near relatives and friends *currente calamo*, and are full of familiar expressions and allusions which may seem trivial and uninteresting to ordinary readers. Those, however, who care to study my sister's character I think cannot fail to trace in these records some of its strongest features; her keen enjoyment of the beauties of Nature,—her love for animals,—for her Home,—her *lares* and *penates*;—and her Friends. Above all that love of God which was the guiding influence of everything she wrote or did. So inseparable was it from her every-day life that readers must not be surprised if they find grave and gay sentences following each other in close succession.

Julie's sense of humour never forsook her, but she was never malicious, and could turn the laugh against herself as readily as against others. I have ventured to insert a specimen of her fun, which I hope will not be misunderstood. In a letter to C. T. G., dated March 13, 1874, she gave him a most graphic picture of the erratic condition of mind that had come over an old friend, the result of heavy responsibilities and the rush of London life. Julie had no idea when she wrote that these symptoms were in reality the subtle beginnings of a breakdown, which ended fatally, and no one lamented the issue more truly than she; but she could not resist catching folly as it flew, and many of the flighty axioms became proverbial amongst us.

The insertion of Bishop Medley's reply to my sister, April 8, 1880, needs no apology, it is so interesting in itself, and gives such a charming insight into the friendship between them.

The *List of Mrs. Ewing's Works* at the end of the Memoir was made before the publication of the present Complete Edition ; this, therefore, is only mentioned in cases where stories have not been published in any other book form. All Mrs. Ewing's Verses for Children, Hymns, and Songs for Music (including two left in MS.) are included in Volume IX.

Volume XVII., " Miscellanea," contains *The Mystery of a bloody hand* together with the Translated Stories, and other papers that had appeared previously in Magazines.

In Volume XII., " Brothers of Pity and other tales of men and beasts," will be found *Among the Merrows ; A Week spent in a Glass Pond; Tiny's Tricks and Toby's Tricks; The Owl in the Ivy Bush, and Owlhoots I. II.*, whilst *Sunflowers and a Rushlight* has been put amongst the Flower Stories in Vol. XVI., *Mary's Meadow*, etc.

The Letter with which this volume concludes was one

of the last that Julie wrote, and its allusion to Gordon's translation seemed to make it suitable for the End.

After her death the readers of *Aunt Judy's Magazine* subscribed enough to complete the endowment (£1000) of a Cot at the Convalescent Home of the Hospital for Sick Children, *Cromwell House, Highgate.* This had been begun to our Mother's memory, and was completed in the joint names of *Margaret Gatty* and *Juliana Horatia Ewing.* So liberal were the subscriptions that there was a surplus of more than £200, and with this we endowed two £5 annuities in the *Cambridge Fund for Old Soldiers* —as the " Jackanapes," and " Leonard " annuities.

Of other memorials there are the marble gravestone in Trull Churchyard, and Tablet in Ecclesfield Church, both carved by Harry Hems, of Exeter, and similarly decorated with the double lilac primrose,—St. Juliana's flower.

In Ecclesfield Church there is also a beautiful stained window, given by her friend, Bernard Wake. The glass was executed by W. F. Dixon, and the subject is Christ's Ascension. Julie died on the Eve of Ascension Day.

Lastly, there is a small window of jewelled glass, by C. E. Kempe, in St. George's Church, South Camp, Aldershot, representing St. Patrick trampling on a three-headed serpent, emblematical of the powers of evil, and holding the Trefoil in his hand—a symbol of the Blessed Trinity.

HORATIA K. F. EDEN.

Rugby, 1896.

The frontispiece portrait of Mrs. Ewing is a photogravure produced by the Swan Electric Engraving Company, from a photograph taken by Mr. Fergus of Largs.

All the other illustrations are from Mrs. Ewing's own drawings, except the tail-piece on p. 136. *This graceful ideal of Mrs. Ewing's grave was an offering sent by Mr. Caldecott shortly after her death, with his final illustrations to* " Lob Lie-by-the-Fire."

1 *

ALL hearts grew warmer in the presence
  Of one who, seeking not his own,
Gave freely for the love of giving,
  Nor reaped for self the harvest sown.

Thy greeting smile was pledge and prelude
  Of generous deeds and kindly words :
In thy large heart were fair guest-chambers,
  Open to sunrise and the birds !

The task was thine to mould and fashion
  Life's plastic newness into grace ;
To make the boyish heart heroic,
  And light with thought the maiden's face.

          *   *   *   *

O friend ! if thought and sense avail not
  To know thee henceforth as thou art,
That all is well with thee forever,
  I trust the instincts of my heart.

Thine be the quiet habitations,
  Thine the green pastures, blossom sown,
And smiles of saintly recognition,
  As sweet and tender as thy own.

Thou com'st not from the hush and shadow
  To meet us, but to thee we come ;
With thee we never can be strangers,
  And where thou art must still be home.

              " *A Memorial.*"—JOHN G. WHITTIER.

JULIANA HORATIA EWING

AND HER BOOKS.

———◇———

PART I.

I HAVE promised the children to write something for them about their favourite story-teller, Juliana Horatia Ewing, because I am sure they will like to read it.

I well remember how eagerly I devoured the Life of my favourite author, Hans Christian Andersen; how anxious I was to send a subscription to the memorial

statue of him, which was placed in the centre of the
public Garden at Copenhagen, where children yet play
at his feet ; and, still further, to send some flowers to
his newly-filled grave by the hand of one who, more
fortunate than myself, had the chance of visiting the
spot.

I think that the point which children will be most
anxious to know about Mrs. Ewing is how she wrote
her stories.   Did she evolve the plots and characters
entirely out of her own mind, or were they in any way
suggested by the occurrences and people around her ?

The best plan of answering such questions will be
for me to give a list of her stories in succession as they
were written, and to tell, as far as I can, what gave
rise to them in my sister's mind ; in doing this we shall
find that an outline biography of her will naturally
follow.   Nearly all her writings first appeared in the
pages of *Aunt Judy's Magazine*, and as we realize
this fact we shall see how close her connection with it
was, and cease to wonder that the Magazine should
end after her death.

Those who lived with my sister have no difficulty
in tracing likenesses between some of the characters in
her books, and many whom she met in real life ; but
let me say, once for all, that she never drew " portraits "
of people, and even if some of us now and then caught
glimpses of ourselves under the clothing she had robed

us in, we only felt ashamed to think how unlike we really were to the glorified beings whom she put before the public.

Still less did she ever do with her pen, what an artistic family of children used to threaten to do with their pencils when they were vexed with each other, namely, to " draw you ugly."

It was one of the strongest features in my sister's character that she "received but what she gave," and threw such a halo of sympathy and trust round all with whom she came in contact, that she seemed to see them " with larger other eyes than ours," and treated them accordingly.   On the whole, I am sure this was good in its results, though the pain occasionally of awakening to disappointment was acute ; but she generally contrived to cover up the wound with some new shoot of Hope.   On those in whom she trusted I think her faith acted favourably.   I recollect one friend whose conscience did not allow him to rest quite easy under the rosy light through which he felt he was viewed, saying to her : " It's the trust that such women as you repose in us men, which makes us desire to become more like what you believe us to be."

If her universal sympathy sometimes led her to what we might hastily consider "waste her time " on the petty interests and troubles of people who appeared to us unworthy, what were we that we should blame her? The value of each soul is equal in God's sight; and when the books are opened there may be more entries than we now can count of hearts comforted, self-respect restored, and souls raised by her help to fresh love and trust in God,—ay, even of old sins and deeds of shame turned into rungs on the ladder to heaven by feet that have learned to tread the evil beneath them. It was this well-spring of sympathy in her which made my sister rejoice as she did in the teaching of the now Chaplain-General, Dr. J. C. Edghill, when he was yet attached to the iron church in the South Camp, Aldershot. "He preaches the gospel of Hope," she said—hope that is in the latent power which lies hidden even in the worst of us, ready to take fire when touched by the Divine flame, and burn up its old evil into a light that will shine to God's glory before men. I still possess the epitome of one of these "hopeful" sermons, which she sent me in a letter after hearing the chaplain preach on the two texts : "What meanest thou, O sleeper? arise, call upon thy God"; "Awake, thou that sleepest, and arise from the dead, and Christ shall give thee light."

It has been said that, in his story of "The Old Bachelor's Nightcap," Hans Andersen recorded something of his own career. I know not if this be true, but certainly in her story of "Madam Liberality"*

* Reprinted in "A Great Emergency and other Tales."

Mrs. Ewing drew a picture of her own character that can never be surpassed. She did this quite unintentionally, I know, and believed that she was only giving her own experiences of suffering under quinsy, in combination with some record of the virtues of One whose powers of courage, uprightness, and generosity under ill-health she had always regarded with deep admiration. Possibly the virtues were hereditary,— certainly the original owner of them was a relation; but, however this may be, Madam Liberality bears a wonderfully strong likeness to my sister, and she used to be called by a great friend of ours the "little body with a mighty heart," from the quotation which appears at the head of the tale.

The same friend is now a bishop in another hemisphere from ours, but he will ever be reckoned a " great " friend. Our bonds of friendship were tied during hours of sorrow in the house of mourning, and such as these are not broken by after-divisions of space and time. Mrs. Ewing named him " Jachin," from one of the pillars of the Temple, on account of his being a pillar of strength at that time to us. Let me now quote the opening description of Madam Liberality from the story :—

It was not her real name ; it was given to her by her brothers and sisters. People with very marked qualities of character do sometimes get such distinctive titles to rectify the indefiniteness of those they inherit and those they receive in baptism. The ruling peculiarity of a character is apt to show itself early in life, and it showed itself in Madam Liberality when she was a little child.

Plum-cakes were not plentiful in her home when Madam Liberality was young, and, such as there were, were of the "wholesome" kind—plenty of breadstuff, and the currants and raisins at a respectful distance from each other. But, few as the plums were, she seldom ate them. She picked them out very carefully, and put them into a box, which was hidden under her pinafore.

When we grown-up people were children, and plum-cake and plum-pudding tasted very much nicer than they do now, we also picked out the plums. Some of us ate them at once, and had then to toil slowly through the cake or pudding, and some valiantly dispatched the plainer portion of the feast at the beginning, and kept the plums to sweeten the end. Sooner or later we ate them ourselves, but Madam Liberality kept her plums for other people.

When the vulgar meal was over—that commonplace refreshment ordained and superintended by the elders of the household—Madam Liberality would withdraw into a corner, from which she issued notes of invitation to all the dolls. They were "fancy written" on curl-papers, and folded into cocked hats.

Then began the real feast. The dolls came and the children with them. Madam Liberality had no toy tea-sets or dinner-sets, but there were acorn-cups filled to the brim, and the water tasted deliciously, though it came out of the ewer in the night-nursery, and had not even been filtered. And before every doll was a flat oyster-shell covered with a round oyster-shell, a complete set of complete pairs which had been collected by degrees, like old family plate. And, when the upper shell was raised, on every dish lay a plum. It was then that Madam Liberality got her sweetness out of the cake. She was in her glory at the head of the inverted tea-chest, and if the raisins would not go round the empty oyster-shell was hers, and nothing offended her more than to have this noticed. That was her spirit, then and always.

She could "do without" anything, if the wherewithal to be hospitable was left to her.

When one's brain is no stronger than mine is, one gets very much confused in disentangling motives and nice points of character. I have doubted whether Madam Liberality's besetting virtue were a virtue at all. Was it unselfishness or love of approbation, benevolence or fussiness, the gift of sympathy or the lust of power, or was it something else? She was a very sickly child, with much pain to bear, and many pleasures to forego. Was it, as the doctors say, "an effort of nature" to make her live outside herself, and be happy in the happiness of others?

All my earliest recollections of Julie (as I must call her) picture her as at once the projector and manager of all our nursery doings. Even if she tyrannized over us by always arranging things according to her own fancy, we did not rebel, we relied so habitually and entirely on her to originate every fresh plan and idea; and I am sure that in our turn we often tyrannized over her by reproaching her when any of what we called her "projukes" ended in "mulls," or when she paused for what seemed to us a longer five minutes than usual in the middle of some story she was telling, to think what the next incident should be!

It amazes me now to realize how unreasonable we were in our impatience, and how her powers of invention ever kept pace with our demands. These early stories were influenced to some extent by the books that she then liked best to read—Grimm, Andersen, and Bechstein's fairy tales; to the last writer I believe we owed her story about a Wizard, which was one of our chief favourites. Not that she copied Bechstein in any way, for we read his tales too, and would not have submitted to anything approaching a recapitulation ; but the character of the little Wizard was one which fascinated her, and even more so, perhaps, the quaint picture of him, which stood at the head of the tale ; and she wove round this skeleton idea a rambling romance from her own fertile imagination.

I have specially alluded to the picture, because my sister's artistic as well as literary powers were so strong that through all her life the two ever ran side by side, each aiding and developing the other, so that it is difficult to speak of them apart.*

Many of the stories she told us in childhood were inspired by some fine woodcuts in a German " A B C book," that we could none of us then read, and in later years some of her best efforts were suggested by illustrations, and written to fit them. I know, too, that in arranging the plots and wording of her stories she followed the rules that are pursued by artists in composing their pictures. She found great difficulty in preventing herself from " overcrowding her canvas " with minor characters, owing to her tendency to throw herself into complete sympathy with whatever creature she touched ; and, sometimes,—particularly in tales which came out as serials, when she wrote from month to

* Letter, May 14, 1876.

month, and had no opportunity of correcting the composition as a *whole*,—she was apt to give undue prominence to minor details, and throw her high lights on

POST MILL, DENNINGTON.

to obscure corners, instead of concentrating them on the central point. These artistic rules kept her humour and pathos,—like light and shade,—duly balanced,

XVIII. 2

and made the lights she "left out" some of the most
striking points of her work.

But to go back to the stories she told us as children.
Another of our favourite ones related to a Cavalier who
hid in an underground passage connected with a
deserted Windmill on a lonely moor.   It is needless to
say that, as we were brought up on Marryat's *Children
of the New Forest,* and possessed an aunt who always
went into mourning for King Charles on January 30,
our sympathies were entirely devoted to the Stuarts'
cause ; and this persecuted Cavalier, with his big hat
and boots, long hair and sorrows, was our best beloved
hero.   We would always let Julie tell us the " Windmill Story" over again, when her imagination was at
a loss for a new one.   Windmills, I suppose from their
picturesqueness, had a very strong attraction for her.
There were none near our Yorkshire home, so, perhaps,
their rarity added to their value in her eyes ;   certain
it is that she was never tired of sketching them, and
one of her latest note-books is full of the old mill at
Frimley, Hants, taken under various aspects of sunset
and storm.   Then Holland, with its low horizons and
rows of windmills, was the first foreign land she chose
to visit, and the "Dutch Story," one of her earliest
written efforts, remains an unfinished fragment ; whilst
"Jan of the Windmill" owes much of its existence to
her early love for these quaint structures.

It was not only in the matter of fairy tales that Julie reigned supreme in the nursery, she presided equally over our games and amusements. In matters such as garden-plots, when she and our eldest sister could each have one of the same size, they did so; but, when it came to there being *one* bower, devised under the bending branches of a lilac bush, then the laws of seniority were disregarded, and it was "Julie's Bower." Here, on benches made of narrow boards laid on inverted flower-pots, we sat and listened to her stories; here was kept the discarded dinner-bell, used at the funerals of our pet animals, and which she introduced into "The Burial of the Linnet." * Near the Bower we had a chapel, dedicated to St. Christopher, and a sketch of it is still extant, which was drawn by our eldest sister, who was the chief builder and caretaker of the shrine; hence started the funeral processions, both of our pets and of the stray birds and beasts we found unburied. In "Brothers of Pity" † Julie gave her hero the same predilection for burying that we had indulged in.

She invented names for the spots that we most frequented in our walks, such as "The Mermaid's Ford," and "St. Nicholas.". The latter covered a space including several fields and a clear stream, and over

* "Verses for Children, and Songs for Music."
† "Brothers of Pity, and other Tales of Beasts and Men."

this locality she certainly reigned supreme ; our gathering
of violets and cowslips, or of hips and haws for jam,
and our digging of earth-nuts were limited by her
orders.   I do not think she ever attempted to exercise
her prerogative over the stream ; I am sure that, whenever we caught sight of a dark tuft of slimy *Batracho-
spermum* in its clear depths, we plunged in to secure it
for Mother, whether Julie or any other Naiad liked it
or no !   But " the splendour in the grass and glory in
the flower" that we found in "St. Nicholas" was very
deep and real, thanks to all she wove around the spot
for us.   Even in childhood she must have felt, and
imparted to us, a great deal of what she put into the
hearts of the children in "Our Field." *   To me this
story is one of the most beautiful of her compositions,
and deeply characteristic of the strong power she
possessed of drawing happiness from little things, in
spite of the hindrances caused by weak health.   Her
fountain of hope and thankfulness never ran dry.

Madam Liberality was accustomed to disappointment.

From her earliest years it had been a family joke, that poor
Madam Liberality was always in ill-luck's way.

It is true that she was constantly planning ; and, if one builds
castles, one must expect a few loose stones about one's ears now
and then.   But, besides this, her little hopes were constantly
being frustrated by Fate.

If the pigs or the hens got into the garden, Madam Liberality's
bed was sure to be laid waste before any one came to the rescue.

---

* " A Great Emergency, and other Tales."

When a picnic or a tea-party was in store, if Madam Liberality
did not catch cold, so as to hinder her from going, she was pretty
sure to have a quinsy from fatigue or wet feet afterwards.   When
she had a treat, she paid for the pleasurable excitement by a
head-ache, just as when she ate sweet things they gave her toothache.

But, if her luck was less than other people's, her courage
and good spirits were more than common.   She could think
with pleasure about the treat when she had forgotten the headache.

One side of her face would look fairly cheerful when the
other was obliterated by a flannel bag of hot camomile flowers,
and the whole was redolent of every possible domestic remedy
for toothache, from oil of cloves and creosote to a baked onicn
in the ear.   No sufferings abated her energy for fresh exploits,
or quenched the hope that cold, and damp, and fatigue would
not hurt her "this time."

In the intervals of wringing out hot flannels for her quinsy
she would amuse herself by devising a desert island expedition,
on a larger and possibly a damper scale than hitherto, against
the time when she should be out again.

It is a very old simile, but Madam Liberality really was
like a cork rising on the top of the very wave of ill-luck that had
swallowed up her hopes.

Her little white face and undaunted spirit bobbed up after
each mischance or malady as ready and hopeful as ever.

Some of the indoor amusements over which Julie
exercised great influence were our theatricals.   Her
powers of imitation were strong ; indeed, my mother's
story of " Joachim the Mimic " was written, when
Julie was very young, rather to check this habit which
had early developed in her.   She always took what
may be called the " walking gentleman's " part in our

plays. Miss Corner's Series came first, and then Julie was usually a Prince; but after we advanced to farces, her most successful character was that of the commercial traveller, Charley Beeswing, in "Twenty Minutes with a Tiger." "Character" parts were what she liked best to take, and in later years, when aiding in private theatricals at Aldershot Camp, the piece she most enjoyed was "Helping Hands," in which she acted Tilda, with Captain F. G. Slade, R.A., as Shockey, and Major Ewing as the blind musician.

The last time she acted was at Shoeburyness, where she was the guest of her friends Colonel and Mrs. Strangways, and when Captain Goold-Adams and his wife also took part in the entertainment. The terrible news of Colonel Strangways' and Captain Goold-Adams' deaths from the explosion at Shoebury in February 1885, reached her whilst she was very ill, and shocked her greatly; though she often alluded to the help she got from thinking of Colonel Strangways' unselfishness, courage, and submission during his last hours, and trying to bear her own sufferings in the same spirit. She was so much pleased with the description given of his grave being lined with moss and lilac crocuses, that when her own had to be dug it was lined in a similar way.

But now let us go back to her in the Nursery, and recall how, in spite of very limited pocket-money, she was always the presiding Genius over birthday and Christmas-tree gifts; and the true 'St. Nicholas' who filled the stockings that the "little ones" tied, in happy confidence, to their bed-posts. Here the description must be quoted of Madam Liberality's struggles between generosity and conscientiousness:—

It may seem strange that Madam Liberality should ever have been accused of meanness, and yet her eldest brother did once shake his head at her and say, "You're the most meanest and the *generousest* person I ever knew!" And Madam Liberality wept over the accusation, although her brother was then too young to form either his words or his opinions correctly.

But it was the touch of truth in it which made Madam Liberality cry. To the end of their lives Tom and she were alike, and yet different in this matter. Madam Liberality saved, and pinched, and planned, and then gave away, and Tom gave away without the pinching and the saving. This sounds much handsomer, and it was poor Tom's misfortune that he always believed it to be so ; though he gave away what did not belong to him, and fell back for the supply of his own pretty numerous wants upon other people, not forgetting Madam Liberality. Painful experience convinced Madam Liberality in the end that his way was a wrong one, but she had her doubts many times in her life whether there were not something unhandsome in her own decided talent for economy. Not that economy was always pleasant to her. When people are very poor for their position in life, they can only keep out of debt by stinting on many occasions when stinting is very painful to a liberal spirit. And it requires a sterner virtue than good nature to hold fast the truth that it is nobler to be shabby and honest than to do things handsomely in debt.

But long before Tom had a bill even for bull's-eyes and Gibraltar rock, Madam Liberality was pinching and plotting, and saving bits of coloured paper and ends of ribbon, with a thriftiness which seemed to justify Tom's view of her character. The object of these savings was twofold,—birthday presents and Christmas-boxes. They were the chief cares and triumphs of Madam Liberality's childhood. It was with the next birthday or the approaching Christmas in view that she saved her pence instead of spending them, but she so seldom had any money that she chiefly relied on her own ingenuity. Year by year it became more difficult to make anything which would "do for a boy;" but it was easy to please Darling, and "Mother's" unabated appreciation of pin-cushions, and of needle-books made out of old cards, was most satisfactory.

Equally characteristic of Julie's moral courage and unselfishness is the incident of how Madam Liberality suffered the doctor's assistant to extract the tooth fang which had been accidentally left in her jaw, because her mother's "fixed scale of reward was sixpence for a tooth without fangs, and a shilling for one with them," and she wanted the larger sum to spend on Christmas-tree presents.

When the operation was over,

Madam Liberality staggered home, very giddy, but very happy. Moralists say a great deal about pain treading so closely on the heels of pleasure in this life, but they are not always wise or grateful enough to speak of the pleasure which springs out of pain. And yet there is a bliss which comes just when pain has ceased, whose rapture rivals even the high happiness of unbroken health ; and there is a keen pleasure about small pleasures hardly earned, in which the full measure of those who can afford anything they want is sometimes lacking. Relief is certainly one of the most delicious sensations which poor humanity can enjoy !

The details which can be traced in Julie's letters

after undergoing the removal of her tonsils read very much like extracts from Madam Liberality's biography. During my sister's last illness she spoke about this episode, and said she looked back with surprise at the courage she had exercised in going to London alone, and staying with friends for the operation. Happily, like Madam Liberality, she too earned a reward in the relief which she appreciated so keenly ; for, after this event, quinsies became things of the past to her, and she had them no more.

On April 14, 1863, she wrote—

"My Dearest Mother,—I could knock my head off when I think that *I* am to blame for not being able to send you word yesterday of the happy conclusion of this affair ! ! * * I cannot apologize enough, but assure you I punished myself by two days' suspense (a letter had been misdirected to the surgeon which delayed his visit). I did intend to have asked if I might have spent a trifle with the flower-man who comes to the door here, and bring home a little adornment to my flower-box as a sugar-plum after my operation * * now I feel I do not deserve it, but perhaps you will be merciful !

"It was a tiresome operation—so choking ! He (Mr. Smith, the surgeon) was about an hour at it. He was more kind and considerate than can be expressed ; when he went I said to him, 'I am very much obliged to you, first for telling me the truth, and secondly for waiting for me.' For when I got 'down in the mouth,' he waited, and chatted till I screwed up my courage again. He said, ' When people are reasonable it is barbarous to hurry them, and I said you were that when I first saw you.' "

April 16, 1863. "Thank you so much for letting me bring home a flower or two ! I do love them so much."

As Julie emerged from the nursery and began to take an interest in our village neighbours, her taste for "projects" was devoted to their interests. It was her energy that established a Village Library in 1859, which still remains a flourishing institution; but all her attempts were not crowned with equal success. She often recalled, with great amusement, how, the first day on which she distributed tracts as a District Visitor, an old lady of limited ideas and crabbed disposition called in the evening to restore the tract which had been lent to her, remarking that she had brought it back and required no more, as—"My 'usband does *not* attend the public-'ouse, and we've no unrewly children!"

My sister gave a series of Lessons * on the Liturgy in the day-school, and on Sunday held a Class for Young Women at the Vicarage, because she was so often prevented by attacks of quinsy from going out to school; indeed. at this time, as the mother of some of her ex-pupils only lately remarked, "Miss Julie were always cayling."

The first stories that she published belong to this so-to-speak "parochial" phase of her life, when her interests were chiefly divided between the nursery and the village. "A Bit of Green" came out in the *Monthly Packet* in July 1861; "The Blackbird's

* Letter, August 19, 1864.

SOUTH SCREEN, ECCLESFIELD CHURCH.

Nest" in August 1861; "Melchior's Dream" in
December 1861; and these three tales, with two
others, which had not been previously published
("Friedrich's Ballad" and "The Viscount's Friend "),
were issued in a volume called "Melchior's Dream
and other Tales," in 1862. The proceeds of the
first edition of this book gave "Madam Liberality"
the opportunity of indulging in her favourite virtue.
She and her eldest sister, who illustrated the stories,
first devoted the "tenths" of their respective earnings
for letterpress and pictures to buying some hangings
for the sacrarium of Ecclesfield Church, and then
Julie treated two of her sisters, who were out of health,
to Whitby for change of air.   Three years later, out of
some other literary earnings, she took her eldest brother
to Antwerp and Holland, to see the city of Rubens'
pictures, and the land of canals, windmills, and fine
sunsets.*   The expedition had to be conducted
on principles which savoured more of strict integrity
and economy than of comfort; for they went in a
small steamer from Hull to Antwerp, but Julie feasted
her eyes and brain on all the fresh sights and sounds
she encountered, and filled her sketch-book with
pictures.

"It was at Rotterdam," wrote her brother, "that I
left her with her camp-stool and water-colours for a

* Letters, September 1865.

moment in the street, to find her, on my return, with
a huge crowd round her, and before—a baker's man
holding back a blue veil that would blow before her
eyes—and she sketching down an avenue of spectators,
to whom she kept motioning with her brush to stand
aside. Perfectly unconscious she was of *how* she
looked, and I had great difficulty in getting her to pack
up and move on. Every quaint Dutch boat, every
queer street, every peasant in gold ornaments, was a
treasure to her note-book. We were very happy!"

I doubt, indeed, whether her companion has
experienced greater enjoyment during any of his later
and more luxurious visits to the same spots ; the
first sight of a foreign country must remain a unique
sensation.

It was not the intrinsic value of Julie's gifts to us
that made them so precious, but the wide-hearted
spirit which always prompted them. Out of a moderate income she could only afford to be generous from
her constant habit of thinking first for others, and
denying herself. It made little difference whether the
gift was elevenpence three-farthings' worth of modern
Japanese pottery, which she seized upon as just the
right shape and colour to fit some niche on one of
our shelves, or a copy of the *edition de luxe* of "Evan-
geline," with Frank Dicksee's magnificent illustrations,
which she ordered one day to be included in the

parcel of a sister, who had been judiciously laying out a small sum on the purchase of cheap editions of standard works, not daring to look into the tempting volume for fear of coveting it. When the carrier brought home the unexpectedly large parcel that night, it was difficult to say whether the receiver or the giver was the happier.

My turn came once to be taken by Julie to the sea for rest (June 1874), and then one of the chief enjoyments lay in the unwonted luxury of being allowed to choose my own route. Freedom of choice to a wearied mind is quite as refreshing as ozone to an exhausted body. Julie had none of the petty tyranny about her which often mars the generosity of otherwise liberal souls, who insist on giving what they wish rather than what the receiver wants.

I was told to take out Bradshaw's map, and go exactly where I desired, and, oh! how we pored over the various railway lines, but finally chose Dartmouth for a destination, as being old in itself, and new to us, and really a "long way off." We were neither of us disappointed; we lived on the quay, and watched the natives living in boats on the harbour, as is their wont; and we drove about the Devon lanes, all nodding with foxgloves, to see the churches with finely-carved screens that abound in the neighbourhood, our driver being a more than middle-aged woman,

with shoes down at heel, and a hat on her head. She
was always attended by a black retriever, whom she
called "Naro," and whom Julie sketched. I am
afraid, as years went on, I became unscrupulous about

"THE LADY WILL DRIVE!"

accepting her presents, on the score that she "liked"
to give them!—and I only tried to be, at any rate, a
gracious receiver.

There was one person, however, whom Julie found
less easy to deal with, and that was an Aunt, whose

liberality even exceeded her own. When Greek met Greek over Christmas presents, then came the tug of war indeed! The Aunt's ingenuity in contriving to give away whatever plums were given to her was quite amazing, and she generally managed to baffle the most careful restrictions which were laid upon her; but Julie conquered at last, by yielding—as often happens in this life!

"It's no use," Julie said to me, as she got out her bit of cardboard (not for a needle-book this time!) —"I must make her happy in her own way. She wants me to make her a sketch for somebody else, and I've promised to do it."

The sketch was made,—the last Julie ever drew, —but it remained amongst the receiver's own treasures. She was so much delighted with it, she could not make up her mind to give it away, and Julie laughed many times with pleasure as she reflected on the unexpected success that had crowned her final effort.

I spoke of "Melchior's Dream" and must revert to it again, for though it was written when my sister was only nineteen, I do not think she has surpassed it in any of her later *domestic* tales. Some of the writing in the introduction may be rougher and less finished than she was capable of in after-years, but the originality, power, and pathos of the Dream itself

are beyond doubt. In it, too, she showed the talent
which gives the highest value to all her work—that of
teaching deep religious lessons without disgusting her
readers by any approach to cant or goody-goodyism.

During the years 1862 to 1868, we kept up a MS.
magazine, and, of course, Julie was our principal con-
tributor. Many of her poems on local events were
genuinely witty, and her serial tales the backbone of
the periodical. The best of these was called "The
Two Abbots: a Tale of Second Sight," and in the
course of it she introduced a hymn, which was afterwards set to music by Major Ewing and published in
Boosey's Royal Edition of "Sacred Songs," under the
title "From Fleeting Pleasures."

The words of this hymn, and of two others which
she wrote for the use of our Sunday school children at
Whitsuntide in the respective years 1864 and 1866
have all been published in vol. ix. of the present
Edition of her works.

Some years after she married, my sister again tried
her hand at hymn-writing. On July 22, 1879, she
wrote to her husband:

"I think I will finish my hymn of 'Church of the
Quick and Dead,' and get thee to write a processional
tune. The metre is (last verse)—

'Church of the Quick and Dead,
    Lift up, lift up thy head,

> Behold the Judge is standing at the door !
> Bride of the Lamb, arise !
> From whose woe-wearied eyes
> My God shall wipe all tears for evermore.' "

My sister published very few of the things which she wrote to amuse us in our MS. "Gunpowder Plot Magazine," for they chiefly referred to local and family events; but "The Blue Bells on the Lea" was an exception. The scene of this is a hill-side near our old home, and Mr. André's fantastic and graceful illustrations to the verses when they came out as a book, gave her full satisfaction and delight.

In June 1865 she contributed a short parochial tale, "The Yew Lane Ghosts," to the *Monthly Packet*, and during the same year she gave a somewhat sensational story, called "The Mystery of the Bloody Hand," * to *London Society*. Julie found no real satisfaction in writing this kind of literature, and she soon discarded it; but her first attempt showed some promise of the prolific power of her imagination, for Mr. Shirley Brooks, who read the tale impartially, not knowing who had written it, wrote the following criticism : "If the author has leisure and inclination to make a picture instead of a sketch, the material, judiciously treated, would make a novel, and I especially see in the character and sufferings of the

* Vol. xvii. " Miscellanea."

Quaker, previous to his crime, matter for effective psychological treatment. The contrast between the semi-insane nature and that of the hypocrite might be powerfully worked up; but these are mere suggestions from an old craftsman, who never expects younger ones to see things as veterans do."

In May 1866 my Mother started *Aunt Judy's Magazine for Children,* and she called it by this title because "Aunt Judy" was the nickname we had given to Julie whilst she was yet our nursery story-teller, and it had been previously used in the titles of two of my Mother's most popular books, "Aunt Judy's Tales" and "Aunt Judy's Letters."

After my sister grew up, and began to publish stories of her own, many mistakes occurred as to the authorship of these books. It was supposed that the Tales and Letters were really written by Julie, and the introductory portions that strung them together by my Mother. This was a complete mistake; the only bits that Julie wrote in either of the books were three brief tales, in imitation of Andersen, called * "The Smut," "The Crick," and "The Brothers," which were included in "The Black Bag" in "Aunt Judy's Letters."

Julie's first contribution to *Aunt Judy's Magazine*

* These have now been reprinted in vol. xvii. "Miscellanea."

was " Mrs. Overtheway's Remembrances," and between May 1866 and May 1867 the three first
portions of " Ida," " Mrs. Moss," and " The Snoring
Ghosts," came out. In these stories I can trace many
of the influences which surrounded my sister whilst she
was still the "always cayling Miss Julie," suffering
from constant attacks of quinsy, and in the intervals,
reviving from them with the vivacity of Madam Liberality, and frequently going away to pay visits to her
friends for change of air.

We had one great friend to whom Julie often went,
as she lived within a mile of our home, but on a perfectly different soil to ours. Ecclesfield stands on
clay; but Grenoside, the village where our friend lived,
is on sand, and much higher in altitude. From it we
have often looked down at Ecclesfield lying in fog,
whilst at Grenoside the air was clear and the sun
shining. Here my sister loved to go, and from the
home where she was so welcome and tenderly cared
for, she drew (though no *facts*) yet much of the colouring which is seen in Mrs. Overtheway—a solitary life
lived in the fear of God ; enjoyment of the delights of
a garden ; with tender treasuring of dainty china and
household goods for the sake of those to whom such
relics had once belonged.

Years after our friend had followed her loved ones
to their better home, and had bequeathed her egg-shell
brocade to my sister, Julie had another resting-place in

Grenoside, to which she was as warmly welcomed as to the old one, during days of weakness and convalescence.   Here, in an atmosphere of cultivated tastes and loving appreciation, she spent many happy hours, sketching some of the villagers at their picturesque occupations of carpet-weaving and clog-making, or amusing herself in other ways.   * This home, too, was broken up by Death, but Mrs. Ewing looked back to it with great affection, and when, at the beginning of her last illness, whilst she still expected to recover, she was planning a visit to her Yorkshire home, she sighed to think that Grenoside was no longer open to her.

On June 1, 1867, my sister was married to Alexander Ewing, A.P.D., son of the late Alexander Ewing, M.D., of Aberdeen, and a week afterwards they sailed for Fredericton, New Brunswick, where he was to be stationed.

A gap now occurred in the continuation of "Mrs. Overtheway's Remembrances." The first contributions that Julie sent from her new home were, "An Idyl of the Wood," and "The Three Christmas Trees." † In these tales the experiences of her voyage and fresh surroundings became apparent; but in June 1868, "Mrs. Overtheway" was continued by the story of "Reka Dom."

* Letters, Advent Sunday, 1881, 25th November, 1881, January 18, 1884.

† Letter, 19th Sunday after Trinity, 1867.

In this Julie reverted to the scenery of another English home where she had spent a good deal of time during her girlhood. The winter of 1862-3 was passed by her at Clyst St. George, near Topsham, with the family of her kind friend, Rev. H. T. Ellacombe, and she evolved Mrs. Overtheway's " River House " * out of the romance roused by the sight of quaint old houses, with quainter gardens, and strange names that seemed to show traces of foreign residents in days gone by. " Reka Dom " was actually the name of a house in Topsham, where a Russian family had once lived. Speaking of this house, Major Ewing said:—On the evening of our arrival at Fredericton, New Brunswick, which stands on the river St. John, we strolled down, out of the principal street, and wandered on the river shore. We stopped to rest opposite to a large old house, then in the hands of workmen. There was only the road between this house and the river, and, on the banks, one or two old willows. We said we should like to make our first home in some such spot. Ere many weeks were over, we were established in that very house, where we spent the first year, or more, of our time in Fredericton. We *called* it " Reka Dom," the River House.

For the descriptions of Father and Mother Albatross and their island home, in the last and most beautiful

* Letter, February 3, 1868.

VIEW FROM THE WINDOW OF REKA DOM.

tale of " Kerguelen's Land," she was indebted to her husband, a wide traveller and very accurate observer of nature.

To the volume of *Aunt Judy's Magazine* for 1869 she only sent " The Land of Lost Toys," * a short but very brilliant domestic story, the wood described in it being the " Upper Shroggs," near Ecclesfield, which had been a very favourite haunt in her childhood. In October 1869, she and Major Ewing returned to England, and from this time until May 1877, he was stationed at Aldershot.

Whilst living in Fredericton my sister formed many close friendships. It was here she first met Colonel and Mrs. Fox Strangways. In the society of Bishop Medley and his wife she had also great happiness, and with the former she and Major Ewing used to study Hebrew. The cathedral services were a never-failing source of comfort, and at these her husband frequently played the organ, especially on occasions when anthems, which he had written at the bishop's request, were sung.

To the volume of *Aunt Judy's Magazine* for 1870 she gave " Amelia and the Dwarfs," and " Christmas Crackers," " Benjy in Beastland," and eight † " Old-fashioned Fairy Tales." " Amelia " is one of her

* Letter, December 8, 1868.
† Letter, Sexagesima, 1869.

NO. I HUT, X LINES, SOUTH CAMP.

happiest combinations of real child life and genuine
fairy lore.   The dwarfs inspired Mr. Cruikshank* to
one of his best water-colour sketches : who is the happy
possessor thereof I do not know, but the woodcut
illustration very inadequately represents the beauty and
delicacy of the picture.

Whilst speaking of the stories in this volume of
Aunt Judy's Magazine, I must stop to allude to one of
the strongest features in Julie's character, namely, her
love for animals.   She threw over them, as over everything she touched, all the warm sympathy of her loving
heart, and it always seemed to me as if this enabled
her almost to get inside the minds of her pets, and know
how to describe their feelings.†

Another Beast Friend whom Julie had in New
Brunswick was the Bear of the 22nd Regiment, and
she drew a sketch of him "with one of his pet black
dogs, as I saw them, 18th September, 1868, near the
Officers' Quarters, Fredericton, N.B.   The Bear is at
breakfast, and the dog occasionally licks his nose when
it comes up out of the bucket."

The pink-nosed bull-dog in "Amelia" bears a
strong likeness to a well-beloved "Hector," whom she
took charge of in Fredericton whilst his master had
gone on leave to be married in England.   Hector,
too, was "a snow-white bull-dog (who was certainly

* Letters, August 3, 1880.   † October 20, 1868.

as well bred and as amiable as any living creature
in the kingdom)," with a pink nose that "became
crimson with increased agitation." He was absolutely
gentle with human beings, but a hopeless adept at
fighting with his own kind, and many of my sister's
letters and note-books were adorned with sketches of
Hector as he appeared swollen about the head, and
subdued in spirits, after some desperate encounter ;

THE BULLDOGUE's FORTUNE

or, with cards spread out in front of him, playing, as
she delighted to make him do, at " having his fortune
told." *   But, instead of the four Queens standing for
four ladies of different degrees of complexion, they
represented his four favourite dishes of—1. Welsh
rabbit.   2. Blueberry pudding.   3. Pork sausages.
4. Buckwheat pancakes and molasses ; and " the

* Letter, November 3, 1868.

Fortune " decided which of these dainties he was to have for supper.

Shortly before the Ewings started from Fredericton they went into the barracks, whence a battalion of some regiment had departed two days before, and there discovered a large black retriever who had been left behind. It is needless to say that this deserted gentleman entirely overcame their feelings ; he was at once adopted, named " Trouvé," and brought home to England, where he spent a very happy life, chiefly in the South Camp, Aldershot, his one danger there being that he was such a favourite with the soldiers, they over-fed him terribly. Never did a more benevolent disposition exist, his broad forehead and kind eyes, set widely apart, did not belie him ; there was a strong strain of Newfoundland in his breed, and a strong likeness to a bear in the way his feathered paws half crossed over each other in walking. Trouvé appears as " Nox " in " Benjy," and there is a glimpse of him in " The Sweep," who ended his days as a "soldier's dog " in " The Story of a Short Life." Trouvé did, in reality, end his days at Ecclesfield, where he is buried near " Rough," the broken-haired bull-terrier, who is the real hero in " Benjy." Amongst the various animal friends whom Julie had either of her own, or belonging to others, none was lovelier than the golden-haired collie " Rufus," who was at once the

delight and distraction of the last year of her life at
Taunton, by the tricks he taught himself of very
gently extracting the pins from her hair, and letting it
down at inconvenient moments; and of extracting,
with equal gentleness from the earth, the labels that
she had put to the various treasured flowers in her
" Little Garden," and then tossing them in mid-air on
the grass-plot.

A very amusing domestic story, called " The Snap
Dragons," came out in the Christmas number of the
Monthly Packet for 1870.

"Timothy's Shoes" appeared in AUNT JUDY's
volume for 1871. This was another story of the same
type as "Amelia," and it was also illustrated by Mr.
Cruikshank. I think the Marsh Julie had in her
mind's eye, with a "long and steep bank," is one near
the canal at Aldershot, where she herself used to enjoy
hunting for kingcups, bog-asphodel, sundew, and the
like. The tale is a charming combination of humour
and pathos, and the last clause, where "the shoes go
home," is enough to bring tears to the eyes of every
one who loves the patter of childish feet.

The most important work that she did this year
(1871) was " A Flat-Iron for a Farthing," which ran as
a serial through the volume of *Aunt Judy's Magazine*.
It was very beautifully illustrated by Helen Paterson
(now Mrs. Allingham), and the design where the

"little ladies," in big beaver bonnets, are seated at a
shop-counter buying flat-irons, was afterwards reproduced in water-colours by Mrs. Allingham, and
exhibited at the Royal Society of Painters in Water-
Colours (1875), where it attracted Mr. Ruskin's
attention.* Eventually, a fine steel engraving was
done from it by Mr. Stodart.† It is interesting to
know that the girl friend who sat as a model for
"Polly" to Mrs. Allingham is now herself a well-
known artist, whose pictures are hung in the Royal
Academy.

The scene of the little girls in beaver bonnets was
really taken from an incident of Julie's childhood,
when she and her "duplicate" (my eldest sister) being
the nearest in age, size, and appearance of any of the
family, used to be dressed exactly alike, and were
inseparable companions : *their* flat-irons, I think, were
bought in Matlock. Shadowy glimpses of this same
"duplicate" are also to be caught in Mrs. Overtheway's "Fatima," and Madam Liberality's "Darling."
When "A Flat-Iron" came out in its book form it
was dedicated "To my dear Father, and to his sister,

* The drawing, with whatever temporary purpose executed, is
for ever lovely ; a thing which I believe Gainsborough would
have given one of his own pictures for—old-fashioned as red-
tipped daisies are, and more precious than rubies.—Ruskin,
"Notes on some of the Pictures at the Royal Academy." 1875.

† Published by the Fine Art Society, Bond-street.

my dear Aunt Mary, in memory of their good friend
and nurse, E. B., obiit 3 March, 1872, æt. 83 ; " the
loyal devotion and high integrity of Nurse Bundle
having been somewhat drawn from the " E. B."
alluded to. Such characters are not common, and
they grow rarer year by year. We do well to hold
them in everlasting remembrance.

PART II.

The meadows gleam with hoar-frost white,
  The day breaks on the hill,
The widgeon takes its early flight
  Beside the frozen rill.
From village steeples far away
  The sound of bells is borne,
As one by one each crimson ray
  Brings in the Christmas morn.
Peace to all ! the church bells say,
  For Christ was born on Christmas day.
    Peace to all.

Here, some will those again embrace
  They hold on earth most dear,
There, some will mourn an absent face
  They lost within the year.
Yet peace to all who smile or weep
  Is rung from earth to sky ;
But most to those to-day who keep
  The feast with Christ on high.
Peace to all ! the church bells say,
  For Christ was born on Christmas day.
    Peace to all.
              R. A. GATTY, 1873.

DURING 1871 my sister published the first of her
Verses for Children, "The Little Master to his Big

Dog"; she did not put her name to it in *Aunt Judy's Magazine*, but afterwards included it in one of her Verse Books. Two Series of these books were published during her life, and a third Series was in the press when she died, called "Poems of Child Life and Country Life"; though Julie had some difficulty in making up her mind to use the term "poem," because she did not think her irregular verses were worthy to bear the title.

She saw Mr. André's original sketches for five of the last six volumes, and liked the illustrations to "The Poet and the Brook," "Convalescence," and "The Mill Stream" best.

To the volume of *Aunt Judy's Magazine* for 1872 she gave her first "soldier" story, "The Peace Egg," and in this she began to sing those praises of military life and courtesies which she afterwards more fully showed forth in "Jackanapes," "The Story of a Short Life," and the opening chapters of "Six to Sixteen." The chief incident of the story, however, consisted in the Captain's children unconsciously bringing peace and goodwill into the family by performing the old Christmas play or Mystery of "The Peace Egg." This play we had been accustomed to see acted in Yorkshire, and to act ourselves when we were young. I recollect how proud we were on one

occasion, when our disguises were so complete, that
a neighbouring farmer's wife, at whose door we went to
act, drove us as ignominiously away, as the House-
keeper did the children in the story. " Darkie," who
"slipped in last like a black shadow," and " Pax," who
jumped on to Mamma's lap, " where, sitting facing the
company, he opened his black mouth and yawned,
with ludicrous inappropriateness," are life-like portraits
of two favourite dogs.

The tale was a very popular one, and many children wrote to ask where they could buy copies of the
Play in order to act it themselves. These inquiries
led Julie to compile a fresh arrangement of it, for she
knew that in its original form it was rather too roughly
worded to be fit for nursery use ; so in *Aunt Judy's
Magazine* (January 1884) she published an adaptation of "The Peace Egg, a Christmas Mumming
Play," together with some interesting information
about the various versions of it which exist in different
parts of England.

She contributed "Six to Sixteen" as a serial to the
Magazine in 1872, and it was illustrated by Mrs.
Allingham. When it was published as a book, the
dedication to Miss Eleanor Lloyd told that many of
the theories on the up-bringing of girls, which the
story contained, were the result of the somewhat

desultory, if intellectual, home education which we had received from our Mother. This education Miss Lloyd had, to a great extent, shared during the happy visits she paid us; when she entered into our interests with the zest of a sister, and in more than one point outstripped us in following the pursuits for which Mother gave us a taste. Julie never really either went to school or had a governess, though for a brief period she was under the kind care of some ladies at Brighton, but they were relations, and she went to them more for the benefit of sea breezes than lessons. She certainly chiefly educated herself by the "thorough" way in which she pursued the various tastes she had inherited, and into which she was guided by our Mother. Then she never thought she had learned *enough*, but throughout her whole life was constantly improving and adding to her knowledge. She owed to Mother's teaching the first principles of drawing, and I have often seen her refer for rules on perspective to "My Childhood in Art," * a story in which these rules were fully laid down; but Mother had no eye for colour, and not much for figure drawing. Her own best works were etchings on copper of trees and landscapes, whereas Julie's artistic talent lay more in

* Included in "The Human Face Divine, and other Tales." By Margaret Gatty. Bell and Sons.

colours and human forms.   The only real lessons in
sketching she ever had were a few from Mr. Paul
Naftel, years after she was married.

One of her favourite methods for practising drawing was to devote herself to thoroughly studying the
sketches of some one master, in order to try and
unravel the special principles on which he had worked,
and then to copy his drawings.   She pursued this
plan with some of Chinnery's curious and effective
water-colour sketches, which were lent to her by
friends, and she found it a very useful one.   She
made copies from De Wint, Turner, and others, in
the same way, and certainly the labour she threw into
her work enabled her to produce almost facsimiles of
the originals.   She was greatly interested one day by
hearing a lady, who ranks as one of the best living
English writers of her sex, say that when she was
young she had practised the art of writing in just the
same way that Julie pursued that of drawing, namely,
by devoting herself to reading the works of one writer
at a time, until her brain was so saturated with his
style that she could write exactly like him, and then
passing on to an equally careful study of some other
author.

The life-like details of the " cholera season," in
the second chapter of " Six to Sixteen," were drawn

from facts that Major Ewing told his wife of a similar season which he had passed through in China, and during which he had lost several friends ; but the touching episode of Margery's birthday present, and Mr. Abercrombie's efforts to console her, were purely imaginary.

Several of the "Old-fashioned Fairy Tales" which Julie wrote during this (1872) and previous years in *Aunt Judy's Magazine*, were on Scotch topics, and she owed the striking accuracy of her local colouring and dialect, as well as her keen intuition of Scotch character, to visits that she paid to Major Ewing's relatives in the North, and also to reading such typical books as *Mansie Wauch, the Tailor of Dalkeith*, a story which she greatly admired. She liked to study national types of character, and when she wrote "We and the World," one of its chief features was meant to be the contrast drawn between the English, Scotch, and Irish heroes; thanks to her wide sympathy she was as keenly able to appreciate the rugged virtues of the dour Scotch race, as the more quick and graceful beauties of the Irish mind.

The Autumn Military Manœuvres in 1872 were held near Salisbury Plain, and Major Ewing was so much fascinated by the quaint old town of Amesbury, where he was quartered, that he took my sister afterwards to visit the place. The result of this was that her "Miller's Thumb"* came out as a serial in *Aunt Judy's Magazine* during 1873. All the scenery is

AMESBURY.

drawn from the neighbourhood of Amesbury, and the Wiltshire dialect she acquired by the aid of a friend,

* Letter, August 25, 1872.

who procured copies for her of *Wiltshire Tales* and *A Glossary of Wiltshire Words and Phrases*, both by J. Y. Akerman, F.S.A. She gleaned her practical knowledge of life in a windmill, and a "Miller's Thumb," from an old man who used to visit her hut in the South Camp, Aldershot, having fallen from being a Miller with a genuine Thumb, to the less exalted position of hawking muffins in winter and "Sally Lunns" in summer! Mrs. Allingham illustrated the story; two of her best designs were Jan and his Nurse Boy sitting on the plain watching the crows fly, and Jan's first effort at drawing on his slate. It was published as a book in 1876, and dedicated to our eldest sister, and the title was then altered to "Jan of the Windmill, a Story of the Plains."

Three poems of Julie's came out in the volume of *Aunt Judy's Magazine* for 1873, "The Willow Man," "Ran away to Sea," and "A Friend in the Garden"; her name was not given to the last, but it is a pleasant little rhyme about a toad. She also wrote during this year "Among the Merrows," a fantastic account of a visit she paid to the Aquarium at the Crystal Palace.

In October 1873, our Mother died, and my sister contributed a short memoir of her * to the November

* Included in "Parables from Nature." By Mrs. Alfred Gatty. Complete edition. Bell and Sons.

number of *Aunt Judy's Magazine.* To the December number she gave "Madam Liberality."

For two years after Mother's death, Julie shared the work of editing the Magazine with me, and then she gave it up, as we were not living together, and so found the plan rather inconvenient; also the task of reading MSS. and writing business letters wasted time which she could spend better on her own stories.

At the end of the year 1873 she brought out a book, "Lob Lie-by-the-Fire, and other Tales," consisting of five stories, three of which—"Timothy's Shoes," "Benjy in Beastland," and "The Peace Egg,"—had already been published in *Aunt Judy's Magazine*, whilst "Old Father Christmas" had appeared in *Little Folks;* but the first tale of "Lob" was specially written for the volume.*

The character of McAlister in this story is a Scotchman of the Scotch, and, chiefly in consequence of this fact, the book was dedicated to James Boyn McCombie, an uncle of Major Ewing, who always showed a most kind and helpful interest in my sister's literary work.

He died a few weeks before she did, much to her sorrow, but the Dedication remained when the story came out in a separate form, illustrated by Mr. Caldecott. The incident which makes the tale

* Letter, August 10, 1873.

specially appropriate to be dedicated to so true and
unobtrusive a philanthropist as Mr. McCombie was
known to be, is the Highlander's burning anxiety to
rescue John Broom from his vagrant career.

"Lob" contains some of Julie's brightest flashes
of humour, and ends happily, but in it, as in many
of her tales, "the dusky strand of death" appears,
inwoven with, and thereby heightening, the joys of
love and life. It is a curious fact that, though her
power of describing death-bed scenes was so vivid,
I believe she never saw any one die; and I will
venture to say that her description of McAlister's last
hours surpasses in truth and power the end of
Leonard's "Short Life"; the extinction of the line
of "Old Standards" in Daddy Darwin; the unseen
call that led Jan's Schoolmaster away; and will even
bear comparison with Jackanapes' departure through
the Grave to that "other side" where "the Trumpets
sounded for him."

In order to appreciate the end, it is almost
necessary, perhaps, to have followed John Broom,
the ne'er-do-weel lad, and McAlister, the finest man
in his regiment, through the scenes which drew them
together, and to read how the soldier, who might
and ought to have been a "sairgent," tried to turn
the boy back from pursuing the downward path along
which he himself had taken too many steps; and

then learn how the vagrant's grateful love and agility enabled him to awaken the sleeping sentinel at his post, and save "the old soldier's honour."

John Broom remained by his friend, whose painful fits of coughing, and of gasping for breath, were varied by intervals of seeming stupor. When a candle had been brought in and placed near the bed, the Highlander roused himself and asked:

"Is there a Bible on yon table? Could ye read a bit to me, laddie?"

There is little need to dwell on the bitterness of heart with which John Broom confessed:

"I can't read big words, McAlister!"

"Did ye never go to school?" said the Scotchman.

"I didn't learn," said the poor boy; "I played."

"Aye, aye. Weel ye'll learn when ye gang hame," said the Highlander, in gentle tones.

"I'll never get home," said John Broom, passionately. "I'll never forgive myself. I'll never get over it, that I couldn't read to ye when ye wanted me, McAlister."

"Gently, gently," said the Scotchman. "Dinna daunt yoursel' ower much wi' the past, laddie. And for me—I'm not that presoomtious to think I can square up a misspent life as a man might compound wi's creditors. 'Gin He forgi'es me, He'll forgi'e; but it's not a prayer up or a chapter down that'll stan' between me and the Almighty. So dinna fret yoursel', but let me think while I may."

And so, far into the night, the Highlander lay silent, and John Broom watched by him.

It was just midnight when he partly raised himself, and cried:

"Whist, laddie! do ye hear the pipes?"

The dying ears must have been quick, for John Broom heard nothing; but in a few minutes he heard the bagpipes from the officers' mess, where they were keeping Hogmenay. They were playing the old year out with "Auld Lang Syne," and the Highlander beat the time out with his hand, and his eyes gleamed out of his rugged face in the dim light, as cairngorms glitter in dark tartan.

There was a pause after the first verse, and he grew restless, and turning doubtfully to where John Broom sat, as if his sight were failing, he said : " Ye'll mind your promise, ye'll gang hame ? " And after a while he repeated the last word " Hame ! "

But as he spoke there spread over his face a smile so tender and so full of happiness, that John Broom held his breath as he watched him.

As the light of sunrise creeps over the face of some rugged rock, it crept from chin to brow, and the pale blue eyes shone tranquil, like water that reflects heaven.

And when it had passed it left them still open, but gems that had lost their ray.

Death-beds are not the only things which Julie had the power of picturing out of her inner consciousness apart from actual experience. She was much amused by the pertinacity with which unknown correspondents occasionally inquired after her " little ones," unable to give her the credit of describing and understanding children unless she possessed some of her own. There is a graceful touch at the end of " Lob," which seems to me one of the most delicate evidences of her universal sympathy with all sorts and conditions of men,—and women ! It is similar in character to the passage I alluded to in " Timothy's Shoes," where they clatter away for the last time, into silence.

Even after the sobering influences of middle age had touched him, and a wife and children bound him with the quiet ties of home, he had (at long intervals) his "restless times," when his good "missis" would bring out a little store laid by in one of the children's socks, and would bid him "Be off, and get a breath of the sea air," but on condition that the sock went with him as his purse. John Broom always looked ashamed to go, but he came back the better, and his wife was quite easy in his absence with that confidence in her knowledge of "the master," which is so mysterious to the unmarried.

*   *   *   *   *   *

"The sock 'll bring him home," said Mrs. Broom, and home he came, and never could say what he had been doing.

In 1874 Julie wrote "A Great Emergency" as a serial for the Magazine, and took great pains to corroborate the accuracy of her descriptions of barge life for it.* I remember our inspecting a barge on the canal at Aldershot, with a friend who understood all its details, and we arranged to go on an expedition in it to gain further experience, but were somehow prevented. The allusions to Dartmouth arose from our visit there, of which I have already spoken, and which took place whilst she was writing the tale ; and her knowledge of the intricacies of the Great Eastern Railway between Fenchurch Street Station and North Woolwich came from the experience she gained when we went on expeditions to Victoria Docks, where one of our brothers was doing parochial work under Canon Boyd.

* Letter, July 22, 1874.

During 1874 five of her "Verses for Children" came out in the Magazine, two of which, "Our Garden," and "Three Little Nest-Birds," were written to fit old German woodcuts. The others were "The Dolls' Wash," "The Blue Bells on the Lea," and "The Doll's Lullaby." She wrote an article on "May-Day, Old Style and New Style," in 1874, and also contributed fifty-two brief "Tales of the Khoja," * which she adapted from the Turkish by the aid of a literal translation of them given in Barker's *Reading-Book of the Turkish Language*, and by the help of Major Ewing, who possessed some knowledge of the Turkish language and customs, and assisted her in polishing the stories. They are thoroughly Eastern in character, and full of dry wit.

I must here digress to speak of some other work that my sister did during the time she lived in Aldershot. Both she and Major Ewing took great interest in the amateur concerts and private musical performances that took place in the camp, and the V.C. in "The Story of a Short Life," with a fine tenor voice, and a "fastidious choice in the words of the songs he sang," is a shadow of these past days. The want that many composers felt of good words for setting to music, led Julie to try to write some, and eventually, in 1874, a book of "Songs for Music, by

* "Miscellanea," vol. xvii.

Four Friends," * was published; the contents were
written by my sister and two of her brothers, and the
Rev. G. J. Chester. This book became a standing
joke amongst them, because one of the reviewers said
it contained "songs by four writers, *one* of whom was
a poet," and he did not specify the one by name.

During 1875 Julie was again aided by her husband
in the work that she did for *Aunt Judy's Magazine.*
"Cousin Peregrine's three Wonder Stories"—1. "The
Chinese Jugglers and the Englishman's Hand"; 2.
"The Waves of the Great South Sea"; and 3. "Jack
of Pera"†—were a combination of his facts and her
wording. She added only one more to her Old-
fashioned Fairy Tales, "Good Luck is Better than
Gold," but it is one of her most finished bits of art, and
she placed it first, when the tales came out in a volume.

The Preface to this book is well worth the study of
those who are interested in the composition of Fairy
literature; and the theories on which Julie wrote her
own tales.‡

She also wrote (in 1875) an article on "Little
Woods," and a domestic story called "A very Ill-
tempered Family."

The incident of Isobel's reciting the *Te Deum* is a

* H. King and Co.
† "Miscellanea," vol. xvii.
‡ Letter. Septuagesima, 1869.

touching one, because the habit of repeating it by heart, especially in bed at night, was one which Julie herself had practised from the days of childhood, when, I believe, it was used to drive away the terrors of darkness. The last day on which she expressed any expectation of recovering from her final illness was one on which she said, " I think I must be getting better, for I've repeated the *Te Deum* all through, and since I've been ill I've only been able to say a few sentences at once." This was certainly the last time that she recited the great Hymn of Praise before she joined the throng of those who sing it day and night before the throne of God. The German print of the Crucifixion, on which Isobel saw the light of the setting sun fall, is one which has hung over my sister's drawing-room fire-place in every home of wood or stone which she has had for many years past.

The Child Verse, "A Hero to his Hobby-horse," came out in the Magazine volume for 1875, and, like many of the other verses, it was written to fit a picture.

One of the happiest inspirations from pictures, however, appeared in the following volume (1876), the story of "Toots and Boots," but though the picture of the ideal Toots was cast like a shadow before him, the actual Toots, name and all complete, had a real existence, and his word-portrait was taken from life. He belonged to the mess of the Royal Engineers in the

South Camp, Aldershot, and was as dignified as if he held the office of President. I shall never forget one occasion on which he was invited to luncheon at Mrs. Ewing's hut, that I might have the pleasure of making his acquaintance; he had to be unwillingly carried across the Lines in the arms of an obliging subaltern, but directly he arrived, without waiting even for the first course, he struggled out of the officer's embrace and galloped back to his own mess-table, tail erect and thick with rage at the indignity he had undergone.

"Father Hedgehog and his Friends," in this same volume (1876), was also written to some excellent German woodcuts; and it, too, is a wonderfully brilliant sketch of animal life; perhaps the human beings in the tale are scarcely done justice to. We feel as if Sybil and Basil, and the Gipsy Mother and Christian, had scarcely room to breathe in the few pages that they are crowded into; there is certainly too much "subject" here for the size of the canvas!—but Father Hedgehog takes up little space, and every syllable about him is as keenly pointed as the spines on his back. The method by which he silenced awkward questions from any of his family is truly delightful:

"Will the donkey be cooked when he is fat?" asked my mother.

"I smell valerian," said my father, on which she put out her nose, and he ran at it with his prickles. He always did this when he was annoyed with any of his family ; and though we knew what was coming, we are all so fond of valerian, we could never resist the temptation to sniff, just on the chance of there being some about.

Then, the following season, we find the Hedgehog Son grown into a parent, and, with the "little hoard of maxims " he had inherited, checking the too inquiring minds of his offspring :

"What is a louis d'or?" cried three of my children; and "What is brandy?" asked the other four.

"I smell valerian," said I; on which they poked out their seven noses, and I ran at them with my spines, for a father who is not an Encyclopædia on all fours must adopt *some* method of checking the inquisitiveness of the young.

One more quotation must be made from the end of the story, where Father Hedgehog gives a list of the fates that befell his children:

Number one came to a sad end. What on the face of the wood made him think of pheasants' eggs I cannot conceive. I'm sure I never said anything about them ! It was whilst he was scrambling along the edge of the covert, that he met the Fox, and very properly rolled himself into a ball. The Fox's nose was as long as his own, and he rolled my poor son over and over with it, till he rolled him into the stream. The young urchins swim like fishes, but just as he was scrambling to shore, the Fox caught him by the waistcoat and killed him. I do hate slyness !

It seems scarcely conceivable that any one can sympathize sufficiently with a Hedgehog as to place

himself in the latter's position, and share its paternal
anxieties,—but I think Julie was able to do so, or, at
any rate, her translations of the Hedgepig's whines
were so *ben trovati*, they may well stand until some
better interpreter of the languages of the brute creation
rises up amongst us. As another instance of her
breadth of sympathy with beasts, let us turn to "A
Week Spent in a Glass Pond" (which also came out
in *Aunt Judy's Magazine* for 1876), and quote her
summary of the Great Water-beetle's views on
life :

> After living as I can, in all three—water, dry land, and air,
> —I certainly prefer to be under water.   Any one whose appetite
> is as keen, and whose hind-legs are as powerful as mine, will
> understand the delights of hunting, and being hunted, in a
> pond; where the light comes down in fitful rays and reflections
> through the water, and gleams among the hanging roots of the
> frog-bit, and the fading leaves of the water-starwort, through
> the maze of which, in and out, hither and thither, you pursue
> and are pursued, in cool and skilful chase, by a mixed company
> of your neighbours, who dart, and shoot, and dive, and come
> and go, and any one of whom, at any moment, may either eat
> you or be eaten by you. And if you want peace and quiet,
> where can one bury oneself so safely and completely as in the
> mud?   A state of existence without mud at the bottom, must
> be a life without repose !

I must here venture to remark, that the chief and
lasting value of whatever both my sister and my
mother wrote about animals, or any other objects in
Nature, lies in the fact that they invariably took the

utmost pains to verify whatever statements they made relating to those objects. Spiritual Laws can only be drawn from the Natural World when they are based on Truth.

Julie spared no trouble in trying to ascertain whether Hedgehogs *do* or do not eat pheasants' eggs; she consulted *The Field*, and books on sport, and her sporting friends, and when she found it was a disputed point, she determined to give the Hedgepig the benefit of the doubt. Then the taste for valerian, and the fox's method of capture, were drawn from facts, and the gruesome details as to who ate who in the Glass Pond were equally well founded!

This (1876) volume of the Magazine is rich in contributions from Julie, the reason being that she was stronger in health whilst she lived at Aldershot than during any other period of her life. The sweet dry air of the "Highwayman's Heath"—bared though it was of heather!—suited her so well, she could sleep with her hut windows open, and go out into her garden at any hour of the evening without fear of harm. She liked to stroll out and listen to "Retreat" being sounded at sundown, especially when it was the turn of some regiment with pipes to perform the duty; they sounded so shrill and weird, coming from the distant hill through the growing darkness.

We held a curious function one hot July evening

during Retreat, when, the Fates being propitious, it
was the turn of the 42nd Highlanders to play. My
sister had taken compassion on a stray collie puppy
a few weeks before, and adopted him; he was very
soft-coated and fascinating in his ways, despite his
gawky legs, and promised to grow into a credit to
his race. But it seemed he was too finely bred to

OUR LATEST PET—A REFUGEE PUP, WHOM WE HAVE SAVED FROM THE
COMMON HANGMAN.

survive the ravages of distemper, for, though he was
tenderly nursed, he died. A wreath of flowers was
hung round his neck, and, as he lay on his bier, Julie
made a sketch of him, with the inscription, "The
Little Colley, Eheu! Taken in, June 14. In spite
of care, died July 1. *Speravimus meliora.*" Major

Ewing, wearing a broad Scotch bonnet, dug a grave
in the garden, and as we had no "dinner-bell" to
muffle, we waited till the pipers broke forth at sundown with an appropriate air, and then lowered the
little Scotch dog into his resting-place.

During her residence at Aldershot Julie wrote
three of her longest books—"A Flat Iron for a
Farthing," "Six to Sixteen," and "Jan of the Windmill," besides all the shorter tales and verses that
she contributed to the Magazine between 1870 and
1877. The two short tales which seem to me her
very best came out in 1876, namely, "Our Field"
(about which I have already spoken) and "The Blind
Man and the Talking Dog." Both the stories were
written to fit some old German woodcuts, but they
are perfectly different in style; "Our Field" is told
in the language and from the fresh heart of a Child;
whilst the "Blind Man" is such a picture of life from
cradle to grave—aye, and stretching forward into the
world beyond,—as could only have come forth from
the experiences of Age. But though this be so, the
lesson shown of how the Boy's story foreshadows the
Man's history, is one which cannot be learned too early.

Julie never pictured a dearer dog than the Peronet
whom she originated from the fat stumpy-tailed puppy
who is seen playing with the children in the woodcut
to "Our Field."

People sometimes asked us what kind of a dog he was, but we never knew, except that he was the nicest possible kind. . . Peronet was as fond of the Field as we were. What he liked were the little birds. At least, I don't know that he liked them, but they were what he chiefly attended to. I think he knew that it was our field, and thought he was the watch-dog of it; and whenever a bird settled down anywhere, he barked at it, and then it flew away, and he ran barking after it till he lost it; by that time another had settled down, and then Peronet flew at him, all up and down the hedge. He never caught a bird, and never would let one sit down, if he could see it.

Then what a vista is opened by the light that is "left out" in the concluding words:—

I know that Our Field does not exactly belong to us. I wonder whom it does belong to? Richard says he believes it belongs to the gentleman who lives at the big red house among the trees. But he must be wrong; for we see that gentleman at church every Sunday, but we never saw him in Our Field.

And I don't believe anybody could have such a field of their very own, and never come to see it, from one end of summer to the other.

It is almost impossible to quote portions of the "Blind Man" without marring the whole. The story is so condensed—only four pages in length; it is one of the most striking examples of my sister's favourite rule in composition, "never use two words where one will do." But from these four brief pages we learn as much as if four volumes had been filled with descriptions of the characters of the Mayor's son and Aldegunda,—from her birthday, on which the boy grumbled because "she toddles as badly as she did yesterday, though she's a year older," and "Aldegunda sobbed till she burst the strings of her hat, and the boy had to tie them afresh,"—to the day of their wedding, when the Bridegroom thinks he can take possession of the Blind Man's Talking Dog, because the latter had promised to leave his master and live with the hero, if ever he could claim to be perfectly happy—happier than him whom he regarded as "a poor wretched old beggar in want of everything."

As they rode together in search of the Dog:

Aldegunda thought to herself—" We are so happy, and have so much, that I do not like to take the Blind Man's dog from him "; but she did not dare to say so.　One—if not two—must bear and forbear to be happy, even on one's wedding-day.

And, when they reached their journey's end, Lazarus was no longer " the wretched one . . . miserable, poor, and blind," but was numbered amongst the blessed Dead, and the Dog was by his grave :

"Come and live with me, now your old master is gone,' said the young man, stooping over the dog.　But he made no reply.

" I think he is dead, sir," said the gravedigger.

" I don't believe it," said the young man, fretfully.　" He was an Enchanted Dog, and he promised I should have him when I could say what I am ready to say now.　He should have kept his promise."

But Aldegunda had taken the dog's cold head into her arms, and her tears fell fast over it.

"You forget," she said; "he only promised to come to you when you were happy, if his old master was not happier still: and perhaps——"

"I remember that you always disagree with me," said the young man, impatiently. "You always did so. Tears on our wedding-day, too! I suppose the truth is, that no one is happy."

Aldegunda made no answer, for it is not from those one loves that he will willingly learn that with a selfish and imperious temper happiness never dwells.

The "Blind Man" was inserted in the Magazine as an "Old-Fashioned Fairy Tale," and Julie wrote another this year (1876) under the same heading, which was called "I Won't."

She also wrote a delightfully funny Legend, "The Kyrkegrim turned Preacher," about a Norwegian Brownie, or Niss, whose duty was "to keep the church clean, and to scatter the marsh marigolds on the floor before service," but, like other church-sweepers, his soul was troubled by seeing the congregation neglect to listen to the preacher, and fall asleep during his sermons. Then the Kyrkegrim, feeling sure that he could make more impression on their hardened hearts than the priest did, ascended from the floor to the pulpit, and tried to set the world to rights; but eventually he was glad to return to his broom, and leave "heavier responsibilities in higher hands."

She contributed "Hints for Private Theatricals. In Letters from Burnt Cork to Rouge Pot," which were probably suggested by the private theatricals in which she was helping at Aldershot; and she wrote four of her best Verses for Children: "Big Smith," "House-building and Repairs," "An Only Child's Tea-party," and "Papa Poodle."

"The Adventures of an Elf" is a poem to some clever silhouette pictures of Fedor Flinzer's, which she freely adapted from the German. "The Snarling Princess" is a fairy tale also adapted from the German; but neither of these contributions was so well worth the trouble of translation as a fine dialogue from the French of Jean Macé called "War and the Dead," which Julie gave to the number of *Aunt Judy* for October 1866.* "The Princes of Vegetation" (April 1876) is an article on Palm-trees, to which family Linnæus had given this noble title.

The last contribution, in 1876, which remains to be mentioned is "Dandelion Clocks," a short tale; but it will need rather a long introduction, as it opens out into a fresh trait of my sister's character, namely, her love for flowers.

It need scarcely be said that she wrote as accurately about them as about everything else; and, in addition to this, she enveloped them in such an

* These translations are included in "Miscellanea," vol. xvii.

atmosphere of sentiment as served to give life and
individuality to their inanimate forms. The habit of
weaving stories round them began in girlhood, when
she was devoted to reading Mr. J. G. Wood's graceful
translation of Alphonse Karr's *Voyage autour de
mon Jardin.* The book was given to her in 1856
by her father, and it exercised a strong influence upon
her mind. What else made the ungraceful Buddlæa
lovely in her eyes? I confess that when she pointed
out the shrub to me, for the first time, in Mr. Ellacombe's garden, it looked so like the "Plum-pudding
tree" in the "Willow pattern," and fell so far short of
my expectation of the plant over which the two florists
had squabbled, that I almost wished that I had not
seen it! Still I did not share their discomfiture so
fully as to think "it no longer good for anything but
firewood!"

Karr's fifty-eighth "Letter" nearly sufficed to enclose a declaration of love in every bunch of "yellow
roses" which Julie tied together; and to plant an
"Incognito" for discovery in every bed of tulips she
looked at; whilst her favourite Letter XL., on the
result produced by inhaling the odour of bean flowers,
embodies the spirit of the ideal existence which she
passed, as she walked through the fields of our work-
a-day world:

The beans were in full blossom. But a truce to this cold-hearted pleasantry. No, it is not a folly to be under the empire of the most beautiful—the most noble feelings; it is no folly to feel oneself great, strong, invincible; it is not a folly to have a good, honest, and generous heart; it is no folly to be filled with good faith; it is not a folly to devote oneself for the good of others; it is not a folly to live thus out of real life.

No, no; that cold wisdom which pronounces so severe a judgment upon all it cannot do; that wisdom which owes its birth to the death of so many great, noble, and sweet things; that wisdom which only comes with infirmities, and which decorates them with such fine names—which calls decay of the powers of the stomach and loss of appetite sobriety; the cooling of the heart and the stagnation of the blood a return to reason; envious impotence a disdain for futile things;—this wisdom would be the greatest, the most melancholy of follies, if it were not the commencement of the death of the heart and the senses.

"Dandelion Clocks" resembles one of Karr's "Letters" in containing the germs of a three-volumed romance, but they *are* the germs only—and the "proportions" of the picture are consequently well preserved. Indeed, the tale always reminds me of a series of peaceful scenes by Cuyp, with low horizons, sleek cattle, and a glow in the sky betokening the approach of sunset. First we have "Peter Paul and his two sisters playing in the pastures" at blowing dandelion clocks:

Rich, green, Dutch pastures, unbroken by hedge or wall, which stretched—like an emerald ocean—to the horizon and met the sky. The cows stood ankle-deep in it and chewed the cud, the clouds sailed slowly over it to the sea, and on a dry hillock sat Mother, in her broad sun-hat, with one eye to the cows, and one to the linen she was bleaching, thinking of her farm.

The actual *outlines* of this scene may be traced in the German woodcut to which the tale was written, but the *colouring* is Julie's! The only disturbing element in this quiet picture is Peter Paul's restless, inquiring heart. What wonder that when his bulb-growing uncle fails to solve the riddle of life, Peter Paul should go out into the wider world and try to find a solution for himself? But the answers to our life problems full often are to be found within, for those who will look, and so Peter Paul comes back after some years to find that:

The elder sister was married and had two children. She had grown up very pretty—a fair woman, with liquid misleading eyes. They looked as if they were gazing into the far future, but they did not see an inch beyond the farm. Anna was a very plain copy of her in body; in mind she was the elder sister's echo. They were very fond of each other, and the prettiest thing about them was their faithful love for their mother, whose memory was kept as green as pastures after rain.

Peter Paul's temperament, however, was not one that could adapt itself to a stagnant existence; so when his three weeks on shore are ended, we see him on his way from the Home Farm to join his ship:

Leena walked far over the pastures with Peter Paul. She was very fond of him, and she had a woman's perception that they would miss him more than he could miss them.

"I am very sorry you could not settle down with us," she said, and her eyes brimmed over.

Peter Paul kissed the tears tenderly from her cheeks.

"Perhaps I shall when I am older, and have shaken off a few more of my whims into the sea. I'll come back yet, Leena, and live very near to you, and grow tulips, and be as good an old bachelor-uncle to your boy as Uncle Jacob is to me."

*   *   *   *   *   *

When they got to the hillock where Mother used to sit, Peter Paul took her once more into his arms.

"Good-bye, good sister," he said, "I have been back in my childhood again, and GOD knows that is both pleasant and good for one."

"And it is funny that you should say so," said Leena, smiling through her tears; "for when we were children you were never happy except in thinking of when you should be a man."

And with this salutary home-thrust (which thoroughly common-place minds have such a provoking faculty for giving) Leena went back to her children and cattle.

Happy for the artistic temperament that can profit by such rebuffs!

PART III.

Yet, how few believe such doctrine springs
        From a poor root,
Which all the winter sleeps here under foot,
        And hath no wings
To raise it to the truth and light of things ;
        But is stil trod
By ev'ry wand'ring clod.

O Thou, Whose Spirit did at first inflame
        And warm the dead,
And by a sacred incubation fed
        With life this frame,
Which once had neither being, forme, nor name,
        Grant I may so
Thy steps track here below,

That in these masques and shadows I may see
        Thy sacred way ;
And by those hid ascents climb to that day
        Which breaks from Thee,
Who art in all things, though invisibly,
        "*The Hidden Flower*."
                            HENRY VAUGHAN.

ONE of the causes which helped to develop my
sister's interest in flowers was the sight of the fresh
ones that she met with on going to live in New Brunswick after her marriage.   Every strange face was a

subject for study, and she soon began to devote a note-book to sketches of these new friends, naming them scientifically from Professor Asa Gray's *Manual of the Botany of the Northern United States*, whilst Major Ewing added as many of the Melicete names as he could glean from Peter, a member of the tribe, who had attached himself to the Ewings, and used constantly to come about their house. Peter and his wife lived in a small colony of the Melicete Indians, which was established on the opposite side of the St. John River to that on which the Reka Dom stood. Mrs. Peter was the most skilful embroiderer in beads amongst her people, and Peter himself the best canoe-builder. He made a beautiful one for the Ewings, which they constantly used ; and when they returned to England his regret at losing them was wonderfully mitigated by the present which Major Ewing gave him of an old gun ; he declared no gentleman had ever thought of giving him such a thing before !

Julie introduced several of the North American flowers into her stories. The Tabby-striped Arum, or Jack-in-the-Pulpit (as it is called in Mr. Whittier's delightful collection of child-poems *), appears in "We and the World," where Dennis, the rollicking Irish hero, unintentionally raises himself in the estim-ation of his sober-minded Scotch companion Alister,

* *Child Life.* Edited by J. G. Whittier. Nesbitt and Co.

by betraying that he "can speak with other tongues," from his ability to converse with a squaw in French on the subject of the bunch of Arums he had gathered, and was holding in his hand.

This allusion was only a slight one, but Julie wrote a complete story on one species of Trillium, having a special affection for the whole genus. Trilliums are amongst the North American herbaceous plants which have lately become fashionable, and easy to be bought in England ; but ere they did so, Julie made some ineffectual attempts to transplant tubers of them into English soil ; and the last letter she received from Fredericton contained a packet of red Trillium seeds, which came too late to be sown before she died. The species which she immortalized in " The Blind Hermit and the Trinity Flower," was *T. erythrocarpum*. The story is a graceful legend of an old Hermit whose life was spent in growing herbs for the healing of diseases ; and when he, in his turn, was struck with blindness, he could not reconcile himself to the loss of the occupation which alone seemed to make him of use in the world. " They also serve who only stand and wait " was a hard lesson to learn ; every day he prayed for some Balm of Gilead to heal his ill, and restore his sight, and the prayer was answered, though not in the manner that he desired. First he was supplied with a serving-boy, who became eyes and feet to him, from gratitude for cures which the Hermit had done to the lad himself; and then a vision was granted to the old man, wherein he saw a flower which would heal his blindness :—

TRILLIUM ERYTHROCARPUM.

"And what was the Trinity Flower like, my Father?" asked the boy.

"It was about the size of Herb Paris, my son," replied the Hermit. "But, instead of being fourfold every way, it numbered the mystic Three. Every part was threefold. The leaves were three, the petals three, the sepals three. The flower

was snow-white, but on each of the three parts it was stained
with crimson stripes, like white garments dyed in blood."

A root of this plant was sent to the Hermit by a
heavenly messenger, which the boy planted, and anxi-
ously watched the growth of, cheering his master with
the hope—" Patience, my Father, thou shalt see yet !"
Meantime greater light was breaking in upon the
Hermit's soul than had been there before :

" My son, I repent me that I have not been patient under
affliction.   Moreover, I have set thee an ill example, in that I
have murmured at that which God—Who knoweth best—
ordained for me."

And, when the boy ofttimes repeated, " Thou shalt yet see,"
the Hermit answered, " If God will. When God will. As
God will."

And at last, when the white bud opens, and the
blood-like stains are visible within, he who once was
blind sees, but his vision is opened on eternal Day.

In *Aunt Judy's Magazine* for 1877 there is
another Flower Legend, but of an English plant, the
Lily of the Valley.   Julie called the tale by the old-
fashioned name of the flower, " Ladders to Heaven."
The scenery is pictured from spots near her Yorkshire
home, where she was accustomed to seeing beautiful
valleys blackened by smoke from iron-furnaces, and
the woods beyond the church, where she liked to
ramble, filled with desolate heaps of black shale, the
refuse left round the mouths of disused coal and iron-

ST. MARY'S CHURCH, ECCLESFIELD.

stone pits.   I remember how glad we were when we found the woolly-leaved yellow Mullein growing on some of these dreary places, and helping to cover up their nakedness.   In later years my sister heard with much pleasure that a mining friend was doing what he could to repair the damages he had made on the beauty of the country, by planting over the worked-out mines such trees and plants as would thrive in the poor and useless shale, which was left as a covering to once rich and valuable spots.

"Brothers of Pity" (*Aunt Judy's Magazine*, 1877) shows a deep and minute insight into the feelings of a solitary child, which one fancies Julie must have acquired by the process of contrast with her own surroundings of seven brethren and sisters.   A similar power of perception was displayed in her verses on "An Only Child's Tea-party."

She remembered from experiences of our own childhood what a favourite game "funerals" is with those whose "whole vocation" is yet "endless imitation"; and she had watched the soldiers' children in camp play at it so often that she knew it was not only the bright covering of the Union Jack which made death lovely in their eyes, "Blind Baby" enjoyed it for the sake of the music; and even civilians' children, who see the service devoid of sweet sounds, and under its blackest and most revolting aspect, still are strangely fascinated thereby. Julie had heard about one of these, a lonely motherless boy, whose chief joy was to harness Granny to his "hearse" and play at funeral processions round the drawing-room, where his dead mother had once toddled in her turn.

The boy in "Brothers of Pity" is the principal character, and the animals occupy minor positions. Cock-Robin only appears as a corpse on the scene; and Julie did not touch much on bird pets in any of her tales, chiefly because she never kept one, having too much sympathy with their powers and cravings for flight to reconcile herself to putting them in cages. The flight and recapture of Cocky in "Lob" were drawn from life, though the bird did not belong to her, but her descriptions of how he stood on the window-sill " scanning the summer sky with his fierce eyes, and flapping himself in the breeze, . . . bowed his yellow crest, spread his noble wings, and sailed out into the æther"; . . . and his " dreams of liberty in the tree-tops," all show the light in which she viewed the practice of keeping birds in confinement. Her verses on " Three Little Nest-Birds " and her tale of the Thrush in " An Idyll of the Wood " bear witness to the same feeling. Major Ewing remembers how often she used to wish, when passing bird-shops, that she could "buy the whole collection and set them all free,"—a desire which suggests a quaint

vision of her in Seven Dials, with a mixed flock of
macaws, canaries, parrots and thrushes shrieking and
flying round her head ; but the wish was worthy of her
in (what Mr. Howells called) "woman's heaven-born
ignorance of the insuperable difficulties of doing right."

In this (1877) volume of *Aunt Judy's Magazine*
there is a striking portrait of another kind of animal
pet, the "Kit" who is resolved to choose her own
"cradle," and not to sleep where she is told.   It is
needless to say that she gets her own way, since,—

> There's a soft persistence about a cat
> That even a little kitten can show.

She has, however, the grace to purr when she is
pleased, which all kits and cats have not !

> I'm happy in ev'ry hair of my fur,
> They may keep the hamper and hay themselves.

There are three other sets of verses in the volume,
and all of them were originally written to old woodcuts, but have since been re-illustrated by Mr. André,
and published by the S.P.C.K.

"A Sweet Little Dear" is the personification of a
selfish girl, and "Master Fritz" of an equally selfish
boy ; but his sister Katerina is delicious by contrast,
as she gives heed to his schemes—

> And if you make nice feasts every day for me and Nickel,
>   and never keep us waiting for our food,
> And always do everything I want, and attend to everything
>   I say, I'm sure I shall almost always be good.

And if I'm naughty now and then, it'll most likely be your
  fault : and if it isn't, you mustn't mind ;
For even if I seem to be cross, you ought to know that I
  meant to be kind.

An old-fashioned fairy tale, " The Magician turned
Mischief-maker," came out in 1877 ; and a short
domestic tale called "A Bad Habit"; but Julie was
unable to supply any long contributions this year, as
in April her seven-years home at Aldershot was
broken up in consequence of Major Ewing being
ordered to Manchester, and her time was occupied by
the labour and process of removing.

She took down the motto which she had hung
over her hearth to temper her joy in the comfort
thereof,— *Ut migraturus habita,*—and moved the
scroll on to her next resting-place. No one knew
better than she the depth of Mrs. Hemans' definition,
—" What is home,—and where,—but *with the loving* ɩ '
and most truly can it be said that wherever Julie went
she carried " Home " with her ; freedom, generosity,
and loving welcome were always to be found in her
house,—even if upholstery and carpets ran short ! It
was a joke amongst some of her friends that though
rose-coloured curtains and bevelled-edged looking-
glasses could be counted upon in their bed-rooms,
such commonplace necessities as soap might be forgotten, and the glasses be fastened in artistic corners

of the rooms, rather than in such lights as were best
adapted for shaving by !

Julie followed the course of the new lines in which
her lot was cast most cheerfully, but the "mighty
heart" could not really support the "little body";
and the fatigue of packing, combined with the effects
of the relaxing climate of Bowdon, near Manchester,
where she went to live, acted sadly upon her constitution.   She was able, however, after settling in

SOUTH CAMP, ALDERSHOT.

the North, to pay more frequent visits to Ecclesfield
than before ; and the next work that she did for *Aunt
Judy's Magazine* bears evidences of the renewal of
Yorkshire associations.

This story, "We and the World," was specially intended for boys, and the "law of contrast" in it was
meant to be drawn between the career which Cripple
Charlie spent at home, and those of the three lads who
went out into "the world" together.   Then, too, she

wished, as I mentioned before, to contrast the national types of character in the English, Scotch, and Irish heroes, and to show the good contained in each of them. But the tale seemed to have been begun under an unlucky star. The first half, which came out in the first six numbers of the Magazine for 1878, is excellent as a matter of art ; and as pictures of North-country life and scenery nothing can be better than Walnut-tree Farm and Academy, the Miser's Funeral, and the Bee-master's Visit to his Hives on the Moors, combined with attendance at Church on a hot Sunday afternoon in August (it need scarcely be said that the church is a real one). But, good though all this is, it is too long and "out of proportion," when one reflects how much of the plot was left to be unravelled in the other half of the tale. "The World" could not properly be squeezed into a space only equal in size to that which had been devoted to "Home." If Julie had been in better health, she would have foreseen the dilemma into which she was falling, but she did not, and in the autumn of 1878 she had to lay the tale aside, for Major Ewing was sent to be stationed at York. "We" was put by until the following volume, but for this (1878) one she wrote two other short contributions,—"The Yellow Fly, a Tale with a Sting in it," and "So-so."

To those who do not read between the lines, "So-so" sounds (as he felt) "very soft and pleasant,"

but to me the tale is in Julie's saddest strain, because
of the suspicion of hopelessness that pervades it;—a
spirit which I do not trace in any of her other writings.

"Be sure, my child," said the widow to her little daughter,
"that you always do just as you are told."

"Very well, mother."

"Or at any rate do what will do just as well," said the small
house-dog, as he lay blinking at the fire.

     *   *   *   *   *

"For the future, my child," said the widow, "I hope you
will always do just as you are told, whatever So-so may say."

"I will, mother," said little Joan. (And she did.) But the
house-dog sat and blinked. He dared not speak, he was in
disgrace.

"I do not feel quite sure about So-so. Wild dogs often
amend their ways far on this side of the gallows, and the Faithful sometimes fall, but when any one begins by being only so-so,
he is very apt to be so-so to the end. So-so's so seldom
change."

Before turning from the record of my sister's life at
Manchester, I must mention a circumstance which
gave her very great pleasure there. In the summer of
1875 she and I went up from Aldershot to see the
Exhibition of Water-Colours by the Royal Society of
Painters, and she was completely fascinated by a
picture of Mr. J. D. Watson's, called "A Gentleman of
the Road." It represented a horseman at daybreak,
allowing his horse to drink from a stream, whilst he sat
half-turned in the saddle to look back at a gallows
which was visible on the horizon against the beams of

rising light. The subject may sound very sensational, but it was not that aspect of it which charmed my sister; she found beauty as well as romance in it, and after we returned to camp in the evening she became so restless and engrossed by what she had seen, that she got up during the night, and planned out the headings of a story on the picture, adding—characteristically—a moral or " soul " to the subject by a quotation * from Thomas à Kempis —*Respice finem.* " In all things *remember the end.*"

This " mapped-out " story, I am sorry to say, remains unfinished. The manuscript went through many vicissitudes, was inadvertently torn up and thrown into the waste-paper basket, whence it was rescued and the pieces carefully enclosed in an envelope ready for mending. It was afterwards lost again for many months in a box that was sent abroad, but the fragments have been put together and copied, as they are interesting from the promise that lies in the few words that remain.

A GENTLEMAN OF THE ROAD.

The old schoolmaster sat on a tombstone, an ancient altar-shaped tomb which may have been reared when the yew tree above it was planted. Children clustered round him like bees upon a branch, and he held the book wide open so that, if possible, all might see into it at once. It was not a school-book,

---

* Letter, March 22, 1880.

it was a picture book, the one out of which he told tales to the children on half-holidays. The volume was old and the text was in Latin, a language of which the schoolmaster had some little knowledge.

He could read the dial motto pat,—*Via crucis via lucis.* The Way of the Cross is the Way of Light.

He understood the Latin headings to the Psalms and Canticles better than the clerk, for he could adjust the words to their English equivalents. The clerk took them as they stood, *Nunc dimittis*, or the Song of Simeon. It was put down so in the rubric, he said, as plain as " Here endeth the first lesson."

The schoolmaster made no such blunders. He could say the Lord's Prayer in Latin, and part of the Creed, and from his seat in church he could make out most of the virtues credited to the last account of one Roger Beaufoy, who in this life had been entitled to write Esquire after his name. The name kept the title after it—*Armiger*—though the man himself had long departed to a life with other distinctions. If the tablet were to be believed, he had been a gentle squire too. The schoolmaster was wont to murmur the list of his qualities over to himself : *fortis—mitis—suavis—largus- —urbanus:—desideratissimus* too, and no marvel !—*nobili genere natus*—and *tam corpore quam vultus præclarus !*

It was a goodly list that the schoolmaster muttered over, and when it was done he would add—" His very portrait, every line, every word of it ! " And then he would sigh.

Old as he was, the schoolmaster was not bearing testimony to the truth of the inscription as regarded the man he referred to ; that Roger Beaufoy had gone back with all his virtues and his vices to the Maker of Souls long before the schoolmaster could read what had been written of him by the maker of epitaphs. It was to the character of another Roger—the great-grandson of this squire—that the old man adapted the graceful flattery of the epitaph. It fitted in every fold, and yet he sighed. For in this Roger, as in that, the sterner virtues were lacking. They had not even been supplied upon the marble, though that is a charity not uncommonly granted to the dead. But when the genial virtues abound, the world misses the others so little !

[Here the sheet of paper is torn, but from the words on the part left it is evident that there was a description of the frontispiece in the schoolmaster's book. Apparently the subject of the picture was allegorical, and the figures of " monstrous beasts " were interspersed with " devices " and " scrolls with inscriptions," together with figures]

of kneeling saints, or pilgrims treading the Via Vitæ with sandalled shoes and heavy staves ; and between the lips of dolorous faces in penal fires issued the words *O Æternitas ! Æternitas !*

All these things the schoolmaster duly interpreted, but the rest of the story he made up out of his own head, a custom which had this among other advantages, that the stories were not always the same, which they must have been had the good man been a merely fluent translator.

At the schoolmaster's elbow nestled his little granddaughter. By herself she could not have secured so good a place, for she was fragile and very gentle, and most of the other children were rough and strong. " First come first served " was the motto of their play. First-come was served first because he helped himself, and the only exception to the rule was when Second-come happened to be stronger and took his place.

This fragment at any rate serves to show what a strong impression the picture had made upon Julie's mind, so it will readily be imagined how intensely delighted she was when she unexpectedly made the acquaintance, at Manchester, of Mr. Galloway, who

proved to have bought Mr. Watson's work, and he
was actually kind enough to lend the treasure to her
for a considerable time, so that she could study it
thoroughly, and make a most accurate copy of it.
Mr. Galloway's friendship, and that of some other
people whom she first met at Bowdon, were the
brightest spots in Julie's existence during this period.

In September 1878 the Ewings removed to
Fulford, near York, and, on their arrival, Julie at
once devoted herself to adorning her new home.
We were very much amused by the incredulous
amazement betrayed on the stolid face of an elderly
workman, to whom it was explained that he was
required to distemper the walls of the drawing-room
with a sole colour, instead of covering them with a
paper, after the manner of all the other drawing-rooms
he had ever had to do with. But he was too polite to
express his difference of taste by more than looks;—
and some days after the room was finished, with
etchings duly hung on velvet in the panels of the
door,—the sole-coloured walls well covered with
pictures, whence they stood out undistracted by gold
and flowery paper patterns—the distemperer called,
and asked if he might be allowed, as a favour, to see
the result of Mrs. Ewing's arrangements. I forget if
he expressed anything by words, as he stood in the
middle of the room twisting his hat in his fingers—

but we had learned to read his face, and Julie was fully satisfied with the fresh expression of amazement mixed with admiration which she saw there.

One theory which she held strongly about the decoration of houses was, that the contents ought to represent the associations of the inmates, rather than the skill of their upholsterer; and for this reason she would not have liked to limit any of her rooms to one special period, such as Queen Anne's, unless she had possessed an old house, built at some date to which a special kind of furniture belonged. She contrived to make her home at York a very pretty one; but it was of short duration, for in March 1879 Major Ewing was despatched to Malta, and Julie had to begin to pack her *Lares* and *Penates* once more.

It may, perhaps, be wondered that she was allowed to spend her time and strength on the labour of packing, which a professional worker would have done far better,—but it is easier to see the mistakes of others than to rectify our own! There were many difficulties to be encountered, not the least of these being Julie's own strong will, and bad though it was, in one sense, for her to be physically over-tired, it was better than letting her be mentally so; and to an active brain like hers, "change of occupation" is the only possible form of "rest." Professional packers and road and rail cars represent money, and

XVIII. 7

Julie's skill in packing both securely and economically was undeniably great. This is not surprising if we hold, as an old friend does, that ladies would make far better housemaids than uneducated women do, because they would throw their brains as well as muscles into their work. Julie did throw her brains into everything, big or little, that she undertook; and one of her best and dearest firiends,—whose belief in my sister's powers and "mission" as a writer were so strong that she almost grudged even the time "wasted" on sketching, which might have been given to penning more stories for the age which boasts Gordon as its hero,—and who, being with Julie at her death, could not believe till the very End came that she would be taken, whilst so much seemed to remain for her to do here,—confessed to me afterwards she had learned to see that Julie's habit of expending her strength on trifles arose from an effort of nature to balance the vigour of her mind, which was so much greater than that of her body.

During the six months that my sister resided in York she wrote a few contributions for *Aunt Judy's Magazine*. To the number for January 1879 she gave "Flaps," a sequel to "The Hens of Hencastle."

The latter story was not written by her, but was a free adaptation which Colonel Yeatman-Biggs made from the German of Victor Blüthgen. Julie had been greatly amused by the tale, but, finding that it ended in a vague and unsatisfactory way, she could not be contented, so took up her pen and wrote a *finale*, her chief aim being to provide a happy ending for the old farm-dog, Flaps himself, after whom she named her sequel. The writing is so exactly similar to that of " The Hens," that the two portions can scarcely be identified as belonging to different writers. Julie used often to reproach me for indulging in what John Wesley called " the lust of finishing," but in matters concerning her own art she was as great an offender on this score as any one else !

Julie gave a set of verses on " Canada Home " to the same number as " Flaps," and to the March (1879) number she gave some other verses on " Garden Lore." In April the second part of " We and the World " began to appear, and a fresh character was introduced, who is one of the most important and touching features of the tale. Biddy Macartney is a real old Irish melody in herself, with her body tied to a coffee-barrow in the Liverpool Docks, and her mind ever wandering in search of the son who had run away to sea. Jack, the English hero, comes across Biddy in the docks just before he starts as a stowaway for America, and his stiff, crude replies to her voluble outpourings are essentially British and boy-like :—

" You hope Micky 'll come back, I suppose ? "

" Why wouldn't I, acushla ?   Sure, it was by reason o' that I got bothered with the washin' after me poor boy left me, from my mind being continually in the docks instead of with the clothes.   And there I would be at the end of the week, with the captain's jerseys gone to old Miss Harding, and *his* washing no corricter than *hers*, though he'd more good-nature in him over the accidents, and iron-moulds on the table-cloths, and pocket-handkerchers missin', and me ruined intirely with making them good, and no thanks for it, till a good-natured sowl of a foreigner that kept a pie-shop larned me to make the coffee, and lint me the money to buy a barra, and he says, ' Go as convanient to the ships as ye can, mother : it 'll ease your mind.   My own heart,' says he, laying his hand to it, ' knows what it is to have my body here, and the whole sowl of me far away.' "

" Did you pay him back ? " I asked.   I spoke without thinking, and still less did I mean to be rude ; but it had suddenly struck me that I was young and hearty, and that it would be almost a duty to share the contents of my leather bag with this poor old woman, if there were no chance of her being able to repay the generous foreigner.

" Did I pay him back ? " she screamed.   " Would I be the black-hearted thief to him that was kind to me ?   Sorra bit nor sup but dry bread and water passed me lips till he had his own again, and the heart's blessings of owld Biddy Macartney along with it."

I made my peace with old Biddy as well as I could, and turned the conversation back to her son.

" So you live in the docks with your coffee-barrow, mother, that you may be sure not to miss Micky when he comes ashore ? "

" I do, darlin' !   Fourteen years all but three days !   He'll be gone fifteen if we all live till Wednesday week."

" *Fifteen ?*   But, mother, if he were like me when he went, he can't be very like me now.   He must be a middle-aged man. Do you think you'd know him ? "

This question was more unfortunate than the other, and produced such howling and weeping, and beating of Biddy's knees as she rocked herself among the beans, that I should have thought every soul in the docks would have crowded round us. But no one took any notice, and by degrees I calmed her, chiefly by the assertion—"He'll know you, mother, anyhow."

"He will so, GOD bless him!" said she. "And haven't I gone over it all in me own mind, often and often, when I'd see the vessels feelin' their way home through the darkness, and the coffee staymin' enough to cheer your heart wid the smell of it, and the least taste in life of something better in the stone bottle under me petticoats. And then the big ship would be coming in with her lights at the head of her, and myself would be sitting alone with me patience, GOD helping me, and one and another strange face going by. And then he comes along, cold maybe, and smells the coffee. 'Bedad, but that's a fine smell with it,' says he, for Micky was mighty particular in his aitin' and drinkin'. 'I'll take a dhrop of that,' says he, not noticing me particular, and if ever I'd the saycret of a good cup he gets it, me consayling me face. 'What will it be?' says he, setting down the mug. 'What would it be, Micky, from your mother?' says I, and I lifts me head. Arrah, but then there's the heart's delight between us. 'Mother!' says he. 'Micky!' says I. And he lifts his foot and kicks over the barra, and dances me round in his arms. 'Ochone!' says the spictators; 'there's the fine coffee that's running into the dock.' 'Let it run,' says I, in the joy of me heart, 'and you after it, and the barra on the top of ye, now Micky me son's come home!'"

"Wonderfully jolly!" said I. "And it must be pleasant even to think of it."

There is another new character in the second part of "We," who is also a fine picture:—Alister the blue-eyed Scotch lad, with his respect for "book-learning," and his powers of self-denial and endurance ; but Julie certainly had a weakness for the Irish nation, and the tender grace with which she touches Dennis O'Moore and Biddy shines conspicuously throughout the story. In one scene, however, I think she brings up her Scotch hero neck-and-neck, if not ahead, of her favourite Irishman.

This is in Chapter VII., where an entertainment is being held on board ship, and Dennis and Alister are called upon in turn to amuse the company with a song. Dennis gets through his ordeal well ; he has a beautiful voice, which makes him independent of the accompaniment of a fiddle (the only musical instrument on board), and Julie describes his *simpatico* rendering of " Bendemeer's Stream " from the way in which she loved to hear one of our brothers sing it. He had learned it by ear on board ship from a fellow-passenger, and she was never tired of listening to the melody. When this same brother came to visit her whilst she was ill at Bath, and sang to her as she lay in bed,—" Bendemeer's Stream " was the one strain she asked for, and the last she heard.

Dennis O'Moore's performance met with warm applause, and then the boatswain, who had a grudge against Alister, because the Scotch Captain treated his countryman with leniency, taunted the shy and taciturn lad to " contribute to the general entertainment."

I was very sorry for Alister, and so was Dennis, I was sure, for he did his best to encourage him.

" Sing 'GOD Save the Queen,' and I'll keep well after ye with the fiddle," he suggested.   But Alister shook his head. " I know one or two Scotch tunes," Dennis added, and he began to sketch out an air or two with his fingers on the strings.

Presently Alister stopped him.   "Yon's the Land o' the Leal ? "

" It is," said Dennis.

" Play it a bit quicker, man, and I'll try 'Scots, wha hae.' "

Dennis quickened at once, and Alister stood forward.   He neither fidgeted nor complained of feeling shy, but, as my eyes (I was squatted cross-legged on the deck) were at the level of his knees, I could see them shaking, and pitied him none the less that I was doubtful as to what might not be before *me.*   Dennis had to make two or three false starts before poor Alister could get a note out of his throat, but when he had fairly broken the ice with the word "Scots !" he faltered no more.   The boat-swain was cheated a second time of his malice.   Alister could not sing in the least like Dennis, but he had a strong manly voice, and it had a ring that stirred one's blood, as he clenched his hands and rolled his R's to the rugged appeal—

> Scots, wha hae wi' Wallace bled,
> Scots, wham Bruce has aften led ;
> Welcome to your gory bed,
>   Or to victory !

Applause didn't seem to steady his legs in the least, and he never moved his eyes from the sea, and his face only grew whiter by the time he drove all the blood to my heart with—

> Wha will be a traitor knave ?
> Wha can fill a coward's grave ?
> Wha sae base as be a slave ?
>   Let him turn and flee !

"GOD forbid !" cried Dennis impetuously.   " Sing that verse again, my boy, and give us a chance to sing with ye ! "

which we did accordingly ; but, as Alister and Dennis were rolling R's like the rattle of musketry on the word *turn*, Alister did turn, and stopped suddenly short. The Captain had come up unobserved.

" Go on ! " said he, waving us back to our places.

By this time the solo had become a chorus. Beautifully unconscious, for the most part, that the song was by way of stirring Scot against Saxon, its deeper patriotism had seized upon us all. Englishmen, Scotchmen, and sons of Erin, we all shouted at the top of our voices, Sambo's fiddle not being silent. And I maintain that we all felt the sentiment with our whole hearts, though I doubt if any but Alister and the Captain knew and sang the precise words—

> Wha for Scotland's King and law
> Freedom's sword will strongly draw,
> Freeman stand, or freeman fa' ?
> Let him on wi' me !

The description of Alister's song, as well as that of Dennis, was to some extent drawn from life, Julie having been accustomed to hear " Scots, wha hae " rendered by a Scot with more soul than voice, who always " moved the hearts of the people as one man " by his patriotic fire.

My sister was greatly aided by two friends in her descriptions of the scenery in " We," such as the vivid account of Bermuda and the waterspout in Chapter XI., and that of the fire at Demerara in Chapter XII., and she owed to the same kind helpers also the accuracy of her nautical phrases and her Irish dialect. Certainly this second part of the tale is full of interest, but I cannot help wishing that the

materials had been made into two books instead of
one. There are more than enough characters and
incidents to have developed into a couple of tales.

Julie had often said how strange it seemed to her,
when people who had a ready pen for *writing* consulted her as to what they should *write about!* She
suffered so much from over-abundance of ideas which
she had not the physical strength to put on paper.

Even when she was very ill, and unable to use her
hands at all, the sight of a lot of good German woodcuts, which were sent to me at Bath, suggested so
many fresh ideas to her brain, that she only longed
to be able to seize her pen and write tales to the
pictures.

Before we turn finally away from the subject of her
liking for Irish people, I must mention a little adventure which happened to her at Fulford.

There is one parish in York where a great number
of Irish peasants live, and many of the women used to
pass Julie's windows daily, going out to work in the
fields at Fulford. She liked to watch them trudging
by, with large baskets perched picturesquely on the
tops of their heads, but in the town the " Irishers " are
not viewed with equal favour by the inhabitants. One
afternoon Julie was out sketching in a field, and came
across one of these poor Irish women. My sister's
mind at the time was full of Biddy Macartney, and she

could not resist the opportunity of having a chat with this suggestive " study " for the character.   She found an excuse for addressing the old woman about some cattle which seemed restless in the field, but quickly discovered, to her amusement, that when she alluded to Ireland, her companion, in the broadest brogue, stoutly denied having any connection with the country. No doubt she thought Julie's prejudices would be similar to those of her town neighbours, but in a short time some allusion was inadvertently made to "me father's farm in Kerry," and the truth leaked out. After this they became more confidential ; and when Julie admired some quaint silver rings on her companion's finger, the old woman was most anxious to give her one, and was only restrained by coming to the decision that she would give her a recipe for "real Irish whisky " instead.   She began with " You must take some barley and put it in a poke——" but after this Julie heard no more, for she was distracted by the cattle, who had advanced unpleasantly near ; the Irish woman, however, continued her instructions to the end, waving her arms to keep the beasts off, which she so far succeeded in doing, that Julie caught the last sentence—

"And then ye must bury it in a bog."

"Is that to give it a peaty flavour ? " asked my sister, innocently.

"Oh, no, me dear!—*it's because of the exciseman.*"

When they parted, the old woman's original reserve entirely gave way, and she cried : "Good luck to ye! *and go to Ireland!*"

Julie remained in England for some months after Major Ewing started for Malta, and as he was despatched on very short notice, and she had to pack up their goods; also—as she was not strong—it was decided that she should avoid going out for the hot summer weather, and wait for the healthier autumn season. Her time, therefore, was now chiefly spent amongst civilian friends and relations, and I want this fact to be specially noticed, in connection with the next contributions that she wrote for the Magazine.

In February 1879, the terrible news had come of the Isandlwana massacre, and this was followed in June by that of the Prince Imperial's death. My sister was, of course, deeply engrossed in the war tidings, as many of her friends went out to South Africa—some to return no more. In July she contributed " A Soldier's Children " to *Aunt Judy*, and of all her child verses this must be reckoned the best, every line from first to last breathing how strong her sympathies still were for military men and things, though she was no longer living amongst them :

Our home used to be in the dear old camp, with lots of bands,
    and trumpets, and bugles, and dead-marches, and three
    times a day there was a gun,
But now we live in View Villa, at the top of the village, and it
    isn't nearly such fun.

The humour and pathos in the lines are so closely
mixed, it is very difficult to read them aloud without
tears ; but they have been recited—as Julie was much
pleased to know — by the " old Father " of the
" Queer Fellows " to whom the verses were dedicated,
when he was on a troopship going abroad for active
service, and they were received with warm approbation by his hearers. He read them on other occasions,
also in public, with equal success.

The crowning military work, however, which Julie
did this year was " Jackanapes." This she wrote for
the October number of *Aunt Judy :* and here let me
state that I believe if she had still been living at
Aldershot, surrounded by the atmosphere of military
sympathies and views of honour, the tale would never
have been written. It was not aimed, as some people
supposed, personally at the man who was with the
Prince Imperial when he met his death. Julie would
never have sat in judgment on him, even before he,
too, joined the rank of those Dead, about whom no
evil may be spoken. It was hearing this same man's
conduct discussed by civilians from the standard of
honour which is unhappily so different in civil and

military circles, and more especially the discussion of
it amongst " business men," where the rule of " each
man for himself " is invariable, which drove Julie into
uttering the protest of " Jackanapes." I believe what
she longed to show forth was how the *life* of an army
—as of any other body—depends on whether the
individuality of its members is *dead ;* a paradox which
may perhaps be hard to understand, save in the light
of His teaching, Who said that the saving of a man's
life lay in his readiness to lose it. The merging of
selfish interests into a common cause is what makes
it strong ; and it is from Satan alone we get the axiom,
" Skin for skin, yea, all that a man hath will he give
for his life." Of " Jackanapes " itself I need not
speak. It has made Julie's name famous, and deservedly so, for it not only contains her highest teaching,
but is her best piece of literary art.

There are a few facts connected with the story
which, I think, will be interesting to some of its
admirers. My sister was in London in June 1879,
and then made the acquaintance of Mr. Randolph
Caldecott, for whose illustrations to Washington
Irving's " Bracebridge Hall " and " Old Christmas "
she had an unbounded admiration, as well as for his
Toy Books. This introduction led us to ask him,
when " Jackanapes " was still simmering in Julie's
brain, if he would supply a coloured illustration for it.

But as the tale was only written a very short time
before it appeared, and as the illustration was wanted
early, because colours take long to print, Julie could
not send the story to be read, but asked Mr. Caldecott to draw her a picture to fit one of the scenes in
it.   The one she suggested was a "fair-haired boy on
a red-haired pony," having noticed the artistic effect
produced by this combination in one of her own
nephews, a skilful seven-year-old rider who was accustomed to follow the hounds.

This coloured illustration was given in *Aunt Judy's
Magazine*, with the tale, but when it was republished
as a book, in 1883, the scene was reproduced on a
smaller scale in black and white only.

"Jackanapes" was much praised when it came
out in the Magazine, but it was not until it had been
re-issued as a book that it became really well known.
Even then its success was within a hair's-breadth of
failing.   The first copies were brought out in dull
stone-coloured paper covers, and that powerful vehicle
"the Trade," unable to believe that a jewel could be
concealed in so plain a casket, refused the work of
J. H. E. and R. C. until they had stretched the
paper cover on boards, and coloured the Union Jack
which adorns it !   No doubt "the Trade" under-
stands its fickle child "the Public" better than either
authors or artists do, and knows by experience that it

requires tempting with what is pretty to look at, before it will taste. Certainly, if praise from the public were the chief aim that writers, or any other workers, strove after, their lives for the most part would consist of disappointment only, so seldom is "success" granted whilst the power to enjoy it is present. They alone whose aims are pointed above earthly praise can stand unmoved amidst neglect or blame, filled with that peace of a good conscience which the world can neither give nor take away.

PART IV.

I shall know by the gleam and glitter
  Of the golden chain you wear,
By your heart's calm strength in loving,
  Of the fire they have had to bear.
Beat on, true heart, for ever ;
  Shine bright, strong golden chain ;
And bless the cleansing fire,
  And the furnace of living pain !

ADELAIDE A. PROCTER.

TOWARDS the end of October 1879, Julie started for Malta, to join Major Ewing, but she became so very ill whilst travelling through France that her youngest sister, and her friend, Mrs. R. H. Jelf (from whose house in Folkestone she had started on her journey), followed her to Paris, and brought her back to England as soon as she could be moved.

Julie now consulted Sir William Jenner about her health, and, seeing the disastrous effect that travelling had upon her, he totally forbade her to start again for several months, until she had recovered some strength and was better able to bear fatigue.   This verdict was a heavy blow to my sister, and the next four years were ones of great trial and discomfort to her. A constant succession of disappointed hopes and frustrated plans, which were difficult, even for Madam Liberality, to bear!

She hoped when her husband came home on leave at Christmas, 1879, that she should be able to return with him, but she was still unfit to go ; and then she planned to follow later with a sister, who should help her on the journey, and be rewarded by visiting the island home of the Knights, but this castle also fell to the ground. Meantime Julie was suffering great inconvenience from the fact that she had sent all her possessions to Malta several months before, keeping only some light luggage which she could take with her. Amongst other things from which she was thus parted, was the last chapter of "We and the World," which she had written (as she often did the endings of her tales) when she was first arranging the plot. This final scene was buried in a box of books, and could not be found when wanted, so had to be re-written ; and then my sister's ideas seem to have got into a fresh channel, for she brought her heroes safely back to their Yorkshire home, instead of dropping the curtain on them after a gallant rescue in a Cornish mine, as she originally arranged. Julie hoped against hope, as time went on, that she should become stronger, and able to follow her *Lares* and *Penates*, so she would not have them sent back to her, until a final end was put to her hopes by Major Ewing being sent on from Malta to Ceylon, and in the climate of the latter place the doctors declared it would be impossible for her to live. The goods, therefore, were now sent back to England, and she consoled herself under the bitter trial of being parted from her husband, and unable to share the enjoyment of the new and wonderful scenes with which he was surrounded, by thankfulness for his unusual ability as a vivid and brilliant letter-writer. She certainly practised both in days of joy and sorrow the virtue of being *lætus sorte meâ*, which she afterwards so powerfully taught in her "Story of a Short Life." I never knew her fail to find happiness wherever she was placed, and good in whomsoever she came across. Whatever her circumstances might be they always yielded to her causes for thankfulness, and work to be done with a ready and hopeful heart. That "lamp of zeal," about which Margery speaks in "Six to Sixteen," was never extinguished in Julie, even after youth and strength were no longer hers :—

Like most other conscientious girls, we had rules and regulations of our own devising ; private codes, generally kept in cipher for our own personal self-discipline, and laws common to us both for the employment of our time in joint duties—lessons, parish work, and so forth.

I think we made rather too many rules, and that we re-made them too often. I make fewer now, and easier ones, and let them much more alone. I wonder if I really keep them better? But if not, may GOD, I pray Him, send me back the restless zeal, the hunger and thirst after righteousness, which He gives us in early youth! It is so easy to become more thick-skinned in conscience, more tolerant of evil, more hopeless of good, more careful of one's own comfort and one's own property, more self-satisfied in leaving high aims and great deeds to enthusiasts, and then to believe that one is growing older and wiser. And yet those high examples, those good works, those great triumphs over evil which single hands effect sometimes, we are all grateful for, when they are done, whatever we may have said of the doing. But we speak of saints and enthusiasts for good, as if some special gifts were made to them in middle age which are withheld from other men. Is it not rather that some few souls keep alive the lamp of zeal and high desire which GOD lights for most of us while life is young?

In spite, however, of my sister's contentment with her lot, and the kindness and hospitality shown to her at this time by relations and friends, her position was far from comfortable ; and Madam Liberality's hospitable soul was sorely tried by having no home to which she could welcome her friends, whilst her fragile body battled against constantly moving from one house to another when she was often unfit to do anything except keep quiet and at rest. She was not able to write much, and during 1880 only contributed two poems to *Aunt Judy's Magazine,* " Grandmother's Spring," and " Touch Him if You Dare."

To the following volume (1881) she again was

only able to give two other poems, " Blue and Red ;
or the Discontented Lobster," and "The Mill Stream";
but these are both much longer than her usual Verses
for Children—and, indeed, are better suited for older
readers—though the former was such a favourite with
a three-year-old son of one of our bishops that he
used to repeat it by heart.

In November 1881, *Aunt Judy's Magazine* passed
into the hands of a fresh publisher, and a new series
was begun, with a fresh outside cover which Mr.
Caldecott designed for it.   Julie was anxious to help
in starting the new series, and she wrote " Daddy
Darwin's Dovecot" for the opening number.   All the
scenery of this is drawn from the neighbourhood of
Ecclesfield, where she had lately been spending a
good deal of her time, and so refreshed her memory
of its local colouring.   The story ranks equal to
" Jackanapes " as a work of literary art, though it is
an idyll of peace instead of war, and perhaps, therefore, appeals rather less deeply to general sympathies ;
but I fully agree with a noted artist friend, who, when
writing to regret my sister's death, said, "'Jackanapes'
and ' Daddy Darwin' I have never been able to read
without tears, and hope I never may."   Daddy had
no actual existence, though his outward man may
have been drawn from types of a race of " old
standards " which is fast dying out.   The incident of

ECCLESFIELD HALL.

the theft and recovery of the pigeons is a true one, and happened to a flock at the old Hall farm near our home, which also once possessed a luxuriant garden, wherein Phœbe might have found all the requisites for her Sunday posy. A "tea" for the workhouse children used to be Madam Liberality's annual birthday feast; and the spot where the gaffers sat and watched the "new graft" strolling home across the fields was so faithfully described by Julie from her favourite Schroggs Wood, that when Mr. Caldecott reproduced it in his beautiful illustration, some friends who were well acquainted with the spot, believed that he had been to Ecclesfield to paint it.

Julie's health became somewhat better in 1882, and for the Magazine this year she wrote as a serial tale "Lætus Sorte Meâ; or, the Story of a Short Life." This was not republished as a book until four days before my sister's death, and it has become so well known from appearing at this critical time that I need say very little about it. A curious mistake, however, resulted from its being published then, which was that most of the reviewers spoke of it as being the last work that she wrote, and commented on the title as a singularly appropriate one, but those who had read the tale in the Magazine were aware that it was written three years previously, and that the second name was put before the first, as it was feared the

public would be perplexed by a Latin title. The
only part of the book that my sister added during her
illness was Leonard's fifth letter in Chapter X. This
she dictated, because she could not write. She had
intended to give Saint Martin's history when the story
came out in the Magazine, but was hindered by want
of space.*   Many people admire Leonard's story as
much as that of Jackanapes, but to me it is not quite
so highly finished from an artistic point of view. I
think it suffered a little from being written in detach-
ments from month to month. It is, however, almost
hypercritical to point out defects, and the circumstances of Leonard's life are so much more within the
range of common experiences than those of Jackanapes,
it is probable that the lesson of the Short Life, during
which a V.C. was won by the joyful endurance of
inglorious suffering, may be more helpful to general
readers than that of the other brief career, in which
Jackanapes, after "one crowded hour of glorious life,"
earned his crown of victory.

On on of Julie's last days she expressed a fear
to her doctor that she was very impatient under her
pain, and he answered, " Indeed you are not ; I think
you deserve a Victoria Cross for the way in which you
bear it." This reply touched her very much, for she
knew the speaker had not read Leonard's Story; and

* Letter, Oct. 5, 1882.

we used to hide the proof-sheets of it, for which she was choosing head-lines to the pages, whenever her doctors came into the room, fearing that they would disapprove of her doing any mental work.

In the volume of *Aunt Judy* for 1883 "A Happy Family" appeared, but this had been originally written for an American Magazine, in which a prize was offered for a tale not exceeding nine hundred words in length. Julie did not gain the prize, and her story was rather spoiled by having to be too closely condensed.

She also wrote three poems for *Aunt Judy* in 1883, "The Poet and the Brook," "Mother's Birthday Review," and "Convalescence." The last one and the tale of "Sunflowers and a Rushlight" (which came out in November 1883) bear some traces of the deep sympathy she had learned for ill health through her own sufferings of the last few years; the same may, to some extent, be said of "The Story of a Short Life." "Mother's Birthday Review" does not come under this heading, though I well remember that part, if not the whole of it, was written whilst Julie lay in bed; and I was despatched by her on messages in various directions to ascertain what really became of Hampstead Heath donkeys during the winter, and the name of the flower that clothes some parts of the Heath with a sheet of white in summer.

In May 1883, Major Ewing returned home from Ceylon, and was stationed at Taunton. This change brought back much comfort and happiness into my sister's life. She once more had a pretty home of her own, and not only a home but a garden. When the Ewings took their house, and named it Villa *Ponente*, from its aspect towards the setting sun, the "garden" was a potato patch, with soil chiefly composed of refuse left by the house-builders; but my sister soon began to accumulate flowers in the borders, especially herbaceous ones that were given to her by friends, or bought by her in the market. Then in 1884 she wrote "Mary's Meadow," as a serial for *Aunt Judy's Magazine*, and the story was so popular that it led to the establishment of a "Parkinson Society for lovers of hardy flowers." Miss Alice Sargant was the founder and secretary of this, and to her my sister owed much of the enjoyment of her life at Taunton, for the Society produced many friends by correspondence, with whom she exchanged plants and books, and the "potato patch" quickly turned into a well stocked flower-garden.

Perhaps the friend who did most of all to beautify it was the Rev. J. Going, who not only gave my sister many roses, but planted them round the walls of her house himself, and pruned them afterwards, calling

himself her "head gardener." She did not live long
enough to see the roses sufficiently established to
flower thoroughly, but she enjoyed them by anti-
cipation, and they served to keep her grave bright
during the summer that followed her death.

Next to roses I think the flowers that Julie had
most of were primulas of various kinds, owing to the
interest that was aroused in them by the incident in
"Mary's Meadow" of Christopher finding a Hose-in-
hose cowslip growing wild in the said "meadow."
My sister was specially proud of a Hose-in-hose
cowslip which was sent to her by a little boy in
Ireland, who had determined one day with his
brothers and sisters, that they would set out and
found an "Earthly Paradise" of their own, and he
began by actually finding a Hose-in-hose, which he
named it after "Christopher," and sent a bit of the
root to Mrs. Ewing.

The last literary work that she did was again on
the subject of flowers. She began a series of "Letters
from a Little Garden" in the number of *Aunt Judy*
for November 1884, and these were continued until
February 1885. The Letter for March was left
unfinished, though it seemed, when boxes of flowers
arrived day by day during Julie's illness from distant
friends, as if they must almost have intuitively known
the purport of the opening injunction in her unpub-

lished epistle, enjoining liberality in the practice of cutting flowers for decorative purposes ! Her room for three months was kept so continuously bright by the presence of these creations of GOD which she loved so well :—

"DEAR LITTLE FRIEND,

"A garden of hardy flowers is pre-eminently a garden for cut flowers. You must carefully count this among its merits, because if a constant and undimmed blaze outside were the one virtue of a flower-garden, upholders of the bedding-out system would now and then have the advantage of us. For my own part I am prepared to say that I want my flowers quite as much for the house as the garden, and so I suspect do most women." The gardener's point of view is not quite the same.

"Speaking of women, and recalling Mr. Charles Warner's quaint idea of all his ' Polly' was good for on the scene of his conflicts with Nature, the ' striped bug' and the weed ' Pusley,' —namely, to sit on an inverted flower-pot and ' consult' him whilst he was hoeing,—it is interesting to notice that some generations ago the garden was very emphatically included within woman's ' proper sphere,' which was not, in those days, a wide one."

The Letters were the last things that my sister wrote; but some brief papers which she contributed to *The Child's Pictorial Magazine* were not published until after her death. In the May number "Tiny's Tricks and Toby's Tricks" came out, and in the numbers for June, July, and August 1885, there were three " Hoots " from "The Owl in the Ivy Bush; or the Children's Bird of Wisdom." They are in the form of quaint letters of advice, and my sister adopted the *Spectator's* method of writing as an eye-witness in the first person, so far as was possible in addressing a very youthful class of readers. She had a strong admiration for many of both Steele and Addison's papers.

The list that I promised to give of Julie's published stories is now completed; and, if her works are to be valued by their length, it may justly be said that she has not left a vast amount of matter behind her, but I think that those who study her writings carefully, will feel that some of their greatest worth lies in the wonderful condensation and high finish that they display. No reviewer has made a more apt comparison than the American one in *Every other Saturday*, who spoke of " Jackanapes " as " an exquisite bit of finished work—a Meissonier, in its way."

To other readers the chief value of the books will be in the high purpose of their teaching, and the consciousness that Julie held her talent as a direct gift from GOD, and never used it otherwise than to His glory. She has penned nothing for which she need fear reproach from her favourite old proverb, " A wicked book is all the wickeder because it can never repent." It is difficult for those who admire her writings to help regretting that her life was cut off before she had accomplished more, but to still such regrets we cannot do better than realize (as a kind friend remarked) "how much she has been able to do, rather than what she has left undone." The work which she did, in spite of her physical fragility, far exceeds what the majority of us perform with stronger bodies and longer lives. This reflection has comforted me, though I perhaps know more than others how many subjects she had intended to write stories upon. Some people have spoken as if her *forte* lay in writing about soldiers only, but her success in this line was really due to her having spent much time among them. I am sure her imagination and sympathy were so strong, that whatever class of men she was mixed with, she could not help throwing herself into their interests, and weaving romances about them. Whether such romances ever got on to paper was a matter dependent on outward circumstances and the state of her health.

One of the unwritten stories which I most regret is "Grim the Collier"; this was to have been a romance of the Black Country of coal-mines, in which she was born, and the title was chosen from the description of a flower in a copy of Gerarde's *Herbal*, given to her by Miss Sargant:—

Hieracium hortense latifolium, sine Pilosella maior, Golden Mouseeare, or Grim the Colliar. The floures grow at the top as it were in an vmbel, and are of the bignesse of the ordinary Mouseeare, and of an orenge colour. The seeds are round, and blackish, and are carried away with the downe by the wind. The stalks and cups of the flours are all set thicke with a blackish downe, or hairinesse, as it were the dust of coles; whence the women who keepe it in gardens for novelties sake, have named it Grim the Colliar.

I wish, too, that Julie could have written about sailors, as well as soldiers, in the tale of " Little Mothers' Meetings," which had been suggested to her mind by visits to Liverpool. The sight of a baby patient in the Children's Hospital there, who had been paralyzed and made speechless by fright, but who took so strange a fancy to my sister's sympathetic face that he held her hand and could scarcely be induced to release it, had affected her deeply. So did a visit that she paid one Sunday to the Seamen's Orphanage, where she heard the voices of hundreds of fatherless children ascending with one accord in the words, " I will arise and go to my Father," and realized the Love that watched over them. These scenes were both to have been woven into the tale, and the " Little Mothers " were boy nurses of baby brothers and sisters.

Another phase of sailor life on which Julie hoped to write was the " Guild of Merchant Adventurers of Bristol." She had visited their quaint Hall, and collected a good deal of historical information and local colouring for the tale, and its lesson would have been one on mercantile honour.

I hope I have kept my original promise, that whilst I was making a list of Julie's writings, I would also supply an outline biography of her life ; but now, if the Children wish to learn something of her at its End, they shall be told in her own words :—

Madam Liberality grew up into much the same sort of person that she was when a child. She always had been what is termed old-fashioned, and the older she grew the better her old-fashionedness became her, so that at last her friends would say to her, "Ah, if we all wore as well as you do, my dear ! You've hardly changed at all since we remember you in short petticoats." So far as she did change, the change was for the better. (It is to be hoped we do improve a little as we get older.) She was still liberal and economical. She still planned and hoped indefatigably. She was still tender-hearted in the sense in which Gray speaks—

" To each his sufferings : all are men
        Condemned alike to groan,
     The tender for another's pain,
        The unfeeling for his own."

She still had a good deal of ill-health and ill-luck, and a good deal of pleasure in spite of both. She was happy in the happiness of others, and pleased by their praise. But she was less head-strong and opinionated in her plans, and less fretful when they failed. It is possible, after one has cut one's wisdom-teeth, to cure oneself even of a good deal of vanity, and to learn to play the second fiddle very gracefully ; and Madam Liberality did not resist the lessons of life.

GOD teaches us wisdom in divers ways. Why He suffers some people to have so many troubles, and so little of what we call pleasure in this world, we cannot in this world know. The

heaviest blows often fall on the weakest shoulders, and how
these endure and bear up under them is another of the things
which GOD knows better than we.

Julie did absolutely remain "the same" during
the three months of heavy suffering which, in GOD's
mysterious love, preceded her death. Perhaps it is
well for us all to know that she found, as others do,
the intervals of exhausted relief granted between
attacks of pain were not times in which (had it been
needed) she could have changed her whole character,
and, what is called, " prepare to die." Our days of
health and strength are the ones in which this preparation must be made, but for those who live, as she did,
with their whole talents dedicated to GOD's service,
death is only the gate of life—the path from joyful
work in this world to greater capacities and oppor-
tunities for it in the other.

I trust that what I have said about Julie's religious
life will not lead chidren to imagine that she was
gloomy, and unable to enjoy her existence on earth,
for this was not the case. No one appreciated and
rejoiced in the pleasures and beauties of the world
more thoroughly than she did : no one could be a
wittier and brighter companion than she always was.

Early in February 1885, she was found to be
suffering from a species of blood-poisoning, and as no
cause for this could then be discovered, it was thought

that change of air migh do her good, and she was
taken from her home at Taunton, to lodgings at Bath.
She had been three weeks in bed before she started,
and was obliged to return to it two days after she
arrived, and there to remain on her back ; but this
uncomfortable position did not alter her love for
flowers and animals.

The first of these tastes was abundantly gratified, as
I mentioned before, by the quantities of blossoms
which were sent her from friends ; as well as by the
weekly nosegay which came from her own Little
Garden, and made her realize that the year was
advancing from winter to spring, when crocuses and
daffodils were succeeded by primroses and anemones.

Of living creatures she saw fewer. The only
object she could see through her window was a high
wall covered with ivy, in which a lot of sparrows and
starlings were building their nests. As the sunlight fell
on the leaves, and the little birds popped in and out,
Julie enjoyed watching them at work, and declared the
wall looked like a fine Japanese picture. She made us
keep bread-crumbs on the window-sill, together with
bits of cotton wool and hair, so that the birds might
come and fetch supplies of food, and materials for
their nests.

Her appreciation of fun, too, remained keen as ever,
and, strange as it may seem, one of the very few books
XVIII. 9

which she liked to have read aloud was Mark Twain's
"Adventures of Huckleberry Finn"; the dry humour
of it—the natural way in which everything is told from
a boy's point of view—and the vivid and beautiful
descriptions of river scenery—all charmed her.   One
of Twain's shorter tales, "Aurelia's unfortunate
Young Man," was also read to her, and made her
laugh so much, when she was nearly as helpless as the
"young man" himself, that we had to desist for fear
of doing her harm.   Most truly may it be said that
between each paroxysm of pain "her little white face
and undaunted spirit bobbed up . . . as ready and
hopeful as ever."   She was seldom able, however, to
concentrate her attention on solid works, and for her
religious exercises chiefly relied on what was stored in
her memory.

    This faculty was always a strong one.   She was
catechized in church with the village children when
only four years old, and when six, could repeat many
poems from an old collection called "The Diadem,"
such as Mrs. Hemans' "Cross in the Wilderness," and
Dale's "Christian Virgin to her Apostate Lover"; but
she reminded me one day during her illness of how
little she understood what she was saying in the days
when she fluently recited such lines to her nursery
audience !

    She liked to repeat the alternate verses of the

Psalms, when the others were read to her ; and to the good things laid up in her mind she owed much of the consolation that strengthened her in hours of trial. After one night of great suffering, in which she had been repeating George Herbert's poem, " The Pulley," she said that the last verse had helped her to realize what the hidden good might be which underlaid her pain—

> Let him be rich and weary ; that, at least,
> If goodness lead him not, yet weariness
> May toss him to My breast.

During the earlier part of her illness, when every one expected that she would recover, she found it difficult to submit to the unaccountable sufferings which her highly-strung temperament felt so keenly ; but after this special night of physical and mental darkness, it seemed as if light had broken upon her through the clouds, for she said she had, as it were, looked her pain and weariness in the face, and seen they were sent for some purpose—and now that she had done so, we should find that she would be " more patient than before." We were told to take a sheet of paper, and write out a calendar for a week with the text above, " In patience possess ye your souls." Then as each day went by we were to strike it through with a pencil ; this we did, hoping that the passing days were leading her nearer to recovery, and not knowing that each was in reality "a day's march nearer home."

For the text of another week she had "Be strong and of a good courage," as the words had been said by a kind friend to cheer her just before undergoing the trial of an operation. Later still, when nights of suffering were added to days of pain, she chose— "The day is Thine, the night also is Thine."

Of what may be termed external spiritual privileges she did not have many, but she derived much comfort from an unexpected visitor. During nine years previously she had known the Rev. Edward Thring as a correspondent, but they had not met face to face, though they had tried on several occasions to do so. Now, when their chances of meeting were nearly gone, ·he came and gave great consolation by his unravelling of the mystery of suffering, and its sanctifying power ; as also by his interpretation that the life which we are meant to lead under the dispensation of the Spirit who has been given for our guidance into Truth, is one which does not take us out of the world, but keeps us from its evil, enabling us to lead a heavenly existence on earth, and so to span over the chasm which divides us from heaven.

Perhaps some of us may wonder that Julie should need lessons of encouragement and comfort who was so apt a teacher herself; but however ready she may always have been to hope for others, she was thoroughly humble-minded about herself. On one day near the end, when she had received some letter of warm praise about her writings, a friend said in joke, "I wonder your head is not turned by such things"; and Julie replied : "I don't think praise really hurts me, because, when I read my own writings over again they often seem to me such 'bosh'; and then, too, you know I lead such a useless life, and there is so little I *can* do, it is a great pleasure to know I may have done *some* good."

It pleased her to get a letter from Sir Evelyn Wood, written from the Soudan, telling how he had cried over *Lætus ;* and she was almost more gratified to get an anonymous expression from "One of the Oldest Natives of the Town of Aldershot" of his "warm and grateful sense of the charm of her delightful references to a district much loved of its children, and the emotion he felt in recognizing his birthplace so tenderly alluded to." Julie certainly set no value on her own actual MSS., for she almost invariably used them up when they were returned from the printers, by writing on the empty sides, and destroying them after they had thus done double duty. She was quite amused by a relation who begged for the sheets of "Jackanapes," and so rescued them from the flames !

On the 11th of May an increase of suffering made

it necessary that my sister should undergo another
operation, as the one chance of prolonging her life.
This ordeal she faced with undaunted courage, thanking God that she was able to take chloroform easily,
and only praying He would end her sufferings speedily,
as He thought best, since she feared her physical
ability to bear them patiently was nearly worn out.

Her prayer was answered, when two days later,
free from pain, she entered into rest. On the 16th
of May she was buried in her parish churchyard of
Trull, near Taunton, in a grave literally lined with
moss and flowers;—so many floral wreaths and
crosses were sent from all parts of England, that
when the grave was filled up they entirely covered it,
not a speck of soil could be seen; her first sleep in
mother earth was beneath a coverlet of fragrant white
blossoms. No resting-place than this could be more
fitting for her. The church is deeply interesting from
its antiquity, and its fine oak-screen and seats, said
to be carved by monks of Glastonbury, whilst the
churchyard is an idyllically peaceful one, containing
several yew-trees; under one of these, which over-
shadows Julie's grave, the remains of the parish stocks
are to be seen—a quaint mixture of objects, that
recalls some of her own close blendings of humour
and pathos into one scene. Here, "for a space, the
tired body lies with feet towards the dawn," but I

must hope and believe that the active soul, now it is
delivered from the burden of the flesh, has realized
that Gordon's anticipations were right when he wrote:
"The future world must be much more amusing,
more enticing, more to be desired, than this world,—
putting aside its absence of sorrow and sin.   The
future world has been somehow painted to our minds
as a place of continuous praise, and, though we may
not say it, yet we cannot help feeling that, if thus, it
would prove monotonous.   It cannot be thus.   It
must be a life of activity, for happiness is dependent
on activity: death is cessation of movement; life is
all movement."

If Archbishop Trench, too, was right in saying:

> The tasks, the joys of earth, the same in heaven will be ;
> Only the little brook has widen'd to a sea,

have we not cause to trust that Julie still ministers to
the good and happiness of the young and old whom
she served so well whilst she was seen amongst them?
Let her, at any rate, be to us one of those who shine
as the stars to lead us unto God :

> God's saints are shining lights : who stays
>   Here long must passe
> O'er dark hills, swift streames, and steep ways
>   As smooth as glasse ;
> But these all night,
>   Like Candles, shed
> Their beams, and light
>   Us into bed.

They are, indeed, our pillar-fires,
　　Seen as we go ;
They are that Citie's shining spires
　　We travel to.
A sword-like gleame
　　Kept man for sin—
First *out*, this beame
　　Will guide him *In*.

"If we still love those we lose, can we altogether lose those we love?"

" *The Newcomes*," Chap. vii.

(*The last entry in J. H. E.'s Commonplace Book.*)

LIST OF MRS. EWING'S WORKS.

TITLE.	FIRST PUBLISHED IN:	SUBSEQUENTLY.	PUBLISHER.
A Bit of Green ...	*Monthly Packet,* July,1861	"Melchior's Dream, and other Tales"	Bell & Sons, 1862.
The Blackbird's Nest ...	— August, 1861...	"	"
Melchior's Dream ...	— December, 1861	"	"
Friedrich's Ballad ...	---	"	"
The Viscount's Friend...			
The Mystery of the Bloody Hand ...	*London Society,* January and February, 1865	"Miscellanea," vol. xvii. ...	S.P.C.K."
The Yew Lane Ghosts ...	*Monthly Packet,* June,1865	"Melchior's Dream, and other Tales"	Bell & Sons, 1885.
The Brownies	*Monthly Packet,* 1865 ...	"The Brownies, and other Tales"	"
Mrs. Overtheway's Remembrances—			
Ida	*Aunt Judy's Magazine,* May, 1866	"Mrs. Overtheway's Remembrances"	"
Mrs. Moss	— June and July, 1866		
The Promise	— July, 1866 ...	"Verses for Children," vol. ix. ...	S.P.C.K."
		"Songs for Music, by Four Friends"	H. King & Co.
The Burial of the Linnet ...	September, 1866	"Papa Poodle, and other Pets" ...	S.P.C.K.
		"Verses for Children," vol. ix. ...	"
Christmas Wishes	December, 1866 ...		
Mrs. Overtheway's Remembrances—			
The Snoring Ghosts ...	December, 1866; Jan. and February, 1867	"Mrs. Overtheway's Remembrances"	Bell & Sons.
An Idyll of the Wood ...	September, 1867 ...	"The Brownies, and other Tales"	"
Three Christmas Trees ...	December, 1867 ...	"	"
Mrs. Overtheway's Remembrances—			
Reka Dom	June, July, August, September, and Oct. 1868	"Mrs. Overtheway's Remembrances"	"
Kerguelen's Land ...	October, 1868 ...	"	"

Title	Date / Source	Collection	Publisher
The Land of Lost Toys	March and April, 1869	"The Brownies, and other Tales"	Bell & Sons.
Kind William and the Water Sprite	November, 1869	"Old-fashioned Fairy Tales"	S.P.C.K.
Christmas Crackers	December, 1869; Jan. 1870	"The Brownies, and other Tales"	Bell & Sons.
Amelia and the Dwarfs	February and March, 1870	,,	,,
The Cobbler and the Ghosts	February, 1870	"Old-fashioned Fairy Tales"	S.P.C.K.
The Nix in Mischief	April, 1870	,,	
Benjy in Beastland	May and June, 1870	"Lob Lie-by-the-Fire, and other Tales"	Bell & Sons.
The Hillman and the Housewife	Aunt Judy's Magazine, May, 1870	"Old-fashioned Fairy Tales"	S.P.C.K.
The Neck	June, 1870	,,	,,
Under the Sun	July, 1870		
The First Wife's Wedding Ring	August, 1870	"Old-fashioned Fairy Tales"	S.P.C.K.
The Magic Jar	September, 1870	,,	,,
Snap Dragons	Monthly Packet, Christmas Number, 1870	"Snapdragons" ,,	,,
Timothy's Shoes	Aunt Judy's Magazine, November, December, 1870; January, 1871	"Lob Lie-by-the-Fire, and other Tales"	Bell & Sons.
A Flat Iron for a Farthing	November, 1870, to October, 1871	"A Flat Iron for a Farthing"	,,
The Widows and the Strangers	February, 1871	"Old-fashioned Fairy Tales"	S P.C.K.
The Laird and the Man of Peace	April, 1871	,,	,,
The Blind Hermit and the Trinity Flower	Monthly Packet, May, 1871	"Dandelion Clocks" ,,	,,
The Ogre Courting	Aunt Judy's Magazine, June, 1871	"Old-fashioned Fairy Tales"	,,
The Six Little Girls and the Five Little Pigs	August, 1871		
The Little Master to his Big Dog	September, 1871	"Papa Poodle, and other Pets"	S.P.C.K.
The Peace Egg	December, 1871	"Lob Lie-by-the-Fire, and other Tales"	Bell & Sons.
Six to Sixteen	January to October, 1872	"Six to Sixteen"	,,

TITLE.	FIRST PUBLISHED IN:	SUBSEQUENTLY.	PUBLISHER.
Murdoch's Rath	February, 1872	"Old-fashioned Fairy Tales"	S.P.C.K.
The Magician's Gifts	March, 1872	"	"
Knave and Fool	June, 1872		Bell & Sons.
The Miller's Thumb	November, 1872, to October, 1873	"Jan of the Windmill. A Story of the Plains"	"
Ran Away to Sea	November, 1872	"Songs for Music, by Four Friends."	King & Co.
Among the Merrows	November, 1872	"Brothers of Pity, and other Tales"	S.P.C.K.
The Willow Man	December, 1872	"Tongues in Trees"	"
The Fiddler in the Fairy Ring	January, 1873	"Old-fashioned Fairy Tales"	"
A Friend in the Garden	January, 1873	"Verses for Children," vol. ix.	
In Memoriam—Margaret Gatty	November, 1873	"Parables from Nature." (Complete edition.)	Bell & Sons.
Madam Liberality	*Aunt Judy's Magazine*, December, 1873	"A Great Emergency, and other Tales"	"
Old Father Christmas	*Little Folks*	"Lob Lie-by-the-Fire, and other Tales," 1873	"
Lob Lie-by-the-Fire		(Illustrated by R. Caldecott.)	"
Our Garden	*Aunt Judy's Magazine*, March, 1874	"Our Garden"	S.P.C.K.
Dolly's Lullaby	April, 1874	"Baby, Puppy, and Kitty"	"
The Blue Bells on the Lea	May, 1874	"The Blue Bells on the Lea"	"
May Day, Old Style and New Style	May, 1874	"Miscellanea," vol. xviii.	
A Great Emergency	June to October, 1874	"A Great Emergency, and other Tales"	Bell & Sons
The Dolls' Wash	September, 1874	"The Dolls' Wash"	S.P.C.K.
Three Little Nest-Birds	October, 1874	"Three Little Nest-Birds"	"
A very Ill-tempered Family	December, 1874, to March, 1875	"A Great Emergency, and other Tales"	Bell & Sons.

Songs for Music, by Four Friends ...	"Songs for Music, by Four Friends," H. King & Co., 1874.	"Verses for Children, and Songs for Music," vol. ix. — S.P.C.K
Ah! Would I Could Forget ...		
The Elleree. A Song of Second Sight		
Faded Flowers ...		
Fancy Free. A Girl's Song ...		
From Fleeting Pleasures. A Requiem for One Alive		
How Many Years Ago?		
The Lily of the Lake ...		
Madrigal ...		
Maiden with the Gipsy Look		
My Lover's Gift ...		
Other Stars ...		
The Runaway's Return, or Ran Away to Sea		
Serenade ...		
Speed Well ...		
Teach Me ...		
With a Difference ...		
{Anemones ...} left in MS.		
{Autumn Leaves}	(From the Danish.)	
Cousin Peregrine's Wonder Stories.—	Aunt Judy's Magazine.—	
The Chinese Jugglers ...	March, 1875	"Miscellanea," vol. xvii. — S.P.C.K
Waves of the Great South Sea	—— May, 1875 ...	,,
Jack of Pera ...	—— July, 1875 ...	,,
Little Woods ...	—— August, 1875...	,,
Good Luck is Better than Gold	—— August, 1875...	"Old-fashioned Fairy Tales" ,,
A Hero to his Hobby Horse...	—— October, 1875	"Little Boys and Wooden Horses" ,,
The Kyrkegrim turned Preacher	—— November, 1875	"Dandelion Clocks" ,,
Hints for Private Theatricals	—— November and December, 1875; February, 1876	"The Peace-Egg," vol. x. ,,
Toots and Boots ...	—— January, 1876	"Brothers of Pity, and other Tales of Beasts and Men" ,,
The Blind Man and the Talking Dog	—— February, 1876	"Dandelion Clocks" ,,

TITLE.	FIRST PUBLISHED IN :	SUBSEQUENTLY.	PUBLISHER.
The Princes of Vegetation	April, 1876	"Miscellanea," vol. xvii.	S.P.C.K.
I Won't	April, 1876	"Old-fashioned Fairy Tales"	"
Father Hedgehog and His Neighbours	June to August, 1876	"Brothers of Pity, and other Tales"	"
House Building and Repairs	June, 1876		
An Only Child's Tea-Party	July, 1876	"Doll's Housekeeping"	"
Dandelion Clocks	August, 1876	"Dandelion Clocks, and other Tales"	Bell & Sons.
Our Field	September, 1876	"A Great Emergency, and other Tales"	
Papa Poodle	September, 1876	"Papa Poodle, and other Pets"	S.P.C.K.
A Week Spent in a Glass Pond	October, 1876	"A Week Spent in a Glass Pond"	Wells, Darton, & Co.
Big Smith	October, 1876	"Little Boys and Wooden Horses"	S.P.C.K.
The Magician turned Mischief-Maker	November, 1876	"Old-fashioned Fairy Tales"	"
A Bad Habit	January, 1877	"Melchior's Dream, and other Tales"	Bell & Sons, 1885.
Brothers of Pity	April, 1877	"Brothers of Pity, and other Tales"	S.P.C.K.
Kit's Cradle	April, 1877	"Baby, Puppy, and Kitty"	"
Ladders to Heaven	May, 1877	"Dandelion Clocks," &c.	"
Boy and Squirrel	June, 1877	"Tongues in Trees"	"
Master Fritz	August, 1877	"Master Fritz"	"
A Sweet Little Dear	September, 1877	"A Sweet Little Dear"	"
We and the World	November, 1887, to June, 1878, and April to October, 1879	"We and the World"	Bell & Sons.
The Yellow Fly	December, 1877	"Baby, Puppy, and Kitty"	S.P.C.K.
So-so	September, 1878	"Dandelion Clocks," &c.	"
Flaps	Aunt Judy's Magazine, January, 1879	"Brothers of Pity, and other Tales"	"
Canada Home	January, 1879	"Verses for Children," &c, vol. ix.	"
Garden Lore	March, 1879		"
A Soldier's Children	July, 1879	"A Soldier's Children"	"
Jackanapes	October, 1879	"Jackanapes"	"

Title	Date	Published in	Publisher
Grandmother's Spring...	June, 1880	"Grandmother's Spring"	S.P.C.K.
Touch Him if You Dare	July, 1880	"Touch Him if you Dare"	,,
The Mill Stream	August, 1881...	"The Mill Stream"	,,
Blue and Red; or, the Discontented Lobster	September, 1881	"Blue and Red," &c....	,,
Daddy Darwin's Dovecote	November, 1881	"Daddy Darwin's Dovecote"	,,
Laetus Sorte Meâ: or, the Story of a Short Life	May to October, 1882	"The Story of a Short Life"	,,
Sunflowers and a Rushlight	November, 1882	"Mary's Meadow," &c., vol. xvi.	,,
The Poet and the Brook	January, 1883	"The Poet and the Brook"	,,
Mother's Birthday Review	April, 1883	"Mother's Birthday Review"	,,
Convalescence ...	May, 1883	"Convalescence" ...	,,
A Happy Family	September, 1883	"Melchior's Dream, and other Tales"	Bell & Sons.
Mary's Meadow	November, 1883, to March, 1884	"Mary's Meadow, and other Tales"	S.P.C.K.
The Peace Egg. A Christmas Mumming Play	January, 1884	"The Peace Egg," &c.	,,
Letters from a Little Garden	November, 1884, to February, 1885	"Mary's Meadow, and other Tales"	,,
Tiny's Tricks and Toby's Tricks	Child's Pictorial Magazine, May, 1885	"Brothers of Pity, and other Tales," vol. xii.	,,
The Owl in the Ivy Bush; or, the Children's Bird of Wisdom.—Introduction	June, 1885	,,	,,
— Owlhoot I.	July, 1885	,,	,,
— Owlhoot II.	August, 1885...	,,	,,

TRANSLATIONS.

Title	Source	Published in
A Child's Wishes	From the German of R. Reinick	Aunt Judy's Magazine, 1866.
War and the Dead	From the French of Jean Macé	October, 1866.
Tales of the Khoja	From the Turkish	April to December, 1874.
The Adventures of an Elf	Adapted from the German	November and December, 1875.
The Snarling Princess	Adapted from the German	December, 1875.
The Little Parsnip Man	Adapted from the German	January, 1876.

LETTERS

To Miss E. Lloyd.

Ecclesfield. August 19, 1864.

My Dearest Eleanor,

It is with the greatest pleasure that I "sit down" and square my elbows to answer one question of your letter. The one about the Liturgical Lessons. Nothing (I find) is more difficult in this short life than to emulate John's example—and "explain my meaning!" but I will do my best. Beloved! In the first place I am going to do what I hope will be more to your benefit than my credit! Send you my rough notes. If you begin at the first page and read straight ahead to where allusion is made to the Apocryphal Lessons, you will have my first Course, and you will see that I was working by degrees straight through the Morning Prayer. But then (like the Turnip Tom-toddies!) we found that "the Inspector was coming"—and though the class was pretty well getting up "Matins"—it knew very little about the Prayer-book—so then I took a different tack. We left off minutiæ and Bible references and took to a sort of general sketch of the whole Prayer-book. For this I did not make fresh notes at the time—but when the Inspector came and I being too ill to examine them—M. did it—I wrote out in a hurry the questions and answers that follow the Apocrypha point for her benefit. My dear old Eleanor—I am such a bad hand myself—that I feel it perfectly ludicrous to attempt to help you—but here are a few results of my limited experience which are probably all wrong—but the best I have to offer!

Don't teach all the school.

Make up a "Liturgical Class" (make a favour of it if possible) of mixed boys and girls.

Have none that cannot read.

XVIII. 10

Tell them to bring their Prayer-books with them on the "Liturgy Day."

If any of them say they have none—let nothing induce you to supply them.

Say "Well, you must look over your neighbour, but you ought to have one for yourself—I can let you have one for 2*d*., so when you go home, 'ask Papa,' and bring me the 2*d*. next time."

Never give the Prayer-book "in advance"——! (I never *pressed* the Prayer-books on them, or insisted on their having them. But gradually they all wanted to have them, and I used to take them with me, and they brought up their 2*d*.'s if they wanted any. The class is chiefly composed of Dissenters, but they never have raised any objection, and buy Prayer-books for children who never come to Church. The first prize last time was very deservedly won by the daughter of the Methodist Minister.)

If you know any that cannot afford them, give them in private.

Deal round the School Bibles to the Class for reference.

One's chief temptation is to attempt too much. The great art is to make a good *skeleton* lesson of the leading points, and fill in afterwards.

Wait a long time for your answers.

Repeat the question as simply as possible, and keep saying—Now *think—think.* One generally gets it in time.

Lead up to your answer: thus—

Eleanor. "S. Augustine was a missionary Priest from—now answer all together?"

The whole Class. Rome.

Eleanor. "Now who was S. Augustine?—All together."

The result probably will be that one or perhaps two will give the whole answer—and then you can say—

"That's right. But I want you all to say it. Now all together. Who was S. Augustine?"

Then you will get it from all.

If you don't mind it, the black board is often of great use, In this way—

[*Sketch.*] **X** represents the black board.

Suppose you have undertaken for the day's lesson (a *long* one!) to begin at the question of whether we know the exact date of the first introduction of Christianity into England and to go on to S. Augustine's Consecration. When you first arrive take your chalk and write—

S. PAUL

and draw a line ;

then

ARLES	.	.	.	. 314
NICÆA	.	.	.	. 323

AUGUSTINE
ROME
ARCHBISHOP OF CANTERBURY
597

Make them read everything as you write it, telling them the words till they are familiar. Then "lead up to" the written words in your questions and point with the stick, so that they will finish the answer by reading it *all together*. Thus—"The Council of—— (stick to Arles) in the year—— (stick to 314)."

When you are *teaching* a thing, make them answer all together. When you are examining what you have taught before, let those answer who can.

Of course my *notes* give no idea of the way one teaches. I mean of course one has perpetually to use familiar examples, and go back and back—and *into* things.

Put the more backward children *behind* the others, and never let any of the *front row* answer till the back row have tried.

If they are very young or backward, perhaps before you attempt anything like Church History, you might *familiarize* them with the Prayer-book services—by making them find the places in their proper rotation—turn quickly to the Psalms for the Day. Make them find the Lessons for the Day, for Holy-days—Collect for the week—Baptism Service. In fact I should advise you to *begin* so. Say for the first Lesson you take a CHRISTMAS DAY Service—make them look out everything in succession. Ask them what a Collect is—where the Lessons come from—who wrote the Psalms, etc. Make them understand how the Holy Communion is administered—suppose a Baptism—and make them explain—the two 'Sacraments in the words of the Catechism. (Never mind whether they understand it—one can't explain everything at once!)

Indeed I strongly advise you to go on this tack for some time.

Say that for the first lesson or two (the above is too advanced) you take *the Psalms*. Ask them what Book they were taken from, etc.—make them find them for the day, and show them where and how to find the Proper Psalms. In succeeding lessons, if you like, you can explain that the Psalms are translations—and why the Bible and Prayer-book versions are different—show which are the seven Penitential—(the three Morning and three Evening for Ash Wednesday and the 51st). Point out the latter as used as a general confession in the Commination Service—having been written on the occasion of David's fall. Also the Psalms of Degrees (the most exquisite of all I think!), which were used to be sung as the Jews came up from all parts of the land to Jerusalem—" I was glad when they said unto me," etc.

Tell them of any Psalms authentically connected with History—and any anecdotes or traditions that you can meet with connected with them. How S. Augustine and his band of missionaries first encountered the King with his choristers carrying the Cross and chanting Psalms to those Gregorians that Gregory (birch in hand!) had taught him in Rome, etc., etc.

I find they like stray anecdotes—and they are *pegs* to hang things on. (Trevor says that our Blessed Lord is supposed to have repeated the *whole* of the twenty-second Psalm on the Cross.) The " Hymn " sung before they went out after the Last Supper was a Psalm. (See marginal Bible notes.) You can do no greater kindness than give them an appreciation and interest in that inexhaustible store of " Prayer and Penitence and

Praise"—that has put words into the mouth of the whole Church of God from the days of David to the present time, which is used by every Church (however else divided) in common—and rejected by no sect however captious!

Point out what Psalms are used in the course of the services —(like the *Venite*, etc.)

Don't be alarmed if the Psalms last you for months! you can't do better—and you must go over and over unless your bairns are Solomons! Make them understand that they were intended, and are adapted for singing.

Get up your lessons beforehand—but teach as familiarly and as much with no book but the Prayer-book and Bible as you can.

Then you might take the Lessons in a similar fashion, and the Collects, etc.

Excuse all this ramble. I have no doubt I have bored you with a great deal of chaff—but I hardly know quite what you want to know. As to the subject—it is a Hobby with me— so excuse rhapsodies!

I don't believe you can confer a greater kindness than to make them well acquainted with their Prayer-books. I believe you may teach every scrap of necessary theology from it—the Life of Jesus in the Collects, and special services from Advent to Trinity—Practical duties and the *morale* of the Gospel in the twenty-five Sundays of Trinity. Apostles—Martyrs—the Communion of Saints—and the Ministry of Angels in the rest. As to the History of Liturgies—it is simply the History of the Church. I believe the Prayer-book contains Prayer, Praise, Confession, Intercession and Ejaculation fitted to every need and occasion of all conditions of men!—with very rare if any exceptions. I believe in *ignorance* of the Prayer-book the poor lose the greatest fund of instruction and consolation next to the Bible (and it is our best Commentary on that!) that is to be got at. And people's ignorance of it is *wonderful!* You hear complaints of the shifting of the services—the arrangement of the Lessons—and a precious muddle it must seem to any one who does no know—that Isaiah is skipped in the reading of the Old Testament—that as the Evangelical Prophet he may be read at the Advent and Nativity of Christ—that we dip promiscuously into the Apocrypha on Saints' Days—because those books are read "for example of life and instruction of manners" —and not to establish doctrine, etc., etc. Somebody has compiled a straight ahead Prayer-book, and I fancy it will be found very useful—about the same time that we get a royal road to learning—or that services compiled on the most comprehensive and comprehensible system by men of the highest and devoutest intellect for every age, class, sex, and succeeding generations of the Church of a whole country, can be made at the same time to fit the case of every ignoramus who won't take the trouble to do more than lick his thumb and turn over a page ! ! ! If people would but understand that the shortest way to anything is to get at the first principles ! ! When one humbles oneself to learn those, the arrangement of the Liturgy becomes as beautiful and lovable a piece of machinery as that of Nature or God's Providence almost ! and is just as provocative of ignorant complaint and sarcasm if one doesn't.

Oh! Eleanora! What *will* you say to this sermon ! !— My "lastly" is—teach your bairns the "why" their great-great-great- (very great!) Grandfathers put all these glorious Prayers together in their present order—and "when they are old they will not" . . . need any modern wiseacres to help them to get blindfold from the *Venite* to the Proper Psalms.

Adieu, beloved. Post time almost—and another letter to write. I have had a sort of double quinsy—but am better, thank God.

Your devoted and prosy,
JULIANA HORATIA GATTY.

The Books I have used are *Wheatley on the Common Prayer*, Hook's *Lives of the Archbishops*, and *Church Dictionary*, and anything I could get hold of. Get any decent book on the Psalms—compare the two versions—read the *prefaces*, *rubrics*, etc.—above all. Have you the Parker Society edition of Edward VI. Prayer-book ?

To H. K. F. G.

Hotel de l'Europe, Anvers.
September 22, 1865.

MY DEAREST D——,

"Here we are again!" at the Hotel Dr. Harvey recommended. The Captain of our boat said it was cheaper and better than S. Antoine. You must excuse a not very lively letter, for I am still so ill from the voyage. I can't get over it somehow at present, but shall be all right to-morrow. We enjoyed our day in Hull immensely! you will be amused to hear. At night we went to the Harvest Thanksgiving service at S. Mary's. Nice service, capital sermon, and crammed congregation. The decorations were scarlet geraniums, corn, evergreen, and grapes. The *Alster* wasn't to time, but they said she would sail at four, so we slept on board. We "turned over" an awful night. R. and I wandered over the ship, and finally settled on the saloon benches. Then, however, the Captain came, and said he couldn't allow us to sleep there, so we sat up, for I couldn't breathe in the berth, and at last I think the Captain saw I really couldn't stand it, and told me to lie down again. At six we went on deck, and it was awfully jolly going up the Humber. At eight we got into the sea, and I didn't get my "shore legs" again till we got into the Scheldt this morning. At about three this morning I went on deck, and R. and I enjoyed it immensely, splendidly starlight, and we were just off Flushing, and the lights looked wonderful with the flat shore and a black windmill. Then the Captain gave me tea and packed me up in the saloon, and I slept till six, when T. came out and woke me, and we went "aloft." We were going down the Scheldt, and R. was in fits of delight because every tree you see is exactly like the trees in boxes of toys. Not a bit like English trees. The flat green banks and odd little villages (of which you can only see the *tops* of the houses) were charming.

To M. S. G.

Hotel de l'Europe, Antwerp.
Sunday, September 24, 1865.

MY DEAREST M.,
        We are getting on capitally, and enjoying it immensely.
I hope T. got home pretty well. I miss him dreadfully, tell
him—especially to-day—for both Churches and pictures bore
R. However, I have only taken him into one Church to-
day, that of S. Jacques, where he really was pleased to see
the tomb of Rubens. I have found the whereabouts of two
other celebrated ones, and shall try to slip off without him. He
is utterly happy when he has got a cigar, "tooling" up and
down the streets, turning in at a café, or buying a peach, and
doing "schneeze" with the "Flams." He does a little French
now and then with people in the streets. I got into the
Cathedral just in time to see the glorious Descent from the
Cross, and (which I admire less) the Elevation ditto by Rubens.
I must tell you this morning I went to high mass in the Cathedral. In fact I heard two masses and a *sermon in Flemish*. It
was wonderful. A very intelligent-looking old priest in surplice
and stole, in the huge carved pulpit, preached with the most
admirable dramatic force, in a language that one can *all but*
understand. It is so like English and German. Every now
and then I could catch a word. If you want to have an idea of
the congregation, imagine the *nave* of York Minster (the side aisles
rather filled up by altars, etc.)—covered like a swarm of bees,
with a congregation with really rare exceptions of Flemish poor.
Flam women, men, and children, and a great many common
soldiers. The women are dressed in white caps, and all have
scarves (just like funeral scarves) of fine ribbed black silk ; and,
Flemish prayer-books in hand, they sit listening to the sermon.
Then it comes to an end with some invocation of something, at
which there is a scraping of chairs and everybody goes round to
the Altar. Then organ, fiddles, all sorts of instruments, and a
splendid "company" of singers—the musical Mass began.

*   *   *   *   *

It is all wonderful, and I feel laying up a store of happiness in going over it at home. How I wish some of you were here! I know my letters are very dull, and I am *so* sorry. But though I have a famous appetite, and can walk and "sight-see" like anything, I have not got back my *nerve*. Somehow I can't describe it, but you must excuse my stupidity. I hope R. is happy. He says he is, and dreads it coming to an end!!! I am very glad, for I feel a heavy weight on *him*, and *he* feels like reposing on a floating soap-bubble! We are as jolly as possible really, and nothing is left in me, but a rather strained nervous feeling, which will soon be gone. You would have laughed to see R. buying snuff to-day, and cigars. He goes in, lays his finger on the cigars, and says—"Poor wun frank?" To which the woman replies—"treize," and he buys six and sneezes violently, on which she produces snuff, fills his box, and charges a trifle, and he abuses her roundly in English, with a polite face, to his own great enjoyment. We mean to make the cash hold out if possible to come home in the *Alster*. If it runs short, we shall give up Ghent and Bruges—this place alone is worth coming for.

Your ever loving sister, J. II. G.

To H. K. F. G.

Hotel de Vieux, Doellen, The Hague.
September 27, 1865.

DEAREST D——,

This morning we had a great treat! We took an open carriage and drove from the Hague to Scheveningen on the coast. All the way you go through an avenue of elms, which is lovely. It is called "the Wood," and to the left is Sorgoliet, where the Queen mother lives, and which was planted, the man says, by Jacob Cats. He lived there. Scheveningen is a bare-looking shore, all sand, and bordered with sandbanks, or Dunes. It was *fiercely* hot, scorching, and not an atom of shade to be had; but in spite of sun, slipping sandbank-seat, sand-fleas, and a hornet circling round, I did make a sketch,

which I hope to finish at home. Both Regie and I bathed, and
it was *delicious*—an utterly calm sea, and I enjoyed it thoroughly.
The bathing machines seem to be a Government affair. They
and the towels are marked with a *stork*, and you take a ticket
and get your gown and towels from a man at a "bureau" on
the sands. I must tell you, this morning when we came down,
we found breakfasting in the *salle-à-manger* our Dutch friend,
the bulb merchant. We had our breakfast put at his table, and
had a jolly chat. It was so pleasant! Like meeting an old
friend. He has gone, I am sorry to say, but I have made great
friends with Stephanie's father; he cannot speak a word of
English, so we can only talk in such French as I can muster;
but he is very pleasant, and his children are so nice! eight—four
boys and four girls. The wife is Dutch, and I do not think can
speak French, so I do not talk to her. After dinner the *maître
d'hôtel* asked us if we would not go to "the Wood" (on the
road to Scheveningen), and hear the military band—so we
went. I can't describe it. It was like nothing but scenes in
a theatre. Pitch dark in all the avenues, except for little lamps
like tiny tumblers fixed on to the trees, and so [*Sketch*] on to
the Pavilion, which was lighted up by chains of similar lamps
like an illumination—[*Sketch*]—and round which—seated round
little green tables—were gathered, I suppose, about two thousand
people. Their politeness to each other—the perfect good-be-
haviour, the quiet and silence during the music, and the buzz
and movement when it was over, were wonderful. The music
was very good. R. and I had each a tiny cup of coffee, and
a little brandy and water, for it was very cold!! Now I have
come in, and he has gone back, I think. Stephanie was there,
and lots of children. As I lay awake last night I heard the
old watchman go round. He beats two pieces of wood together
and calls the hours of the night. I saw a funeral too, this
morning, and the coachman wears a hat like this—[*Sketch*].
In the streets we have met men in black with cocked hats.
They are "Ansprekers," who go to announce a man's death to
his friends. The jewellery of the common women is marvellous;

Mr. Krelage (our Dutch friend) says they have sometimes
£400 of gold and jewels upon them ! ! ! A common market
woman I saw to-day wore a plate of gold under her cap of this
shape—[*Sketch*]. Then a white [*Sketch*] lace cap. Then a
bonnet highly-trimmed with flowers, and a white feather and
green ribbons; and on her temples filagree gold and pearl,
pins, brooches and earrings; round her neck three gold chains—
one of many little ones together clasped by a gorgeous clasp —
the next supporting a highly-elaborate gold cross—a longer one
still supporting a heart and some other device. She had rings
also, and a short common purple stuff dress which she took up
when she sat down for fear of crushing it ; no shawl and a black
silk apron ! !

Thursday. We have been to the Museum. Below is the
" Royal Cabinet " of curiosities, and above are the pictures.
Some of the former were *very* interesting. The hat, doublet,
etc. in which William the Silent was murdered—the pistol, two
bullets, etc., and a copy of Balthazar Geraardt's condemnation,
and his watch, on which were some beautiful little paintings.
Admiral Ruiter's sabre, armour, chain and medal; Admiral
Tromp's armour; Jacqueline of Bavaria's chair, and locks of her
hair. Also a very curious model—a large baby-house imitating
a Dutch *ménage*, intended by Peter the Great as a present to
his wife. A wonderful toy !! R. was quite at home among
the " relics." Besides historical relics, the cabinet contains the
most marvellous collection of Japanese things. It is a most
choice collection. There were some such funny things—a *fiancé*
and *fiancée* of Japan in costume were killing ! and made up
monsters like life-sized mummies of the most hideous demons!
Besides indescribably exquisite workmanship of all sorts. The
pictures are not so charming a collection as those at Antwerp,
but there are some grand ones. Tell Mother—Paul Potter's
Bull is too indescribable ! His nose, his hair, and a frog at
his feet are wonderful ! There is a portrait by Rubens of his
second wife that would have charmed T. ; she is *lovely*, and
the picture has that *sunshiny* beauty he will remember in

"S. Anne teaching the B. V. M." I suspect she was the model for his most lovable faces.   There is a large and wonderful Rembrandt—a splendid collection of Wouvermans—the most charming Ruisdael I ever saw.   Some beautiful Vandykes—a Van de Velde of Scheveningen, Teniers, Weenix, Snyders, etc. I do so wish M. could see the pictures, she would enjoy them so, and get more out of them than I can.   The collection is *free* to the public, and the utmost good behaviour prevails. After that R. went into the town, and I sat down to a hurried sketch on the "Vyfeiberg," a quiet sort of promenade. But gradually the populace collected, till I was nearly smothered. My veil blew over my face, and I suddenly felt it seized from behind, and looking round, found that a young baker in white had laid hold of it, but only to fasten it out of my way, as he began volubly to explain in Dutch!   I couldn't speak, so remonstrance was impossible, and I let them alone.   Soldiers, boys, women, etc.!   I could hear them recognizing the various places.   They were very polite, kept out of my line of sight, and decided that it was "Photōgeraphēē" like the people in Rotterdam!   When we parted, I bowed to them and they to me!!!   To-morrow we go back to Rotterdam for one night, the next day to Antwerp.

Friday night.   Michaelmas Day.   Hotel Pay Bas, Rotterdam.—Back again! and to-morrow at 8.15 a.m. we go back to dear old Antwerp.   For the solemn fact has made itself apparent, that the money will not hold out till to-morrow week, as we intended.   So we must give up our dear Captain, and come home in the *Tiger!!*   We shall be with you D.V. on Saturday week, starting on Wednesday from Antwerp.   We have been to the Poste Restante, and got dear Mother's letter, to my infinite delight.   I am so glad Miss Yonge likes "the Brownies."

                                        Your ever loving, JUDY

To Mrs. Gatty.

Sevenoaks. January 12, 1866.

My Dear, Dear Mother,

I do humbly beg your pardon for having written such scrappish, snappish, selfish letters! The tide of comfort has begun to set in from Ecclesfield to my infinite delight. So far from being vexed at your being so careful—I earnestly hope you will never be less so. If you had been, *I* should have been dead long ago. I have no more doubt than of my present well-being. And as it is—taking care is so little in my line—that if *you* took to *ignoring* one's delicacy, or fancying it was fancy—I know I should merely (by instinct) hold out to the last gasp of existence, and do *what* I could, *while* I could ! ! . . .

I am cheered beyond anything with these critiques on " The Brownies." I must tell you I have read Aunt Mary the beginning of my new story, and she likes it very much. It will be longer than " The Brownies." . . . I am writing most conscientiously—it will not be a bit longer than it should be, but naturally of itself will spread into a good deal. In fact, it is several stories together—a *Russian* one among them (" Mrs. Overtheway's Remembrances ").

To A. E.

Ecclesfield. May 28, 1866.

I send you a song,* " which is not very long "—and that is about its only merit. I am utterly disgusted with it myself for producing nothing better. . . . However, here it is, and now I must explain it.

I have endeavoured to bear in mind three things—simplicity of idea, few verses, and a musical swing. I have constructed it so that one child's voice may sing for the Child, another child's voice for the Bird, and as many children as you please in the Chorus.

The " Hush! hush! hush! " I thought ought to have a piano effectiveness, and it is a word children enjoy.

---

* " The Promise " : " Verses for Children." Vol. ix. Set to music by Alexander Ewing.—*Aunt Judy's Magazine*, July 1866.

The Promise.

Child.

Five blue eggs hatching,
With bright eyes watching,
Little brown mother, you sit on your nest.

Bird.

Oh ! pass me blindly,
Oh ! spare me kindly,
Pity my terror, and leave me to rest.

Chorus of Children.

Hush ! hush ! hush !
'Tis a poor mother thrush.
When the blue eggs hatch, the brown birds will sing—
This is a promise made in the spring.

Child.

Five speckled thrushes,
In leafy bushes,
Singing sweet songs to the hot summer sky.
In and out twitting,
Here and there flitting,
Happy in life as the long days go by.

Chorus.

Hush ! hush ! hush !
'Tis the song of the thrush :
Hatched are the blue eggs, the brown birds do sing—
Keeping the promise made in the spring.

If you liked, one voice, or half the party, might sing, "When
the blue eggs hatch," and the other, "The brown birds will
sing." Some are doubtful about the last lines, but the word
"promise" had a jubilant musical rhythm in my head. However, you can alter it, if it has not the same in yours. . . . I

don't set up for a versifier, and you may do what you please with this.

There is a certain class of child's song which is always taught in the National system by certificated infant school mistresses. They are semi-theatrical, very pretty, and serve at once as music, discipline, and amusement. Such as "The Clock," in which they beat the hours, swing for the pendulum, etc. There are certain actions in these songs which express listening. . . . I am very fond of the National system for teaching children, and it has struck me that this song is a little of that type. . . . I am doubly vexed it is so poor, because your next thing to "Jerusalem the Golden" ought to be very good. If you can, make your Processional Hymn very grand, and I will do my very best. I have more hope of that. Would the metre of Longfellow's "Coplas de Manrique" be good for music? It would be a fine hymn measure. . . . Don't hamper yourself about the metre. I will fit the words to the music.

To Mrs. Gatty.

S.S. China. June 10, 1867.

I staggered up yesterday morning to have my first sight of an iceberg. . . The sea was dark-blue, a low line of land (Cape Race) was visible, and the iceberg stood in the distance dead white, like a lump of sugar. . . I think the first sight of Halifax was one of the prettiest sights I ever saw. When I first came up there was no horizon, we were in a sea of mist. Gradually the horizon line appeared—then a line of low coast—muddy-looking at first—it soon became marked with lines of dark wood—then the shore dotted with grey huts—then the sun came out—the breeze got milder—and the air became strongly redolent of pine-woods. Nearer, the coast became more defined, though still low, rather bare, and dotted with brushwood, and grey stones low down, and crowned always with "murmuring pines." As we came to habitations, which are dotted, and sparkle along the shore, the effect was what we noticed in Belgium, as if a box of very bright new toys had been put out to play with, red roofs—even red houses—cardboard-looking churches—little bright wooden houses—and stiffish trees mixed everywhere. It looks more like a quaint watering-place than a city, though there are some fine buildings. . . We took a great fancy to the place, which was like a new child's picture book, and I was rather disappointed to learn it is not to be our home. But Fredericton, where we are going, has superior advantages in some respects, and will very likely be quite as pretty.

Halifax. June 19, 1867.

*   *   *   *   *

Rex and I went down to the fish-market that I might see it. Coming back we met an old North American Indian woman. Such a picturesque figure. We talked to her, and Rex gave her something. I do not think it half so degraded-looking a type as they say. A very broad, queer, but I think acute and pleasant-looking face. Since I came in I have made two rather successful sketches of her.* She wore an old common striped shawl, but curiously thrown round her so that it looked like a chief's blanket, a black cap embroidered with beads, black trousers stuffed into moccasins, a short black petticoat, and a large gold-coloured cross on her breast, and a short jacket trimmed with scarlet, a stick and basket for broken victuals. She said she was going to catch the train! It sounded like hearing of Plato engaged for a polka! . . .

---

* See pages 175, 176.

To Miss E. Lloyd.

[*Sketch.*]
Cathedral Church of Fredericton, New Brunswick.

August 23, 1867.

My Dearest Old Eleanora,

I have been a wretch for not having written to you sooner. It seems strange there should remain any pressure of business or hurry of life in this place, where workmen look out of the windows of the house (our house and a fact !); they are repairing nine at a time, and boys swing their buckets and dawdle to the well for water, as if Time couldn't be lounged and coaxed off one's hands ! ! And yet busy I have been, and every mail has been a scramble. Getting into our house was no joke, attending sales and shops, buying furniture—ditto, ditto—as to paying and receiving calls on lovely days with splendid sketching lights—they have been thorns in the flesh—and, worst of all, regular colonial experiences of servants—one went off at a day's notice—and for two or three days we had *nobody* but Rex's *orderly*, such a handy, imperturbable soldier, who made beds, cooked the dinner, hung pictures, and blew the organ with equal urbanity. He didn't know much—and in the imperfect state of our cuisine had few appliances—but he affected to be *au fait* at everything—and what he had not got, he "annexed" from somewhere else. One of our maids uniformly set tumblers and wine-glasses with the tea set, and I found "William" the Never-at-fault cleaning the plate with knife-powder, and brushing his own clothes with the shoe brush. However, we have got a very fair maid now, and are comfortable enough. Our house is awfully jolly, though the workmen are yet about. The drawing-room really is not bad. It is a good-sized room with a day window—green carpet and sofa in the recess—window plant shelf—on one long side of the wall—a writing-table between two book-shelves—and oh ! my dear, I cannot sufficiently say the *pleasure* as well as *use* and *comfort* all my wedding presents have been to me. You can hardly estimate the comforting effect of these dear bits of civilization out here, especially at first when we were less comfortable.   But the *refinements* of comfort, you know, are not to be got here for love or money as we get them at home.   Your dear book and inkstand and weights (uncommonly useful at this juncture of new postage), etc., look so well on my writing-table—on which are also the Longleys' Despatch Box—Frank Smith's blotting book—my Japanese bronzes, Indian box, Chinese ditto, Japanese candlestick and Chinese shoes, etc. of Rex's—our standing photos, table bookstand, etc., etc.   You can't imagine how precious any knickknacks have become.   My mother's coloured photo that Brownie gave me is propped in the centre—and we have bought a mahogany bracket for my old Joan of Arc ! !   We have hired a good harmonium.   Altogether the room really looks pretty with a fawn-coloured paper and the few water colours up—round table, etc., etc.   Our bedroom has a blue and white paper, is a bright, airy, two-windowed room, with a *lovely* eastward view over the river—the willows—and the pine woods.   Our abundant space mocks one's longing to invite a good many dear old friends to visit one !   We have much to be thankful for—which excellent sentiment brings me to the Cathedral.   It would be a fine, well-appointed Church even in Europe.   It stands lovelily looking over the river, surrounded by maples, etc., etc. (and to the left a beautiful group of the "feathered elms" of the country).   There is daily Morning Prayer at 7.30, to which we generally go, and where the Bishop always appears.   There is a fair amateur choir, and a beautiful organ built by a man who died just when he had completed it.   But, my dear, in addition to these privileges, we weekly "sit under" the most energetic, quaint-looking, and dignified of Bishops—who has a clear, soft, penetrating voice that rings down the Cathedral in the Absolution and Benediction, and who preaches such fine, able, practical, learned, and beautiful sermons —as I really do not think Oxon, or Vaughan, or any of our great men much excel.   This would be nearly enough, even if one did not know him ; but when we dined at Government House the other night—rather to my surprise, I was sent in with him, and found him very

amusing, and full of funny anecdotes of the province. Since
when we have rapidly become fast friends. He is very musical,
and when he and Rex get nobbling over the piano and organ—
there they stick!! Rex is appointed supplementary organist,
and to-morrow (being their Annual Festival) he is to play.
Last night we had a grand "practice" at the Bishop's, and it
felt wonderfully like home. He has lots of books, and has put
them at our disposal—and, to crown all, has offered to teach us
Hebrew if we will teach him German this winter. His wife is
very nice too. . . . She is a good practical doctor, kind
without measure, and being a great admirer of Mother's writings, has taken me under her wing—to see that I do nothing
contrary to the genius of the climate! People are wonderfully
kind here. They really keep us in vegetables, and I have a
lovely nosegay on my table at this moment. There is a very
pleasant Regiment (22nd) here, with a lovely band. On my
birthday Rex gave me Asa Gray's *Botany*, a book on botany
generally, and on North American plants in particular. Some
of the wild-flowers are lovely. One (Pigeon Berry) [*sketch*] has
a white flower amid largish leaves—thus. It grows about as large
as wild anemone, in similar places and quantities. When the
flower falls the stamens develop into a thick *bunch* of *berries*,
the size and colour of holly berries, only *brighter* brilliant
scarlet, and patches of pine wood are covered with them.

My dear, you *would* like this place! My best love to all your
people. Isabel's fan could have no more appropriate field for
its exhibition than summer here! Adieu, beloved. (I say nothing
about home news. Z.'s affair bewilders me. I am awfully
anxious for news, but it's useless talking at this distance.) (See
Lamb's Essay on Distant Correspondents in the Elia !!!!!)

Your ever loving,

J. H. EWING.

To Mrs. Gatty.

Fredericton. September 21, 1867.

My Dearest Mother,

The room being rather warm (with a fire!) and having been very busy all day sketching, etc., etc., and having just done my Hebrew lesson in a sleepyish sort of manner—I have turned lazy about working at Mrs. Overtheway to-night, and am going to get on with my letter instead.   Rex is mouthing Hebrew gutturals at my elbow, so don't be astonished if I introduce the "*yatz, yotz, yomah,*" etc., that sound in my ears!   I must tell you we have actually despatched a small parcel to Ecclesfield. We crossed early one day by the ferry, and went to the Indian settlement, where we bought a small and simple basket of a squaw which she had just made, and which shows their work, and will hold a few of your odds and ends.   We send M. a little card-case of Indian work, and R. a cigar-case.   These two things are worked by Huron Indians in stained moose hair. The Melicites who are *here* work in basket-work and in coloured beads.   I got two strips of their coloured bead-work, and Sarah and I "ran up" two red velvet bags and trimmed them with these strips for tobacco bags for A. and S.   I thought you would like to see the different kinds of work.   The MicMacs work in stained porcupine, but I have not sent any of their work.   They are only very little things, but they come from *us!* We have had so much to do, I have got on very badly with my botanizing, but I have sent one or two ferns for you. We were late for flowers.   Tell S. the *Impatiens Fulva* is a wonderful flower.   When you touch (almost when you *shake* with approaching) the seed vessels, they burst and curl up like springs, and fling the seed away.   I mean to try to preserve seed.   The *Chelone Glabra* as pressed by me gives no idea of the beautiful dead-white flower, something like a foxglove only more compact.   I have told you what the parcel contains that you may not expect greater things than will appear from our little Christmas Box ! . . .

To-day has been lovely and we have enjoyed it.   Rex has

been with me all day, though when I speak of his being with me I speak of his bodily presence only. In spirit he is with the conjugations Kal, Highil, etc., etc. He has bought Gesenius' Grammar, and a very fine one it seems. He lives with Gesenius, and if he doesn't take it to bed, it is not that he leaves Hebrew in the drawing-room. He undresses to the tune of the latest exercise, and puts me through the imperfect and perfect of חָתַ before we get up of mornings! (He has just discovered that Eden was about the same latitude as Fredericton!) There is always Morning Prayer and Holy Communion here on Saints' Days, and to-day being S. Matthew, we went to the 11 service. After Church we went a little way up the road, and I did a sepia sketch of "our street," Rex sitting by me and groaning Hebrew. It was gloriously sunny, and such a lovely sky, and such an exquisitely calm river with white-sailed boats on it. I have enjoyed it immensely. . .

Fredericton. 19th Sunday after Trinity, 1867.

* * * * * *

I wonder if I send it by next mail, whether you would have room for a very short Christmas sort of prose Idyll suggested to me by a scene I saw when we were hunting for a sketch the other day. If I can jot it down, I don't suppose it would be more than two or three pages. If I send it at all it will come by the Halifax mail. It will be called "The Two Christmas Trees." . . .

To H. K. F. G.

September 29, 1867.

. . . I have fallen head over ears in love with another dog. Oh! bless his nose! . . . His name is Hector. He is a *white* pure bull-dog. His face is more broad and round—and delicious and ferociously good-natured—and affectionately ogreish —than you can imagine. The moment I saw him I hugged him and kissed his benevolence bump, and he didn't even *gowly powl.* . . .

To Mrs. Gatty.

[Fredericton, 1867 ?]

. . . . Talking of stories, if I only can get the full facts of his history, I think I shall send A. J. M. a short paper on a Fredericton Dog. Did I ever tell you of him? He has the loveliest face I ever saw, I think, *in any Christian.* He knows us quite well when we go up the High Street where he lives. When he gets two cents (1*d.*) given him, he takes it in his mouth to the nearest store and buys himself buscuits. I have seen him do it. If you only give him *one* cent he is dissatisfied, and tries to get the second. The Bishop told me he used to come to Church with his master at one time ; he would come and behave very well—TILL the offertory. Then he rose and *walked after the alms-collectors,* wagging his tail as the money chinked in, because he wanted his penny for his biscuits ! ! ! He is a large dog—part St. Bernard, and has magnificent eyes. But (my *poor !*) they shaved him this summer like a poodle ! There is a bear in the officers' quarters here—he belongs to the regiment. I have patted him, but he catches at one's clothes. To see him *patting* at my skirts with his paw was delicious—but I don't like his *head,* he looks very sly !

January 2, 1868.

. . . Indeed it is hard not to be able to see each other at any moment and to be "parted" even for a time. But to us all, who all enjoy everything to be seen and heard, and heard of in new places and among other people ; the fact that I have to lead a traveller's life gives us certain great pleasures we could not have had if Rex had been a curate at Worksop (we'll say), and we couldn't even afford a trip to the Continent ! Also if I have any gift for writing it really *ought* to improve under circumstances so much more favourable than the narrowing influence of a small horizon. . . I only wish my gift were a little nearer *real* genius ! ! As it is, I do hope to improve gradually ; and as I *do* work slowly and conscientiously, I may honestly look forward with satisfaction to the hope of being able to turn a few honest pennies to help us out : and it *is* a satisfaction, and a blessing I am thankful for. I only wish I could please myself better ! However, small writers are wanted as well as big ones, and there is no reason why donkey-carts shouldn't drive even if there are coaches on the road ! . . .

[*Fredericton.*] February 3, 1868.

*   *   *   *   *   *

I am so infinitely obliged to you for your wisdom *in re* Reka Dom, and very thankful for the criticisms, to which I shall attend. I mean to compress it very much. I will keep the river part, though that is really the shadow of some of my best writing, I think, in the *Dutch* tale describing that scene at Topsham. I wrote a good bit last night, and was much wishing for the returned MS. But the sight of the proof will help me more than anything. I lose all judgment of my own work in MS. I feel as if it must be as laborious to read as it has been to write. Whereas in print it comes freshly on me, and I can criticize it more fairly. It will not be very long when all is done, I think, and I am so anxious to make it good, I hope it will be satisfactory. A little praise really does help one to work, and I don't think makes one a bit less conscientious.

It has been a very jolly mail this time, though the Lexicon has not come. The Bishop's is getting worn with use, for Rex does his daily chapter with unfailing regularity, and is murmuring Hebrew at my elbow at this moment as usual. Mr. James McCombie, the uncle who lives in Aberdeen, the lawyer, has sent me such a pretty book of photographs of Aberdeen ! with a kind message about my letter to the poor old Mother, and asking me to write to them. I had asked for a photo of the old Cathedral graveyard where Rex's parents and brother and sister are buried, and there is a lovely one of it, but it is a set of views of Aberdeen, very good photos, and a very pretty book. All Rex's old haunts. Isn't it nice?

[*Sketch of Old Machar Cathedral.*]

*   *   *   *   *

[*Fredericton.*]   April 4, 1868.

I hoped to have sent you the whole of Reka Dom this mail. But a most unexpected fall of snow has made the travelling so insecure that it is considered a risk to wait till Monday, and I must send off what I can to-day. It is so nearly done that I am not now afraid to send off the first part (which will be more than you will want for May), and you may rely on the rest by next mail; and the remainder of Mrs. O. as rapidly as possible. It has certainly given me a wonderful amount of bother this time, and I was disappointed in the feeling that Rex did not think it quite up to my other things. But to-day in reading it all, and a lot that he had not seen before, I heard him laughing over it by himself, and he thinks it now one of my best, so I am in great spirits, and mean to finish it with a flourish if possible. I have cut and carved and clipped till I lost all sense of what was fit to remain, and Rex has insisted on a good deal being replaced.

*   *   *   *   *

Fredericton.   April 17, 1868.

*   *   *   *   *

The Squaw has been making the blotting-case, and Peter brought it to-day, and I am very much pleased with it and hope M. will like it. I would like to have got an envelope case and a canoe, but they are so difficult to pack, and it would be so aggravating to have them broken, so we got a few flat things. The blotting-case and moccasins, and a cigar-case for F., and a tiny pair of snow-shoes. The blotting-case is a good specimen, as it is made of the lovely birch bark; and they were all got direct from Indians we know. A squaw with a sad face of rather a nigh type called to beg the other day. She could hardly speak English. She said, "Sister, me no ate to-day;" so I gave her some bread-and-butter, which she gave at once to the boy with her, and went away.

We have had some splendid Auroras lately. They are not *rosy* here, but very beautiful otherwise, and very capricious in shape, long grand tongues of light shooting up into the sky.

* * * * * *

We are beginning now to talk of "Mayflower expeditions." I think I shall give one to a few select friends. I had thought of a child's one, but a nice old school-mistress here gives one for children, and I think one raid of the united juvenile population on the poor lovely flowers is enough. The Mayflower is a lovely wax-like ground creeper with an exquisite perfume. It is the first flower, and is to be found before the snow has left the woods. . . .

May 12, 1868.

. . . I have a wonderful lot of gardening on my shoulders, for we have no *gardener*—only get a soldier to work in the kitchen garden—so I have had to make my plans and arrange my crops for the kitchen garden, as well as look after my own. We have really two *charming* bits—a little, hot, sunny, good soil, vegetable plot—and quite away from this—by the house, my flower garden. Two round beds and four borders, with a high fence and two little gates. I have nearly got this tidy. The last occupant had never used it. It is a *great* enjoyment to me, and does me great good, I think, by keeping me out of doors. Rexie has given me a dear little set of tools—French ones, like children's toys, but quite enough for me. They form the subject of one of the little rhymes that Hector and I make together, and that I croon to the bull-doge to his great satisfaction.

> " The little Missus with the little spade
> Two little beds in the little garden has made.

The Bull-doge watches (for he can't work)
How she turns up the earth with her little fork.
Then she takes up the little hoe
And into the weeds doth bravely go.
At last with the smallest of little rakes
Quite smooth and tidy the beds she makes."

Another that was made in bed on the occasion of one of his
raids on my invalid breakfast was—

"'Tis the voice of the Bull-doge, I hear him complain,
'You have fed me but lately : I must grub again.'
As a pauper for pudding—so he for his meat—
Gapes his jaws, and there's nothing a Bull-doge can't eat."

We sing these little songs together—and then I let him look
in the glass, when he gowly powls and barks dreadfully at the
rival *doge*. . .

To H. K. F. G.

May 18, 1868.

. . . I am awfully busy with my garden, and people are
very kind in giving me things. To-morrow we go to the
Rowans, and I am to ransack *his* garden ! I do think the exchange of herbaceous perennials is one of the joys of life. You
can hardly think how delicious it feels to *garden* after six
months of frost and snow. Imagine my feelings when Mrs.
Medley found a bed of seedling bee larkspurs in her garden,
and gave me at least two dozen ! ! ! I have got a whole row of
them along a border, next to which I *think* I shall have migno-
nette and scarlet geraniums alternately. It is rather odd after
writing Reka Dom, that I should fall heir to a garden in which
almost the only "fixture" is a south border of lilies of the
valley ! . . .

To MISS E. LLOYD.

Fredericton, N.B. June 2, 1868.

MY DEAREST ELEANOR—

    *   *   *   *   *   *

I can hardly tell you what a pleasure it is to me to have a garden. The place has never felt so like a home before ! I went into my little flower garden (a separate plat from the other— fenced round, and simply composed of two round beds, and four wooden-edged borders ! and one elm tree) [*sketch*] early this morn- ing, and it seemed so jolly after the long winter. My jonquils are just coming out, and one or two other things. In the elm tree two bright yellow birds were cheeping. I mean to plant scarlet-runners to attract the humming birds. It is something to see fireflies and humming birds in the flesh, one must admit !

    *   *   *   *   *   *

I cannot echo your severe remarks on the Queen, though I am *quite* willing to second your praise of the Prince Consort. Her Most Gracious Majesty is—excuse me—a subject I feel rather strongly about. We are not—as an age—guilty of much weakness in the way of over loyalty to anything or any person, and I cannot help at times thinking that it must be a painful enough reflection to a woman like Queen Victoria, who at any rate is as well read in the history and constitution of England as most of us, to know what harvests of love and loyalty have been reaped by Princes who lived for themselves and not for their people, who were fortunate in the accidents of more power and less conscience, and of living in times when you couldn't get your sovereign's portrait for a penny, or suggest to the loyal and well-behaved Commons that if the King's health was not equal to all that you thought fit, you would rather he abdicated. When one thinks of all that noble hearts bled and suffered and held their peace for—to prop up the throne of Stuart—of all the vices that have been forgiven, the weaknesses that have been covered, the injustice that has been endured from Kings—when one thinks—if *she* thinks !—of all that has been suffered from successive mistresses and favourites of royalty a thousand times

more easily than she can be forgiven for (grant it !) a weak and
selfish grief for a noble husband—it is enough to make one
wonder if nations are not like dogs—better for beating. If the
Queen could cut off a few more heads, and subscribed to a few
less charities, if she were a little less virtuous, and a little more
tyrannical, if she borrowed her subjects' plate and repudiated her
debts, instead of reducing her household expenses, and regulating
court mournings by the interests of trade, I am very much afraid
we should be a more loyal people ! If we had a slender-limbed
Stuart who insisted upon travelling with his temporary favourite
when the lives and livelihoods of the best blood of Britain were
being staked for his throne whilst he amused himself, I suppose
we should wear white favours, and believe in the divine right of
Kings. It must be impossible for her to forget that the Prince,
whom death has proved to be worthy of the praise most people
now accord him, was far from popular in his lifetime, and the
pet gibe and sport of *Punch*. I suppose when she is dead or
abdicated we shall discover that England has had few better
sovereigns—and one can only hope that the reflection may not
be additionally stimulated by the recurrence of her successor to
some of the more popular—if not beneficial—peculiarities of
former reigns. It is true that then we might kick royalty over-
board altogether, but, judging by the United States, I don't
know that we should benefit even on the points where one might
most expect to do so. In truth, I believe that the virtue of
loyalty is extinct and must be—except under one or two conditions. Either more royal prerogative than we have—or in the
substitution of a loyal affection that shall in each member of the
commonwealth cover and be silent over the weak points which
the publicity of the present day exposes to vulgar criticism—for
the spirit which used to give the blood and possessions which
are not exacted of us. This is why the Queen's books do not
trouble *my* feelings about her. She is no great writer certainly,
and has perhaps made a mistake in thinking that they would do
good. I think they will do good with a certain class, perhaps
they lower her in the eyes of others. I do think myself that the

virtues she (and even her books incidentally) display are so great, and her weaknesses comparatively so small, that one's loyalty must be little indeed if one cannot honour her. " Them's my sentiments." I am ashamed to have bored you with them at such length.

I wonder whether you thought of us yesterday ? But I know you did ! We had planned a Johnny Gilpin out for the day, but it proved impossible. So we spent it thus—A.M. Full Cathedral Service with the Holy Communion, which was very nice, though, as it was a Feast Day, the service was later than usual, so it took all our morning. Rex played the organ. We spent most of the afternoon in tuning the organ, and then R. went off to mesmerize a man for neuralgia, and I went up town to try and get something good for dinner !

I am very happy, though at times one *longs* to see certain faces. But GOD is very good, and I have all that I can desire almost.

The Spring flowers are very lovely, some of them. I must go out. Adieu.

Best love to your Mother and all, to Lucy especially.

Your ever affectionate, J. II. E.

To MRS. GATTY.

Fredericton. June 8, 1868.

MY DEAREST MOTHER,

Does the above sketch give you the faintest idea of what it is to paddle up and down these lovely rivers with their smaller tributaries and winding creeks, on a still sunny afternoon ? It really is the most fascinating amusement we have tried yet. Mr. Bliss took us out the other day, it being the first time either of us was in a canoe, and Rex took one of the paddles, and got on so well that we intend to have a canoe of our own. Peter Poultice is building it, and I hope soon to send you a sketch of Rex paddling his own canoe! Of us, I may say, for I tried a paddle to-day, and mean to have a little one of my own to give *my* valuable assistance in helping the canoe

along. Next month when Rex can get away we think of going
up the river to "Grand Falls" (the next thing to Niagara, they
say) by steamer, taking our canoe with us, and then paddling
ourselves home with the stream. About eighty miles. Of
course we should do it bit by bit, sleeping at stopping-places.
One art Rex has not yet acquired, and it *looks* awful! A sort
of juggler's trick, that of *carrying* his canoe. Imagine taking
hold of the side of a canoe that would hold six people, throwing
it up and overturning it neatly on your head, without injuring
either your own skull or the canoe's bottom. . . This canoeing
is really a source of great pleasure to us, and will more than
double the enjoyment of summer to me. With a canoe Rex
can "pull" me to a hundred places where a short walk from
the shore will give me sketching, botanizing, and all I want!
Moreover, the summer heat at times oppresses my head, and
then to get on the water gives a cool breeze, and *freshens one up*
in a way that made me think of what it must be to people in
India to get to "the hills." I have never wished for some
of you more than on this lovely river, gliding about close to
the water (you sit on the very bottom of the canoe), all the trees
just bursting into green, and the water reflecting everything
exquisitely. Kingfishers and all kinds of birds flitting about
and singing unfamiliar songs; bob-o-links going "twit-twit,"
little yellow birds, kingbirds, crows, and the robin-thrushes
everywhere. I landed to-day at one place, and went into a
wood to try and get flowers. I only got one good one, but it
was very lovely! Two crows were making wild cries for the
loss of one of their young ones which some boys had taken, and
as I went on I heard the queer chirrup (like a bird's note) of
Adjidaumo the squirrel! and he ran across my path and into a
hollow tree. It is a much smaller squirrel than ours, about the
size of a water rat, and beautifully striped.

The only drawback to the paddling is that the beloved
Hector cannot go with us. He would endanger the safety of
the canoe. One has to sit very still. . . .

June 16, 1868.

MY DEAREST MOTHER,

We sent off the first part of "Kerguelen's Land" yesterday. . . . Rex is so much pleased with the story that I am quite in spirits about it, and hope you may think as favourably. He thinks if you read the end bit before you get the rest you will never like it, and yet I am very anxious to take the chance of the first part's having gone, as I want a proof—so if you do not get the first part, please put this by till you do, and don't read it.

Would it be possible for Wolf to illustrate it? If he knows the breeding islands of the Albatross he would make a lovely thing of it. This is the last *story*. There will only be a *conclusion* now. I have got my "information" from Rex, and "Homes without Hands."——The only point I am in doubt about is whether the parent birds would have remained on the island so *long*—I mean for *months*. Do you know any naturalist who would tell you this? When they are not breeding they seem to have no home, as they follow ships for weeks.

How we miss Dr. Harvey, and his *fidus Achates*—poor old Dr. Fisher!—I so often want things "looked up"—and we do lack books here! . . .

Fredericton. November 3, 1868.

. . . I *must* tell you what Mrs. Medley said to me this evening as we came out of church. She said, "It is an odd place to begin in about it, but I must thank you for the end of Mrs. Overtheway. The pathos of those old Albatrosses! The Bishop and I cried over them. I suppose it's the highest compliment we can pay you to say it is equal to anything of your Mother's, and that you are a worthy daughter of your Mother." Wasn't that a splendid bit of praise to hear all these miles away from one's dear old wonderful old Mother? . . .

XVIII. 12

To H. K. F. G.

Fredericion, N.B.
Tuesday, December 8, 1868.

. . . Tell the dear Mother, please, that I got dissatisfied with my story, and *recast it*, and began again—and got on awfully well, and was very well satisfied with it. But Rex read what was done and doesn't care for it a bit—in fact quite the reverse, which has rather upset my hopes. However, he says he cannot properly judge till it is finished, so I am going to finish it off, and if he likes it better then, I shall send it next mail. It is a regular child's story—about Toys—not at all sentimental—in fact meant to be amusing ; but as Rex read it with a face for a funeral, I don't know how it will be. I don't somehow think the idea is bad. It is (roughly) this : A pickle of a boy with a very long-suffering sister (I hope you won't object to her being called Dot. You know it's a very common pet name, and it "shooted" so well) gets all her toys and his own and makes an "earthquake of Lisbon" in which they are all smashed. From which a friend tells them the story of a dream she is supposed to have had (but I flattered myself the dream was rather neatly done up) of getting into fairyland to the Land of Lost Toys—where she meets all her old toys that she destroyed in her youth. Here she is shown in a kind of vision Dutch and German people making these toys with much pains and industry, and is given a lot of material and set to do the like. Failing this she is condemned to suffer what she inflicted on the toys, each one passing its verdict upon her. Eventually a doll (MY Rosa ! ! ! !) that she had treated very well rescues her, and the story reverts to the sister and brother, who takes to amusing himself by establishing himself as toy-mender to the establishment, instead of cultivating his bump of destructiveness. I sketch the idea because (if the present story fails) if you think the *idea* good I would try to recast it again. If I send it as it is, it is pretty sure to come by the Halifax mail next week. . . . I do miss poor dear old Dr. Fisher so! I very much wanted some statistics about toy-making. You never read anything about the making of common Dutch toys did you? . . .

Fredericton. December 8, 1868.

*   *   *   *   *   *

Tell Mother I think she ought to get *Henry* Kingsley to write for *Aunt Judy's Magazine.* The *children* and the *dogs* in his novels are the best part of them. They are utterly first-rate! I am sure he would make a hit with a child and dog story.

I told you that Bishop Ewing had written me such a charming letter, and sent me a sermon of his? This mail he sent us a number of the *Scottish Witness* with "Jerusalem the Golden" in Gaelic in it. . . .

To Mrs. GATTY.

Fredericton, N.B.
Easter Monday, 1869.

*   *   *   *   *   *

You are very dear and good about our ups and downs, and it makes me doubly regret that I cannot reward you by conveying a perfectly truthful *impression* of our life, etc. here to your mind. I trace in your very dearness and goodness about it, in your worrying more about discomfort for me in our moves than about your own hopes of our meeting at Home, how little able one is to do so by mere letters. I wish it did not lead you to the unwarrantable conclusion that it is because you are "weak and old" that you do not appreciate the uncertainties of our military housekeeping, and can only "admire" the coolness with which I look forward to breaking up our cosy little establishment, just when we were fairly settled down. You can hardly believe how well I understand your feelings for me, *because I have so fully gone through them for myself.* I never had D.'s "spirit" for a wandering life, and it is out of the fulness of my experience that I *know,* and wish unspeakably that I could convey to you, how very much of one's shrinking dread has all the *unreality* of fear of an *unknown* evil. When I look back to all I looked forward to with fear and trembling in reference to all the strangenesses of my new life, I understand your feelings better than you think. I am too much your daughter not to be strongly tempted to "beat my future brow," much more so than to be over-hopeful. Rex is given that way too in his own line; and we often are brought to say together how inexcusable it is when everything turns out so much better than we expected, and when "God" not only "chains the dog till night," but often never lets him loose at all! Still the natural terrors of an untravelled and not herculean woman about the ups and downs of a wandering, homeless sort of life like ours are not so comprehensible by him, he having travelled so much, never felt a qualm of sea-sickness, and less than the average of home-sickness, from circumstances. It is one among my many reasons for wishing to come Home soon, that one chat would put you in possession of more idea of our passing home, the nest we have built for a season, and the wood it is built in, and the birds (of many feathers) amongst whom we live, than any *letters* can do. . . . You can imagine the state of (far from blissful) ignorance of military life, tropical heat, Canadian inns, etc., etc., in which I landed at Halifax after such a sudden wrench from the old Home, and such a very far from cheerful voyage, and all the anecdotes of the summer heat, the winter cold, the spring floods, the houses and the want of houses, the servants and the want of servants, the impossibility of getting anything, and the ruinous expense of it when got! which people pour into the ears of a new-comer just because it is a more sensational and entertaining (and *quite* as stereotyped) a subject of conversation as the weather and the crops. The points may be (isolatedly) true; but the whole impression one receives is alarmingly false! And I can only say that my experience is so totally different from my fears, and from the cook-stories of the "profession," that I don't mean to request Rex to leave Our Department at present! . . .

To Mrs. Gatty.

Fredericton. Septuagesima, 1869.

. . . . I am sending you two fairy stories for your editorial consideration. They are not intended to form part of "The Brownies" book— they are an experiment on my part, and *I do not mean to put my name to them.*

You know how fond I have always been of fairy tales of the Grimm type. Modern fairy tales always seem to me such *very* poor things by comparison, and I have two or three theories about the reason of this. In old days when I used to tell stories to the others, I used to have to produce them in considerable numbers and without much preparation, and as that argues a *certain* amount of imagination, I have determined to try if I can write a few fairy tales of the genuine "uninstructive" type by following out my theories in reference to the old traditional ones. Please *don't* let out who writes them (if you put them in, and if any one cares to inquire !), for I am very anxious to hear if they elicit any comments from your correspondents to confirm me in my views. In one sense you must not expect them to be original. *My aim is* to imitate the "old originals," and I mean to stick close to orthodox traditions in reference to the proceedings of elves, dwarfs, nixes, pixies, etc., and if I want them to use such "common properties of the fairy stage"—as unscrupulous foxes, stupid giants, successful younger sons, and the traditional "fool"—with much wisdom under his folly (such as Hans in Luck)—who suggests the court fools with their odd mixture of folly and shrewdness. *One* of my theories is that all real fairy tales (of course I do not allude to stories of a totally different character in which fairy machinery is used, as your Fairy Godmothers, my "Brownies," etc., etc.), that all real "fairy tales" should be written as if they were oral traditions taken down from the lips of a "story teller." This is where modern ones (and modern editions of Grimm, *vide* "Grimm's Goblins," otherwise a delicious book) fail, and the extent to which I have had to cut out reflections, abandon epithets, and shorten sentences, since I began, very much confirms my ideas.

I think the Spanish ones in *Aunt Judy's Magazine* must have been so obtained, and the contrast between them and the "Lost Legends" in this respect is marked. There are plenty of children who can appreciate "The Rose and the Ring," "The Water Babies," your books, and the most poetical and suggestive dreams of Andersen. But (if it can be done) I think there is also a strong demand for new combinations of the Step-mother, the Fox, the Luck Child, and the Kings, Princesses, Giants, Witches, etc. of the old traditions. I say combinations advisedly, for I suppose *not* half of Grimm's Household Stories have "original" plots. They are palpable "*réchauffées*" of each other, and the few original germs might, I suspect, be counted on one's fingers, even in fairy-lore, and then traced back to a very different origin. Of course the market is abundantly stocked with modern versions, but I don't think they are done the right way. This is, however, for the Editorial ear, and to gain your unbiased criticism. But, above all, don't tell any friends that they are mine for the present. Of course if they DID succeed, I would republish and add my name. But I want to be incognito for the present—1st, to get free criticism ; 2nd, to give them fair play ; 3rd, not to do any damage to my reputation in another "walk" of story-writing. I do not in the least mean to give up my own style and take to fairy tale-telling, but I would like to try this experiment. . . . . . .

Monday, April 19, 1869.

. . . . I have two or three *schemes* in my head.

"Mrs. Overtheway" (*2nd series*), "Fatima's Flowers," etc.

"The Brownies (and other Tales)."

"Land of Lost Toys," "Three Christmas Trees," "Idyll," etc.

"Boneless," "Second Childhood," etc., etc.

"The Other Side of the World," etc., etc.

"Goods and Chattels" (quite vague as yet).

"A Sack of Fairy Tales" (in abeyance).

"A Book of *weird queer* Stories" (none written yet).

"Bottles in the Sea," "Witches in Eggshells," "Elephants in Abyssinia," etc.

And (a dear project) a book of stories, chiefly about Flowers and Natural History associations (*not scientific, pure fiction*), "The Floating Gardens of Ancient Mexico," the "Dutch Story," "Immortelles," "Mummy Peas," etc., etc. (none even planned yet!) . . .

To H. K. F. G.

[Undated, *Fredericton.*]

. . . How well I know what you say about the truth of Mother's sayings of the soothing effects of Nature! I used to feel it about gardening also so much. Visions of three yellow, three white, and three purple crocuses blooming in one pot beguile the mind from less happy fancies—perhaps too the *largeness* and *universality* of Nature disperse the selfishness of personal cares and worries. Then I think the smell of *earth* and *plants* has a physical anodyne about it somehow! One cannot explain it. . .

To MRS. GATTY.

Fredericton, N.B.
5th Sunday after Trinity, 1869.

. . . We have another "dogue." . . . *Trouvé* is the name of Hector's successor. 'Cos for why, we found him locked up in one of the barrack rooms, when I was with Rex on one of his inspections. He is a "left behind" either of the 1st Battalion 22nd, or the 4th Battalion 60th Rifles, we do not know which. He has utterly taken to us, and is especially fond of me I think. He is a big, black fellow, between a Newfoundland and a retriever. In the "Sweep" line, but not so big. He is wonderfully graceful and well-mannered (barring a trifling incident yesterday, when he got into my little cupboard, ate about two pounds of cheese and all the rolls, and *snuffed* the butter). And another trifling occurrence to-day. We chained him to the sofa,

which, during our absence, he *dragged* (exactly as the dogs
dragged *Mons. Jabot's bed*) across the room, upset the ink on to
the carpet, threw my photo-book down by it, and established
himself in Rex's arm-chair. It was most ludicrous, for the
other day he slipped his collar, and *chose the sofa* to lie on, but
because he was tied to the sofa, with full permission to use it,
he chose the chair ! and must nearly have lugged his own head
off. He does wonderfully little damage with his pranks ; there
were wine-glasses, bottles, pickles, &c., in the cupboard when
he got the cheese ; but he extracted his supper as daintily as a
cat, and not a thing was upset ! Oddly enough, when we are
with him, he never thinks of getting into cushions and chairs
like that blessed old sybarite the Bull-dogue. But if we leave
him tied up, he plays old gooseberry with the furniture. I had
been fearing it would be rather a practical difficulty in the way
of his adoption, the question of where he should sleep ; but he
solved it for himself. He walks up-stairs after us, flops on to
the floor, gives two or three sighs, and goes gracefully to sleep.
. . . I wish you could have seen him lying in perverse dignity
in the arm-chair, with the sofa attached to the end of his chain
like a locket ! ! !

To H. K. F. G.
                                    12th Sunday after Trinity.
                          Fredericton, N.B. August 16, 1869.

    . . . We had a great scene with Peter yesterday. Rex has
two guns, you must know--a rifle, and an old fowling-piece—
good enough in its way, but awfully *old-fashioned* (not a breech-
loader), and he determined to make old Peter a present of this,
for he is a good old fellow, and does not *cheat* one, and we had
resolved to give him something, and we knew this would delight
him. I wish you *could* have seen him. He burst out laughing,
and laughed at intervals from pure pleasure, and went away with
it laughing. But with the childlike *enjoyment* (which negroes have
also), the Indians have a power and grace in " expressing their
sentiments" on such an occasion which far exceeds the attempts of

our ' poor people," and is most dignified. His first *speech* was an
emphatic (and *always slow*) " *Too* good ! Too much ! " and when
Rex assured him it was very old, not worth anything, etc., etc.,
he hastily interrupted him with a *thoroughly* gentlemanlike air,
almost Grandisonian, "Oh ! oh ! as good as new to me. Quite
as good as new." They were like two Easterns ! For not to
be outdone in courtesy, Rex warned him not to put too large
charges of powder for fear the barrel should burst—being so
old. A caution which I believe to be totally unnecessary, and
a mere hyperbole of depreciation—as Peter seemed perfectly to
understand ! He told me it was "The first present I ever
receive from a gentleman. Well—well—I never forget it, the
longest day I live." The graceful candour with which he said,
"I am very thankful to you," was quite pretty.

To Mrs. Gatty.

[*Aldershot.*]   February 23, 1870.

My Darling Mother,

I was by no means sensible of your iniquities in not
acknowledging my poor Neck,* for I had entirely forgotten his
very existence ! Only I was thinking it was a long time since I
heard from you—and hoping you were not ill. I am *very* glad
you like the Legend—I was doubtful, and rather anxious to hear
till I forgot all about it. The " Necks " are Scandinavian in
locality, and that desire for immortal life which is their dis-
tinguishing characteristic is very touching. There is one lovely
little (real) Legend·in Keightley. The bairns of a Pastor play
with a Neck one day, and falling into disputes they taunt him
that he will never be saved—on which he flings away his harp
and weeps bitterly. When the boys tell their father he reproves
them for their want of charity, and sends them back to unsay
what they had said. So they run back and say, " Dear Neck,
do not grieve so ; for our father says that your Redeemer liveth
also," on which the Neck was filled with joy, and sat on a wave

* The Neck in " Old-fashioned Fairy Tales."

and played till the sun went down. He appeared like a boy with long fair hair and a red cap. They also appear in the form of a little old man wringing out his beard into the water. I ventured to give my Neck both shapes according to his age. All the rest is *de moi-même.* . . .

[*Aldershot.*] March 22, 1870.

MY DARLING MOTHER,

    I am so very much pleased that you think better of Benjy * now. As I have plenty of time, I mean to go through it, and soften Benjy down a bit. He is an awful boy, and I think I can make him less repulsive. The fact is the story was written *in fragments*, and I was anxious to show that it was not a little boyish roughness that I meant to make a fuss and "point a moral" about—nor did I want to go into fine-drawn questions about the cruelties of sport, and when I came to join the bits into a whole and copy out, I found I had overproved my point and made Benjy a *fearful* brute. But there *are* some hideously cruel boys, and I do think a certain devilish type of cruelty is generally combined with a certain *lowness* and *meanness* of general style—even in born gentlemen—and though quite curable, I would like to hear what the boys think of it, if it would not bore them to read it. But I certainly shall soften Benjy down—and will attend to all your hints—and put in the "Mare's Nest" (many thanks!). Tell D. I do not know how I could alter about Rough—unless I take out his death altogether—but beg her to observe that he was not the least neglected as to food, etc. ; what he died of was joy after his anxiety. . . .

[*Aldershot.*] May Day, 1870.

    . . . I have got some work into my head which has been long seething there, and will, I think, begin to take shape. It is about *flowers*—the ancestry of flowers; whether the flowers will

---

* Included in "Lob Lie-by-the-Fire, and other Tales," vol. vii.

tell their own family records, or what the *plot* will be I have not
yet planned, and it will take me some time to collect my data,
but the family histories of flowers which came originally from
old Mexico in the days of Montezuma, and the floating gardens,
and the warriors who wore nosegays, and the Indians who
paddled the floating gardens on which they lived up the waters
of that gorgeous city with early vegetables for the chiefs—would
be rather weird! And then the strange fashions and universal
prevalence of Japanese gardening. The wistaria rioting in the
hedges, and the great lilies wild over the hills. Ditto the
camellias. With all the queer little thatched Japanese huts that
always have lumps of *iris* on the top, which the Japanese ladies
use for bandoline. Then the cacti would have queer legends of
South America, where the goats climb the steep rocks and dig
them up with their horns and roll them down into the valley,
and kick and play with them till the *spines* get rubbed off, and
then devour them at leisure. I give you these instances in case
anything notable about flowers comes in your way, "when found
to make a note of" for me. . . .

To Mrs. Elder.

Ecclesfield. October 25, 1871.

My Dearest Aunt Horatia,

Your letter *was* shown to me, and I cannot tell you how
much obliged to you I am for the prospect of the gold thimble,
a thing I have always wished to possess.

I—(if it fits !!! But, as I told Charlie, if it is too big I *can*
wrap a sly bit of rag round my finger, but if it's too small, unless
I cut the tip, as Cinderella's sisters cut their heels, I don't know
how I can secure it!) shall additionally value it as a testimony
of your approval of my dear old Hermit,* for that is one of my
greatest favourites amongst my efforts. Miss Yonge prefers it,
I believe, to anything I have ever done, and Rex nearly so. . . .

Your loving niece, J. H. E.

* "The Blind Hermit and the Trinity Flower," vol. xvi.

TO C. T. GATTY.

Aldershot.   Holy Innocents, 1871.

. . . I had the very latest widow here for two days "charring." She is the lady alluded to by Rex when he told Stephen that she had been weighed, and was found wanting. In justice to her physique, I must say that this was not according to avoirdupois measure ! ! but figurative. She whipped about as nimbly as an elephant. She was rather given to panting and groaning. You can fancy her. [*Sketch.*] " Mrs. Hewin, ma'am, *don't* soil your 'ands ! *Let* me ! As I says to the parties at the ' Imperial' at Folkstone, ladies thinks an elderly person can't get through their work, but they can do a deal more than the young ones that has to be told every—Using the table-cloth to wipe the dishes am I? Tst, tst ! so I ham ! M'm ! Hemma ! where's your kitchen cloths? I don't know where things his yet, Mrs. Hewin. But I've 'ad a 'Ome of my own, Mrs. Hewin, and been use to take care of things "—(" Take care, Mrs. Plumridge") —" Well now ! 'owever did *that* slip through my fingers now ? Tst ! tst ! tst ! There must have been a bit of butter on the hunder side I think. Eh ! deary dear ! Ah—! Oh—!" Pause—Solo recitative—" Eh, dear ! If my poor 'usband was but alive, I shouldn't be wanting now ! I Ope I give you satisfaction, Mrs. Hewin. If I'm poor, I'm honest. I ope I give satisfaction in hevery way, Mrs. Hewin. Your property is safe in *my* 'ands, Mrs. Hewin ! What do you think of my papers, Mrs. Hewin? One lady as see them said she didn't know what more *hany* one. could require." (Said papers chiefly consisting of baptism registers of the little Plumridges. Marriage lines of Mrs. P., and forms in reference to the late Mr. P., a pensioner.)

SEQUEL.

" Emma, where's the water-can?"

" Please 'm, Mrs. Plumberridge, she left it outside of the door yesterday, and some one's took it."

There is yet a later widow, but I do *not* think of taking her into the house. The Widow Bone has taken to *boning* her daughter's clothes, so *she* is forbidden the house. . . .

To A. E.

Brighton. April 17, 1872.

. . . I got here all right, and wonderfully little tired, though the train shook a good deal the latter part of the way.

Oh! the FLOWERS! The cowslips, the purple orchids, the kingcups, the primroses! And the grey, drifting cumuli with gaps of blue, and the cinnamon and purple woods, broken with yellowish poplars and pale willows, with red farms, and yellow gorse lighted up by the sun!!! The oaks just beginning to break out in yellowish tufts. [*Sketch.*] I can't tell you what lovely sketches I passed between Aldershot and Redhill!

On to Brighton I took charge of a small boy being sent by a fond mother to school. When I mention that he was nine years old,—and informed me—that he had got "a jolly book," which proved to be *A School for Fathers*, that his own school.wasn't *much of a one*, and he was going to leave, and ate hard-boiled eggs and crystallized oranges by the way—you will see how this generation waxes apace !!

Ecclesfield. May 27, 1872.

. . . The weather is very nice now. I stayed till the end of the Litany in church yesterday, and then slipped out by the organ door and sat with Mother. I sat on the Boy's school side of the chancel, where a little lad near me was singing *alto* (not a "second" of thirds !) strong and steady as a thrush in a hedge!! The music went very well.

The country looks lovely, *but for the smoke.* If it had but our blue distance it would be grand. But the

> " wreathed smoke afar
> That o'er the town like mist upraised
> Hung, hiding sun and star,"

gets worse every year! And when I think of our lovely blue and grey folds of distance, and bright skies, and tints, I feel quite *Ruskinish* towards mills and manufactories.

To C. T. GATTY.

X Lines, South Camp, Aldershot.
August 10, 1873.

MY VERY DEAR OLD CHARLIE,

Don't you suppose your sister is forgetting you. Two causes have delayed your drawings.

1. I have been working—-oh *so* hard! It was because Mr. Bell announced that he wanted a "volume," and that for the Xmas Market one must begin at once in July!

Such is competition!

He had an idea that something which had not appeared in any magazine would be more successful than reprints. *So* I have written "Lob Lie-by-the-Fire, or the Luck of Lingborough," and you will recognize your *Cockie* in it! I have taken no end of pains with it, and it has been a matter of seven or eight hours a day lately. I mean the last few days. Rather too much. It knocked me off my sleep, and reduced "my poor back" to the consistency of pith. But I am picking up, partly by such gross material aid as *bottled stout* affords! and any amount of fresh air blowing in full draughts over my bed at night!!

2. I *have* been at work for you, but I get so horribly dissatisfied with my things. No; I must do some real steady *work* at it. One can't jump with a little "nice feeling" and plenty of theories into what can give any lasting pleasure to oneself or any one else. I will send you shortly (I hope) a copy of one of Sir Hope Grant's Chinnerys, and perhaps a wee thing of Ecclesfield. The worst of drawing is, it wants mind as well as hands. One can't go at it *jaded* from headwork, as one could "sew a long white seam" or any mechanical thing! . . .

When D—— was with me, we went to a *fête* in the North Camp Gardens, and I was talking to Lady Grant about the

Chinnerys, and the "happy thought" struck her to introduce me to a Mr. Walkinshaw. They live somewhere in this country, and Mrs. Walkinshaw came up afterwards to ask if she might call on me, as they have a Chinnery collection (gathered in China), and Mr. Walkinshaw would show them to me! . . . I mean to collect all possible information on the subject, and either to write myself, or *prime you* to write an article on him some day !

To C. T. GATTY.

X Lines. August 20, 1873.

DEAR OLD BOY,

. . . I enjoyed your letter very much, and am so glad you keep "office hours." It is very good of you not to be angry with my good advice ! "Experientia does it," as Mr. 'Aughton would say. . . . *I* break down about once in three months like clockwork—from sheer overwork. I certainly am never happy idle ; but I have too often to sit in sackcloth in the depths of my heart—whilst everybody is beseeching me to be "idle"— from a consciousness that, not from doing nothing, but by doing B when I should have done A, and C when I should have done B, a kind of indolence at the critical moment, I have *wasted* my strength and time, not MERELY overworked myself. Also that on *many* things—drawing, languages, etc.—I have spent in my life a great deal of labour with little result, because it has not been consecutive and methodical. One would like one's own failures to be one's friends' stepping-stones. I *may* say too that I have an excuse which, thank GOD, you can't plead now— ill-health. It is not always easy, even for oneself, to judge when languor at the precise instant of recurring duty is spine-ache from brain work, and the sofa is the remedy,—or when it is what (in reference to an unpublished—indeed unwritten—story on this head) I call Boneless on the spine ! MY back is apt to ache in any case ! . . . I am trying to teach myself that if one *has* been working, one has not necessarily been working to good purpose, and that one may waste strength and forces of all sorts, as well as time!

Curious that *you* and D—— should both have quoted that saying of J. H. Newman to me in one week! I also will adopt it! Indeed "bit by bit" is the only way *I* feel equal to improve in *anything*, and I do think it is GOD's way of teaching and leading us all as a rule, and it is the principle on the face of all His creation—*Gradual* growth. The art of being happy was never difficult to me. I think I am permitted an unusual *intensity* of joy in common cheap pleasures and natural beauties—fresh air, colour, etc., etc., to compensate for some ill-health and deprivations.

Herewith comes my "Portrait by Spoker," and a copy of a Chinnery. The first-fruits of "regular" work at drawing an hour a day!!!

Farewell, Beloved. . . . Ever your very loving old sister,

JULIANA HORATIA EWING.

TO A. E.

Ecclesfield Vicarage, Sheffield.
Sunday, Oct. 5, 1873.

. . . It is all over. She *is* with your Father and Mother, and the dear Bishop, and my two brothers, and many an old friend who has "gone before." Had she been merely a friend she is one of those whose loss cannot but be felt more as years and experience make one realize the value of certain noble qualities, and their rarity; but if GOD has laid a heavy cross upon us in this blow,—which seems such a blow in spite of long preparing!—He has given us every comfort, every concession to the weaknesses of our love in the accidents of her death. . . . It was an ideal end. GOD Who had permitted her to suffer so sorely in body, and to be often visited in old times—by dread of death and of "death-agonies," parted the waves of the last Jordan, and she "went through dryshod!" . . . The sense of her higher state is so overwhelming, one *cannot* indulge a *common* sorrow. For myself I can only say that I feel as if I were a child again in respect of her. She is as much with *me* now, as with any of her children, even if I am in Jamaica or Ceylon. *Now* she knows and sees my life, and I have a feeling as if she were an ever-present *conscience* to me (as a mother's *presence* makes a child alive to what is right and what is wrong), which I hope by GOD's grace may never leave me and may make me more worthy of having had such a Mother. . . .

TO C. T. GATTY,

R Lines, South Camp. January 4, 1874.

DEARLY BELOVED,

What *would* I give to have a visit from you! I fear you did not get home at Xmas! Thank you a thousand times for your card—I think it almost the very prettiest I ever saw!

. . . As I am not prompt *to time* with my Xmas Box I may as well be appropriate in kind. Is there any trifle you are "in want" of?

"Price ner object," as Emmanuel Eaton (the old Nursery man) (very appropriately) named his latest Fuchsia, when he saw us children turning down the Wood End Lane in the Donkey Carriage on a birthday, flush of coppers—and bashful about abating prices!

. . . I was on the border of sending you a nice collection of poetry—and a shadow crossed my brain that you have said you "don't care about poetry"—"Lives there a man with soul so dead"—or does the great commercial whirl weary out the brain? —If I am wrong and you like it—will you have (if you don't possess) Trench's fine collection of poems of all dates?

Your ever devoted

J. H. E.

To C. T. GATTY,

X Lines, South Camp.   March 13, 1874.

MY DEAREST CHARLIE,

I am *quite a brute* not to have written before. I didn't, because (to say the truth !) I had a "return compliment" in the Valentine line in my head, and I never got time to do it ! You know what the *pressure* of work is, and I have had a lot in hand, and been *very* far from well.

It was VERY good of you to send me a Val., and much appreciated.

I also owe you thanks for a copy of the "fretful" Porcupine [*Sketch*] duly received. I was very glad to get it—for you have greatly, wonderfully improved in your writing. I liked your article extremely, and was so very glad to see the marked improvement. . . .

I am *not*, when I speak of improvement in the art of English composition, alluding solely to the time when you wrote as follows (italics and caps your own) :

"Mr. Gatty thinks that Messrs. Fisher & Holmes has sent more than he desired *he said* 2*s*. or 2*s*. 6*d*. and he thinks there is here more than that he hopes he will answer and tell me what price the LOT is and how many plants I may take for 2*s*. or 2*s*. 6*d*. by return of post or by Cox which will be better Ecclesfield June 1866."

I wouldn't part with the original of the above under a considerable sum of money ! It always refreshes my brain to go back to it—and I laugh as often as one laughs and re-laughs at Pickwick !—the way the pronouns become entangled and after making an imperfectly distinctive stand at "*he said*," jump desperately to the pith of the matter in "what price the LOT is." All difficulties of punctuation being disposed of by the process of omitting stops entirely—like old Hebrew—written without points !

(What an autograph for collectors if ever you're the "King Cole" of Liverpool !)

*   *   *   *   *   *

. . . I have been staying with M. M. I wish I could impart my mental gleanings. I made several experiments on her intellect. I tried to *pin her* again and again—but QUITE without success—or (on *her* part) sense of failure. I tried to remember what she had said afterwards—and I could not succeed. I couldn't carry a single sentence.

Generally speaking I gather that—

"The Kelts are destroying themselves—the Teuton Element MUST prevail—one feels—genius—the thing—Herr Beringer—Dr. Zerffi—but whatever one may FEEL—so it is! Every other nation COMMENCED where we LEAVE OFF. WE BEGAN with the DRAMA and left off with the Epic—Milton's—what-is-it? But there you have Hamlet—where do you find a character like Hamlet?—NOWHERE! That's the beauty of it. The young lady's maid never reads anything—but Macbeth. ANNE I *can* trust with Faust. I read Lessing myself—and the Greek Testament (not the Epistles—don't let me exaggerate)—with a bit of dry toast and a cup of tea without a saucer or anything. I never sit down till the Easter holidays—before breakfast—I ought to feel—what is it—PROUD. Dr. Zerffi says he'll show A. B.'s papers at any University against the first-class men—and they won't understand a word of them. What were those girls when they came? There's the Duchess of Somerset's 15th coz twice removed. *It's all blood.* My father drove four-in-hand down this very hill in the old *coaching* days (!!!)—and there's not another school in England where the young ladies read Bopp before breakfast. But the Vedas are a mine of—you know what—*Sanskrit* is *English*—change the letters and I could make myself understood by a Parsee better than by half the young ladies of this establishment. We're all Indians!"

If her conversation is what it was—and *more so,* her hospitality, her generosity—and her admirable management of the girls and the house is as A1 as ever. I never saw a prettier, jollier, nicer set of girls. H—— is growing *very* charming, I think. I believe the secret of her success, in spite of that extraordinary fitful intellect of hers, is that one never learns anything *well* but

what one learns *willingly*, and that she makes life so much
more pleasant and reasonable that the girls work themselves,
and so get on.

It's getting late! Good-night. I wish we met oftener!
Ever your very loving sister,
J. H. E.

Have you seen March *A. J. M.?* I particularly want you to
read a thing of mine called " Our Garden." I'll send it if you
can't get it.

For Private Circulation Only.

(Oh, Charles! Charles!)

Time, 2 p.m. Julie in bed for the sake of "perfect quiet."
M. M. " without a moment to spare."

" I SEE I'm tiring you—I shall NOT stop—I haven't a moment
—I can't speak—I've given lessons on the mixed Languages
this morning—and paid all my bills—Mr. B—— has called—
he's better-looking than I thought, but too much hair—and the
BREWER all over—you look very white—you're killing yourself—why DO you DO it?—and U——'s as bad—I mean D——.
Dear me! what a pleasure it has been! When I THINK of
Ecclesfield!!!! You are NOT to kill yourself—I forbid it—why
should you work for daily bread as I have to do?—Our bread bill
doesn't exceed £4 a week—I mean a month—TEN pounds a
month for groceries and wine—spirits we never have in the
house—you've seen all that we have—when I was senseless and
Dr. F—— called—when the other doctors came he left his card
and retired, but we've employed him since—he ordered gin
cloths—they sent out—when the bill came in I said Brown!
BROWN! BROWN!!—*what's this?* GIN! GIN! GIN! WHO's
'ad GIN! They said YOU! Such is life!

" Dear, dear, IT is a pleasure to see you—but I see your
head's bad and I'm going—I MUST dress.—May I ring your bell
for the maid—a black silk, Julie, good and well cut is economical,

my dear. No *underground to Whiteley's* for me ! Lewis and
Allenby—they dress me—I order nothing—I know nothing—I
haven't a rag of clothing in the world—they line the bodices
with silk and you can darn it down to the last—I eat nothing—
I drink nothing—I only *work*—I never sleep—I read German
classics in bed—Lessing—and the second part of Schiller's *Faust*
—I give lessons on it before breakfast in my dressing-gown—this
morning the young ladies hung on my lips—I *know* the lesson
was a good one—It was the Sorrows of Goethe. Last week
Dr. Zerffi said—' All religions are one and one religion is all—
particularly the Brahmas.' It was splendid ! and none of the
young ladies knew it before they came. But Poor Mrs. S——!
She didn't seem one bit wiser. I sent him a Valentine on the
14th—designed by the young ladies. He said ' I *knew* where
it came from—by the word BOPP. Zis is ze only establishment
in England where the word BOPP is known.' He's a great
man—and the Teutonic element *must* prevail. The Kelts are
very charming, but they will GO. We've the same facial angle as
the Hindoo, but poor Mrs. S—— can't see it. Dr. A—— says I
must have some sleep—so I've given up Sanscrit—You can't do
everything even in bed. And it's *English* when all's done—and
Brown speaks it as well as I do !! *Go* to India, Julie, if ever
you have the chance, and talk to the natives—they'll understand
you. They understand me. Signor Ricci sometimes does NOT.
But then he speaks the modern—the base—Italian, and *I*—the
classic. He said, ' I do not understand you, Mees M——' I
said, ' E vero, Signor—I know you don't. But that's because I
speak *classic* Italian. All the organ-boys understand me.' And
he smiled. Dear, dear ! How pleasant it is to see a Gatty—
but I wish you didn't look so white—when I see other people
suffer, and think of all the years of health I've enjoyed, I never
can be thankful enough—and when I've paid my monthly bills
I'm the happiest woman in England. When I think of how
much I have and how little I deserve, I don't know what to do
but say my prayers. Dear, I'm sorry I told you that story about
X——. If she sent this morning for £10 I must let her have it,

if I had to go out and borrow it. I am going out—the Dr. says I must. In the holidays I go on the balcony—and look down into the street—and see the four-in-hands—and the policemen— and the han(d)som cabmen (they're most of them gentlemen— and some of them Irish gentlemen), and I say—'Such is life!' And poor Mrs. S—— says '*Is it*, Miss M——?' and I know I speak sharply to her, which I should *not do*. And I go into Kensington Gardens—and see the Princess—and the Ducks in the water—and the little ragged boys going to bathe—and I say 'This is a glorious world!' I saw Lord—Lord—dear me! I know his name as well as my own—Lord—Lord—Oh Lord! he believes in Tichborne—K——, that's it—Lord K—— in the Row. He always asks after me. HE married a woman—well. No more about that. He couldn't get a divorce. HER sister married a parson. SHE was the mother of that poor woman—you know— who was murdered by those people—THEY lived two streets off Derby House—the brother—a handsome man—lived opposite Gipsey Hill Station. You know *that? Well*. HIS wife had a bunch of curls behind (I hate curls and bunches behind—keep your hair clean and put it up simply). SHE—got off and so did HE. THEY—that's the parson and his wife—wrote to Lord K—— and said 'Lady K—— is dead.' He said 'Then bury her,' and he married again at once. SHE was a Miss A., and she said—'I marry him because I've been told to'— but that's neither here nor there, and these things occur. ANN! is that you? My dear, how black you are under the eyes—DO, Julie, try and take better care of yourself—and *keep quiet*. If I were Major Ewing I'd *thrash* you if you didn't. Coming, Ann!—What was it?—Oh, Lord K—— and Tichborne —well—just let me shut the door. He IS Tichborne—but *he murdered him*. That's the secret.

"ANN! My black silk—go to my room—murdered who? why—*Castor*.

"Now try and get some sleep. If I find you with papers I'll *burn them*. Oh! there go all the drags and Mr. M—— on the box—and there go the 4.45, 5.15, and 5.25 to Baker St.—The days fly ! But it's a glorious life. Work ! Work !—Keep quiet, dear—I shall be back directly."

To A. E.

"Sheffield House," New Quay, Dartmouth.

June 4, 1874.

. . . The above I find is our *correct* address, though what I sent you is all-sufficient, especially as you can't land without our seeing you out of our window, as we are almost within speaking distance of the steamer. . . .

From Exeter here the line is lovely. Half the way you run along the shore. The fields ploughed and meadowed, and with trees, and cattle come down to the shore. [*Sketch.*]

TORBAY is in this line. The cliffs are a deep red sandstone, the sky deep blue, and the fields deep green ! ! [*Sketch.*]

At Dawlish, Torquay, etc. the jutting rocks of worn-away sandstone mark the points of the little bays with fantastic-looking shapes, like petrified giants. [*Sketch.*]

Looking back from Teignmouth is a very curious one on which the sea-birds sit. Bless their noses ! and their legs ! How they do enjoy the waves ! [*Sketch.*]

Those lazy ripples damp their boots so nicely !

In the Exeter Station sat a ——— [*Sketch*] Bull Dogue. O dear ! He looked so "savidge," and was so nervous ; every train made him tremble in every limb ! I bought him a penny bun, but he was too nervous to eat, though he looked very grateful. The porter promised me to give him plenty of water, and as I gave the porter plenty of coppers I hope he did !

Tell Stephen the flowers on the railway banks give you quite a turn ! Crimson, pale pink, and dead-white Valerian against a deep blue sky in hot sunshine make one not know whether to PAINT or press !

As to Dartmouth itself it is a mixture of Matlock, Whitby and Antwerp ! ! ! The defect is it is really on the river, not on

the sea, but the neighbouring bays are so get-at-able we have
settled here. The town is very old. Some of the streets, or
rather terraces—if a perfectly irregular perching and jumbling
of houses up and down a steep hill can be called a terrace—are
very curious. [*Sketch.*]

Flowers everywhere. . . .

To H. K. F. G.

July 12, 1874.

Dr. Edghill preached a fine sermon this morning on "Friend!
wherefore art thou come?" Terribly didactic on the fate of
Judas, but the practical application was wonderful and *so* like
him! It being chiefly on the "patient love of Christ." Quite
merciless on Judas, and on the coarseness, coldness and
brutalness of betrayal by the tenderest sign of human love.
' But " (plunging head-first among the Engineers !) "if there's
any man sitting here with a heart and conscience every bit as
black as Judas's *in that hour :* to thee, Brother, in this hour—in
thy worst and vilest hour—Jesus speaks—' *Friend !*—You may
have worn out human love, you may try your hardest to wear
out Mine' "—(parenthesis to the A. S. C. and a nautical *hitch* of
half his surplice)—(" and we all try hard enough, *that's* certain !)
—'but *you never can*—Friend, still My Friend ! ' " (Pull up, and
obvious need of bronchial troches. Tonsure mopped and a
re-commencement.) " Then there's the appeal to the *conscience*
as well as to the *heart. Wherefore art thou come ?* what art
thou about—what is thy object? I tell you what, I believe if
Judas had answered this in plain language to himself he would
have stopped short even then. And we should stop short of
many a sin if we'd *face* what we're going to do " (Dangerous
precipitation of the whole Chaplain at the heads of the privates
below.) " Some of you ask yourselves that question to-day—
this evening *as you're walking to Aldershot,* ' Wherefore am I
come?' And don't let the Devil put something else into your
head, but just *answer it,*" etc. etc.

He's not exactly an *equal* or a *finished* preacher for highly educated ears, but that sort of transparent candour which he has makes him *very* affecting when on his favourite topic, the inexhaustible love of God. His face when he quotes—" The Son of God Who loved *Me* and gave Himself for *Me*," is like a man showing the Rock he has clung to himself in shipwreck.

To C. T. G.

X Lines. July 22, 1874.

DEAREST CHARLIE,

It was a *great* disappointment not to see you ! Now don't fail me next week—you scoundrel ! I want you *most* particularly for most selfish reasons. I am just taking my hero * into Victoria Docks, and want to dip my brush in *Couleur locale* with your help. Do come, and we'll go up to London by *barge* and sketch all the way ! ! ! I know an A1 Bargemaster, and we can get beds at the inns *en route*. A two days' voyage ! Or we can go for a shorter period and come home by rail. It won't cost us much.

I am so glad to think of you in the dear *Old—New* Forest.

*　　*　　*　　*　　*　　*

Now mind you come—if only to see my Nelson (bureau) Relic ! ! It is such a comfort to me and *my papers !*

Ever your most loving sister,

J. H. E.

To MRS. ELDER.

X Lines, South Camp. August 7, 1874.

MY DEAR AUNT HORATIA,

I have begged the Tiger Tom for you !

He is the handsomest I ever saw, with such a head ! His name is *Peter*. [*Sketch.*]

---

* " A Great Emergency," vol. xi.

Nothing—I assure you, can exceed his beauty—or the depth of his stripes. . . .

If I had not too many cats already I should have adopted Peter long ago. We always quote William Blake's poem to him when we see him prowling about our garden.

> "Tiger! Tiger! burning bright,
>   In the forest of the night,
>   What immortal Hand and Eye
>   Framed thy fearful symmetry?"

Do you remember it?

I feel *quite a wretch* not to like your "Ploughman"* as well as usual. There is always poetry in your things, but TO ME the *spirit* of this one has not quite that reality which is the highest virtue of "a sentiment"—or at least its greatest strength. But I may be wrong. Only that kind of constant lifting of the soul from the labour of daily drudgery to the Father of our spirits seems to me one of the highest, latest, and most refined Christian Graces in natures farthest removed from "the ape and tiger," and most at leisure for contemplative worship. I know there are exceptions. Rural contemplative saints among shepherds and ploughmen. But that the agricultural labourer as a type seeks "Nature's God" at the plough-tail and in the bosom of his family I fear is *not* the case—and it would be very odd if poverty and ignorance did lead to such results, even in the advantages of an "open-air" life. Perhaps Burns knew such a Cottar on Saturday Nights as he painted—he wasn't *sich* himself! unless you interpret *a neet wi' Burns* by that poem!—and there has been one contemplative Shepherd on Salisbury Plain—though the proverb says—

> "Salisbury Plain
>   Is seldom without a thief or twain."

---

* Sonnet by H. S. Elder, *Aunt Judy's Magazine.*

—*not* I believe supposed to refer to highwaymen !! and agricultural labourers stand (among trades) statistically high (or
low !) for the crime of murder.

But I won't inflict any more rigmarole on you, because of an
obstinate conviction *in my inside* that dear Mother was right in
the idea that it is the learned—not the ignorant—who wonder,
and that the ploughman feels no wonder at all in the glory of
the rising sun—though YOUR mind might overflow with awe and
admiration.   As to the last verse—that a "cot" should ever be
"cheerful" which "serves him for" washhouse, kitchen, nursery
and all—is a triumph of the "softening influence of use"—and
I concede it to you !   But where "he reigns as a king his toils
forgot" is, I am convinced, at the Black Bull with highly-
drugged beer ! ! ! ! !!

Now am I *not* a Brute ?

And yet it is *very* pretty, and—strange to say—the class to
whom I believe it would be acceptable, is the class of whom I
believe it is not (typically) true, and PERHAPS it is good for
every class to have an *ideal* of its own circumstances before its
eyes.   But I don't think it is good for rich people's children to
grow up with the belief that twelve shillings a week, and cider
and a pig, are the wisest and happiest earthly circumstances in
which humanity with large families can be placed for their
temporal and spiritual progress.   I don't think it ever leads to a
wish in the young Squire to exchange with Hodge for the good
of his own soul, but I think it fosters a fixed conviction that
Hodge has nothing to complain of, *plus* being placed at a
particular advantage as to his eternal concerns.

Will you ever forgive me ?   I like the descriptive parts so
much, the "rival cocks at dawn"—the "autumn's mist and
spring's soft rain," the team that "turn in their trace in the
furrow's face," and the life-like descriptions in verse 4.   It is as
true to one's observation as it is graceful. . . .

Your loving niece,

J. H. E.

To A. E.

Ecclesfield.   May 14, 1876.

[*Sketch.*] Do you remember Whitley Hall? I used to be so fond of the place when I was a child, and no one lived there but an old woman—old Esther Woodhouse—with a face like an ideal witch—at the lodge. As you know I always hated *writing down*—but long before I accomplished a tale on paper I wrote a novel *in my head* to Whitley Hall, and used to walk about in the wood there, by the pond—*to think it!*

York.   February 23, 1879.

. . . . Yesterday was sunny though cold, and I had a delicious drive to Escrick and Naburn.   Oh, it *does* send thrills of delight through me, when the hay-coloured hedge-grass begins to mix itself with green, and the hedges have a very brown-madderish tint in the sun, and all the trunks of all the old trees are far greener than the fields, and the earth is turned over, and the rooks hold Parliaments.

        *   *   *   *   *   *

[*York.*]   Easter Day, 1879.

. . . . I went to Church at S. John's, Mr. Wilberforce's Church ; I had never been in it.   That window with S. Christopher, and those strange representations of the Trinity, and the five Master Yorkes kneeling all in blue on one side, and their four sisters on the other, is very wonderful.   One of the most wonderful.   How fascinating these dear old churches are ! Mr. Wilberforce has a fine voice, a most rich and flexible baritone, and sings ballads with a great deal of taste and expression.   I shall for ever love York and its marble-white walls and dear old churches, but "Benedetta sia 'l giorno e 'l mese e 'l anno," when you set your face with your black poodle towards the island called Melita ! This north-east wind which still blows *cruelly* would have made you very ill, I think. . . .

I must tell you of another thing. On Thursday I went to the Blind School to a concert. I went rather against my will, for you know I was sadly impressed before by their *very* unhealthy and miserable look, but oh, dear, they do sing well! and it was very affecting. One of the Barnbys teaches them. They have a good organ, and one of the blind men played very well. They sang very refinedly. No doubt they are well taught, but no doubt also the sense of hearing is delicate with them. . . .

Frimhurst. April 18, 1879.

I got here safely yesterday, though I had a horrid headache on Wednesday, and expected to arrive here in very bad condition. I felt rather bad yesterday morning, but as I drew near, marvellous to relate, my headache went away! Oh! I thought so much of you, as the misty network of pines against the sky—the stretches of moor—the flashes of the canal—and all the dear familiar Heimath Land came nearer and nearer. . . .

It is still "chill April" even here, but wonderfully different from Yorkshire. Sunshine—and green things so much more forward—and birds singing their very throats out.

"Lion," the mastiff, I am rather frightened of, but he loves me and gives me paws over and over again. He is pawing me now and will interrupt.

April 22.

The weather is intensely cold again, though nothing can make this country quite dreary—but cold it is! Still there are all the dear old features. I did not know the Mitchett side (of the Frimhurst bridge) of the canal; but I have been a good way down getting water-weeds—but of course you know it well. It is curiously like bits of the S. John [New Brunswick] River. One could almost see birch-bark canoes at points.

To-day the Jelfs came. It was an affecting meeting, our first since he was so ill in Cyprus, and he said, "It used to

seem so little likely one would ever again see the old faces"
. . . He spoke at once about your calling this country Heimath
Land, saying it seemed the very word.

I am going on Thursday to stay with the Jelfs till Monday;
I shall be so thankful to get a Sunday in the old Tin Tabernacle.

K Lines, South Camp, Heimath Land.
April 25.

It is a sunny sweet day, so that I have been strolling about
in the garden without a jacket.   It is strangely pleasant being
here, the old scenes without, and all Sir Howard Elphinstone's
pretty things within.   The Jelfs are staying in the Elphinstones'
hut.   In the matter of pictures I do not always agree with Sir
Howard, but his decorative taste is very good, and the things
he has picked up in all parts of the world are delightful.   " Et
ego, etc."   We have things and things as it is, and shall pick
up more!   He is so very ingenious, and has made a dado over
the mantelpiece, with a white or coloured border on which he
puts pictures and photographs; in the centre is a square of
coloured material with other things mounted on it.   I foresee
making a similar design for our Malta mantelpiece, with a gold
Maltese cross in the centre and tiles round illustrating the eight
Beatitudes. . . .

I am intensely enjoying this bit here.   Yesterday the Jelfs
and the boys and I had a long wander by the canal where the
larches and the birches are getting their tenderest tints on. . . .
On Thursday evening I went to the Tin Church, with the old
bell *tankling* as I went in, and the mess bugles tootling afar as
I came out.   Bell the schoolmaster and baritone started as if I
were a ghost, and sent me a book for the special hymn.   Not a
soul in the officers' seats—but a good choir and a very fair
congregation of men and barrack families.   Said I to myself,
"I've been living in wealthy Bowdon and in ecclesiastical York,
and not had this.   Well done—the Tug of War and the Tin
Tabernacle and the Camp! and unpaid soldiers and their sons
to sing the Lord's Song in the land of their pilgrimage!"

To-day I went with Mrs. Jelf to a meeting at the Club House about "Coffee Houses." When we got in a "rehearsal" (dramatic) was going on, and the chaff was "Have you come for the rehearsal or the coffee-house?" We "Coffee-housers" adjourned to the Whist Room. Sir Thos. Steele in the chair. I had a long chat with him. He says Music and the Drama have declined dreadfully. The meeting was full of friends. "Mat Irvine" nearly wrung my hand off, and I sat by poor Knollys, who is heart-broken at the death of that dear little soul, Captain Barton. It was a first-rate meeting, mixed military and Aldershot tradesmen—a very "nice feeling" displayed—altogether it was wonderfully pleasant.

Exeter. May 16, 1879.

. . . The weather alternates here between North-Easters and mugginess, and I have never slept without fires yet. All the same I have had some lovely *drives*, which you know are so good for me. When Mrs. Fox Strangways couldn't go the Colonel has taken me alone 12 or 14 miles in the dog-cart with a very "free-going" but otherwise prettily-behaved little mare named Daphne. The tumbledown of hills and dales is very pretty here, and the deep red of the earth, and the whitewashed and thatched cottages. Very pretty bits for sketching if it had been sketching-weather. . . .

I hope to get several things done in London. Jean Ingelow has burst out rather about my writings, and wants me to do something "in the style of Madam Liberality," and let her try to get it into *Good Words*, as she thinks I ought to try for a wider audience. I shall certainly go and see her, and talk over matters. . . . I was *very* much pleased Sir Anthony Home had been so much pleased with "Jan." To draw tears from a V.C. and a fine old Scotch medico is very gratifying! Capt. Patten said their own Dr. Craig had also been delighted with it. When "We and the World" is done I mean to rest well on my oars, and then try and aim at something to give me a better footing if I can. . . .

June 14, 1879.

. . . I am getting as devoted to Browning as you. It is very funny—this sudden and simultaneous light on him !

May 23, 1879.

[*Sketch.*]

Forty-four of these aquatic plant tubs stand in one part of the back premises of Clyst S. George Rectory, full of truly wondrous varieties. The above is a thing like white tassels and purple-pink buds. Fancy how I revel in them, and in the garden, which holds 1640 species of herbaceous perennials all labelled and indexed !! The old Rector (he is 89) is as hard at it as ever. He is so pleased to be listened to, and it is enormously interesting though somewhat fatiguing, and leaves me no time whatever for anything else ! My brain whirls with tiles, mosaics, tesseræ, bell-castings, bell-marks, and mottos, electros, squeezes, rubbings, etc., etc. His latest plant fad is Willows and Bamboos, of which he has countless kinds growing and flourishing !!! He is infirm, but it is very grand to see life rich with interests, and with work that will benefit others—so near the grave !

We'd a funny scene this morning when I went over the church with him, and had to write my name in the book.

Very testily—"The *date*, my dear, put the date ! "

"I have put it."

More testily at being in the wrong—"Then put your address, put your address."

I hesitated, and he threw up his hands : " Bless me ! you've not got one. It has always puzzled me so what made *you* take a fancy to a soldier."

He had been very full of all kinds of ancient Church matters —a wonderful bell dedicated to the Blessed Virgin in a very remarkable inscription, etc.,—so I seized the pen and wrote— *Strada Maria Stella, Malta*—and " I dŭ thenk" (as they say here) it will considerably puzzle the old sexton !!!!!

Soon after sunrise on Ascension Day I was woke clear and

clean by the bells *breaking into song.* You know campanology is his great hobby. They rang changes, with long pauses between. Bells often try me very much, at Ecclesfield *par exemple,* but I really enjoyed these. . . .

May 24, 1879.

. . . A very pathetic bit of private news of poor little MacDowell. He was sent by the General to tell them to strike the tents, and was urging on the ammunition to the front, and encouraging the bandsmen to carry it, when a Zulu shot him. A good and not painful end—God bless him! The Capt. Jones who told this, said also that one little bugler killed three big Zulus with his side-arms before he fell! Also that a private of the 24th saved Chard's life at Rorke's Drift by pushing his head down, so that a bullet went over it!

Woolwich. Whit Monday, 1879.

*   *   *   *   *   *

Don't think you have all the picturesque beggars to yourself! Out in a street of Woolwich with Mrs. O'Malley the other day I saw this— [*Sketch.*] The eyes though very clear and intense-looking decided me at once the man was blind, though he had no dog, and was only walking solemnly on, with a *carved fiddle* of white wood under his arm! I ran back after him, and went close in front of him. He gazed and saw nothing. Then I touched him and said, "Are you blind?" He started and said, " Very nearly." I gave him a penny, for which he thanked me, and then I asked about the fiddle. He carved and made it himself out of firewood in the workhouse! The *handle part* (forgive my barbarism!) is "a bit of ash." It was much about the level of North American Indian *art*, but very touching as to patient ingenuity. He asked if anybody had told me about him. I said, "No. But I've a husband who plays the fiddle," and I gave him the balance of my loose coppers! He said, " Have you? He plays, does he? Well. This has been a lucky day

for me." He was a shipwright—can play the piano, he says—
lives in the workhouse in winter and comes out in summer—
with the flowers—and his fiddle! I knew you would like me to
give something to that *povero fratello*.

Woolwich. June 6, 1879.

. . . *The* painter of the Academy this year is Mrs. Butler!!
I do hope some day somewhere you may see *The Remnants of
an Army* and *Recruits for the Connaught Rangers.* The first is
in the *Academy Notes*, which I send you. The second is at least
as fine. [*Sketch.*] The landscape effect is the opal-like sky
and bright light full of moisture after rain—heavy clouds hang
above—the mountains are a leaden blue—and the sky of all
exquisite pale shades of bright colour. Down the wet moor
road comes the group. Two very tall, dark-eyed Connaught
"boys"—one with a set face and his hands in his pockets
looking straight out of the picture—the other with a yearning of
Keltic emotion looking back at the hills as if his heart was
breaking. The strapping young sergeant looks very grave ; but
an "old soldier" behind is lighting his pipe, and a bugler is
holding back a dog. One of the best faces is that of the
drummer who walks first, and whose 13-year-old face is so
furrowed about the brow with oppressive anxiety — very
truthful!

The Remnants of an Army is of course overpowering by the
mere subject, and it is nobly painted. The man and his horse
are wonderful alike. There is nothing to touch these two. But
I *would* like to steal Peter Graham's *The Seabirds' Resting-
Place.* Such penguins sitting on wet rocks with wet Fucus *growing on* them ! Such myriads more in the *sea-mist* that hides the
horizon-line—sitting on distant rocks !—and *such* green waves—
by the light of a sunbeam into one of which you see Laminaria
fronds and lumps of Fucus tossing up and down. You feel wet
and ozoney to come near it ! There are some very fine men's
portraits, and Orchardson's *Gamblers Hard Hit* is the best thing
of his, I think, that I know . . .

. . . There is a very beautiful old gun in the Arsenal upon a gun-carriage with wheels thus [*Sketch*], and with bas-reliefs of St. Paul and the Viper. It is needless to say the gun came from the island called Melita ! But for cunning workmanship and fine bold designs and delicate execution the Chinese guns are the ones ! I am taking rubbings of the patterns for decorative purposes ! They were taken in the war.

There is yet one picture I must tell you of—*A Musical Story by Chopin* "—the boy playing to a group of lads and a tutor. His utterly absorbed face is *admirable*. It is a very pretty thing. Not marvellous, but very good.

August 5, 1879.

  * * * * * *

I must tell you that it is *on the cards* that Caldecott is going to do a coloured picture for me *to write to*, for the October No. of *A. J. M.* (so that it will bind up with the 1879 volume and be the Frontispiece). He is so fragile he can't "hustle," but he wants to do it. D—— and he became great friends in London, and I think now he would help us whenever he could. We have been bold enough to "speak our minds" pretty freely to him, about wasting his time over second-rate "society" work for *Graphic*, etc., etc., when he has such a genius to interpret humour and pathos for good writers, and no real writing gifts himself. (He has done some things called *Flirtation in France*, supplying both letter-press and sketches !—that are terrible to any one who has gone heart and soul into his House that Jack built ! ! !) I've told him frankly if he " *draws down to me* " in the hopes of making *my* share easy by making his common-place, and gives me a " rising young family in sand-boots and frilled trousers with an over-fed mercantile mamma," my "few brains will utterly congeal," but I have made two suggestions to *him*, so closely on his own lines that if hints help him I think he would find it easy. You know *horses* are really his spécialité.

I have asked him to give me a coloured thing and one or two
rough sketches.   Either
                An Old Coaching Day's Idyll
                or—A Trooper's Tragedy.
The same beginning for either :
    Child learning to ride on
                        hobby-horse
                        rocking-horse
                        donkey
                        pony
                etc.   etc.
Then (if coaching) an old haunted-looking posting-house on
a coaching road (Hog's Back !)—a highwayman—a broken-down
postilion—a girl on a pillion, etc., etc.

Or, if military :
A yokel watching a cavalry regiment in Autumn Manœuvres
over a bridge.
A Horse and Trooper—Riding for life (here or Hereafter !)
with another man across his saddle.

Of course it may only hamper him to have hints (I've not
heard yet), but I hope anyhow he'll do something for me.

          *   *   *   *   *   *

                                        August 9, 1879.

          *   *   *   *   *   *

I was reading again at *Robert Falconer* the other day.
What *grand* bits there are in it ?   With such *bosh* close by.   So
like Ruskin in that, who is ever to me a Giant, half of gold and
half of clay !
When G. Macdonald announces (by way of helping one to
help the problems of life !) that the Gospel denounces the sins
of the rich, but nowhere the sins of the poor, one wonders if he
" has his senses," or knows anything about " the poor."   " The
Gospel" is pretty plain about drunkards, extortioners, thieves,
murderers, cursers, and revilers, false swearers, whoremongers,

and "all liars"—I wonder whether these trifling vices are confined to the Upper Ten Thousand!

But oh, that description to the *son* of what it sounded like when *his father* played the *Flowers of the Forest* on his fiddle, isn't to be beaten in any language I believe! All the Scotch lasses after Flodden doing the work of an agricultural people in the stead of the men who lay on Flodden Field!—" Lasses to reap and lasses to bind—Lasses to stook," etc., etc., and " no a word I'll warrant ye, to the orra lad that didna gang wi' the lave"! ! ! !* and the lad's outburst in reply, " I'd raither be gratten for nor kissed ! "

Poor Z——! They don't teach that at Academies and Staff Colleges, nor in the Penny-a-line of newspaper correspondents and the like—but he should get some woman to soak it into his brains that the men women will love are men who would rather be "gratten for" in honour than be kissed in shame.

    *   *   *   *   *   *

Ecclesfield. August 23, 1879.

    *   *   *   *   *   *

Talking of drawings, what do you think? Caldecott has done me the most *lovely* coloured thing to write a short tale to for October *A. J. M.* It is very good of him. He has simply drawn what I asked, but it is quite lovely !

A village Green, sweet little old Church, and house and oak tree, etc., etc. in distance, a small boy with aureole of fair hair on a red-haired pony, coming full tilt across it blowing a penny trumpet and scattering pretty ladies, geese, cocks and hens from his path. His dog running beside him ! You will be delighted !

    *   *   *   *   *   *

* *Robert Falconer*, chap. xix.

September 1, 1879.

I have done my little story to Caldecott's picture, and I have a strong notion that it will please you.   It is called "Jackanapes." . . . I shall be so *disappointed* if you don't like "Jackanapes." But I think it is just what you will like !! I think you will cry over him !

September 19, 1879.

Isn't it a great comfort that I have finished the serial story, and "Jackanapes"?—so that I am now quite free, and never mean to write against time again.   I know you never cared for the serial ; however, it is done, and tolerably satisfactory I think.   "Jackanapes" I do hope you will like, picture and all.   C—— sent Mr. Ruskin "Our Field," and I am proud to hear he says it is not a mere story—it's a poem !   Great praise from a great man !

October 11, 1879.

      *   *   *   *   *   *

I was knocked up yesterday in a good cause.   We went to see Mr. Ruskin at Herne Hill.   I find him *far* more *personally* lovable than I had expected.   Of course he lives in the incense of an adoring circle, but he is absolutely unaffected himself, and with a GREAT charm.   So much gentler and more refined than I had expected, and such clear Scotch turquoise eyes.

He had been out to buy buns and grapes for *me* (!), carrying the buns home himself very carefully that they might not be crushed !!   We are so utterly at one on some points : it is very delightful to hear him talk.   I mean it is uncommonly pleasant to hear things one has long thought very vehemently, put to one by a Master !!   *Par exemple.*   You know my mania about the indecent-cruel element in French art, and how the Frenchiness of Victor Hugo chokes me from appreciating him : just as we were going away yesterday Mr. Ruskin called out, "There is something I MUST show Aunt Judy," and fetched two photos. One, an old court with bits of old gothic tracery mixed in with a modern tumbledown building—peaceful old doorway, wild vine twisting up the lintel, modern shrine, dilapidated waterbutt, sunshine straggling in—as far as the beauty of contrast and suggestiveness and form and (one could fancy) colour could go, perfect as a picture. (R——— didn't say all this, but we agreed as to the obvious beauty, etc.) Then he brought out the other photo, and said, "but the French artist cannot rest with that, it must be heightened and stained with blood," and there was the court (photo from a French picture), with two children lying murdered in the sunshine.

Another point we met on was my desire to write a tale on Commercial Honour. He was delighted, and will I think furnish me with "tips." His father was a merchant of the old school. And then to my delight I found him soldier-mad!! So we got on very affably, and I hope to go and stay there when I go home next summer.

*   *   *   *   *   *

November 7, 1879.

Friends are truly kind. Miss Mundella sent two season tickets for the Monday "Pop." to D——— and me. I managed to go and stay for most of it. Norman Neruda, Piatti, and *Janotha*—have you heard Janotha play the piano? I think she is *very* wonderful. It is so absolutely without affectation, and so *selfless*, and yet such a mastery of the instrument. Her *rippling* passages are like music writ in water, and she has a singing touch too, and when she accompanies, the subordination and sympathy are admirable. She is not pretty, nor in any way got up, but is elfish and quaint-looking, and quite young. We sat quite near to Browning, who is a nice-looking old man, delightfully *clean*. He seemed to delight in Neruda and Piatti, and followed the music with a score of his own.

Ecclesfield. Saturday, January 31, 1880.

How beautiful a day is to-day I cannot tell you! It does refresh me! . . . Head and spine very shaky this morning so that I could not get warm ; but I wrapped in my fur cloak, and went out into the sunshine, up and down, up and down the churchyard flags. A sunny old kirkyard is a nice place, I always think, for aged folk and invalids to creep up and down in, and "Tombstone Morality" isn't half as wearing to the nerves as the problems of *life!* . . .

       *   *   *   *   *   *

Greno House, Tuesday.

Harry Howard drove me up yesterday. It was *just* as much as I could bear ; but I lay on the sofa till dinner, and went to bed at eight, and though my head kept me awake at first, I did well on the whole. Breakfast in bed, a bigger one than I have eaten for three weeks, and since then I have had an hour's drive. The roughness of the roads is unlucky, but the air *divine!* Such sweet sunshine, and Greno Wood, with yellow remains of bush and bracken, and heavy mosses on the sandstone walls, and tiny streams trickling through boggy bits of the wood, and coming out over the wall to overflow those picturesque stone troughs which are so oddly numerous, and which I had in my head when I wrote the first part of "Mrs. Overtheway."

       *   *   *   *   *   *

January 11, 1880.

       *   *   *   *   *   *

Very dear to me are all your "tender and true" regards for the old home—the grey-green nest (more grey now than green !) a good deal changed and weatherbeaten, but not quite deserted —which is bound up with so much of our lives ! It is one of the points on which we feel very much alike, our love for things, and places, and beasts ! ! ! Another chord of sympathy was very strongly pulled by your writing of the "grey-green fields," and sending your love to them. No one I ever met has, I think, *quite* your sympathy with exactly what the external world of out-of-doors is to me and has been ever since I can remember. From days when the batch of us went-out-walking with the Nurses, and the round moss-edged holes in the roots of gnarled trees in the hedges, and the red leaves of Herb Robert in autumn, and all the inexhaustible wealth of hedges and ditches and fields, and the Shroggs, and the brooks, were happiness of the keenest kind—to now when it is as fresh and strong as ever ; it has been a pleasure which has balanced an immense lot of physical pain, and which (between the affectation of the sort of thing being fashionable—and other people being destitute of the sixth sense to comprehend it—so that one feels a fool either way)—one rarely finds any one to whom one can comfortably speak of it, and be *understanded* of them. It is the one of my peculiarities which you have never doubted or misunderstood ever since we knew each other ! I fancy we must (as it happens) *see* those things very much alike. That grey-green winter tone (for which I have a particular love) has been "on my mind" for days, and it was odd you should send your love to it. Don't think me daft to make so much of a small matter, I am sure it is not so to me. It is what would make me *content* in so many corners of the world ! And I thought when I read your letter, that if we live to be old together, we have a common and an unalienable source of "that mysterious thing felicity" in any small sunny nook where we may end our days—so long as there is a bit of yellow sandstone to glow, or a birch stem to shine in the sun ! . . .

[*Grenoside.*] February 21, 1880.

* * * * * *

I whiled away my morning in bed to-day by going through the *Lay of the Last Minstrel.* There are lovely bits in it.

Reading away at Mrs. Browning lately has very much confirmed my notion that the fault of her things is lack of condensation. They are almost without exception too long. I doubt if one should ever leave less than fifty per cent. of a situation to one's readers' own imagination, if one aims at the

highest class of readers. That swan song to Camöens from his
dying lady would have been very perfect in FIVE verses. As it
is, one gets tired even of the exquisite refrain "Sweetest eyes
were ever seen" (an expression he had used about her eyes in a
song, and which haunts her).

The other night we had Sergeant Dickinson up. He has
lately settled in the village. He was in the Light Cavalry
Charge at Balaklava (17th Lancers), and also at Alma, Inker-
man, and Sebastopol. He has also the Mutiny Medal and
Good Conduct and Service one, so he is a good specimen.
Curious luck, he never had a *scratch* (!). Says he has had far
"worse wounds" performing in Gyms., as he was a good
swordsman, etc. He told us some *dear* tales of old Sir Colin
Campbell. He said his men idolized him, but their wives rather
more so, and if any of them failed to send home remittances,
the spouses wrote straight off to Sir Colin, who had up "Sandy
or Wully " for remonstrance, and stopped his grog "till I hear
again from your wife, man."

On one occasion he saw a drummer-boy drunk, and a
sergeant near. Sir Colin: "Sergeant, does yon boy belong to
your company?"

Sergeant: "He does not, sir."

"Does he draw a rum allowance?"

"He does, sir."

"Well, away to the Captain of his company, and say it's
my orders that the oldest soldier in this bairn's company is to
draw his rum, till he feels convinced it's for the lad's benefit
that he should tak it himsel'—and that'll not be just yet awhile
I'm thinking."

Some brilliant tales too of the wit and gallantry of Irish
comrades, several of whom wore the kilt. And almost neatest
of all, a story of coming across a fellow-villager among the
Highlanders:

"But I were fair poozled. He came from t' same place as
me, and a clever Yorkshireman too, and he were talking as
Scotch as any of 'em. So I says, 'Why I'm beat! what are

YOU talking Scotch for, and you a Knaresborough man?'
'Whisht! whisht! Dickinson,' he says, 'we mun A' be Scotch
in a Scotch regiment—or there's no living.'" . . .

February 19, 1880.

I have been re-reading the *Legend of Montrose* and the
Heart of Midlothian with *such* delight, and poems of both the
Brownings, and Ruskin, and *The Woman in White*, and *Tom
Brown's Schooldays*, etc., etc. !!! I have got two volumes of
The Modern Painters back with me to go at.

What a treat your letters are! Bits are *nearly* as good as
being there. The sunset you saw with Miss C——, and the
shadowy groups of the masquers below in the increasing mists
of evening, painted itself as a whole on to my brain—in the way
scenes of Walter Scott always did. Like the farewell to the
Pretender in *Red Gauntlet*, and the black feather on the quick-
sand in *The Bride of Lammermuir*.

March 1, 1880.

*   *   *   *   *   *

The ball must have been a grand sight, but I think, judging
from the list, that your dress as Thomas the Rhymer stands out
in marked *individuality*. Nothing shows more how few people
are at all *original* than the absence of anything striking or quaint
in most of the characters assumed at a Fancy Ball. This, however, is Pampering the Pride of you members of the Mutual
Admiration Society. You must not become cliquish—no not
Ye Yourselves !!!!

Above all *you* must never lose that gracious quality (for
which I have so often given you a prize) of patience and
sympathy with small musicians and jangling pianos in the houses
of kind and hospitable Philistines. Besides, I like you to be
largely gracious and popular. All the same I confess that it is
a grievance that music (and sherry!) are jointly regarded as
necessary to be supplied by all hosts and hostesses—whether they
can give you them good or not! People do not cram their bad

drawings down your throats in similar fashion. Still what is, is
—and Man is more than Music—and I have never felt the real
mastership you hold in music more than when you have beaten
a march out of some old tub for kindness' sake with a little
gracious bow at the end! Don't you remember my telling you
about that wisp of an organist whom Mr. R— petted till he didn't
know his shock head from his clumsy heels, and the insufferable
airs he gave himself at their party over the piano, and the
audience, and the lights, and silence, and what he would or
would not play to the elderly merchants. And of all the
amateur-and-water performances ! ! ! I have heard enough
good playing to be able to gauge him ! . . .

Incapacity for every other kind of effort is giving me leisure
for a feast of reading and *re-reading* such as I have not indulged
for years. Amongst other things I have read for the first time
Black's *Strange Adventures of a Phaeton*—it is *very* charming
indeed, and if you haven't read it, some time you should. As a
rule I detest German heroes *to English books*, but Von Rosen is
irresistible! and the refrain outbreaks of his jealousy are really
high art, when he unconsciously brings every subject back to the
original motif—" but that young man of Twickenham—he is a
most pitiful fellow—" you feel Dr. Wolff was never more simply
sincere and self-deluded, than Von Rosen's belief that it is an
abstract criticism. Also you know how tedious broken English
in a novel is, as a rule. But Black has very arristically managed
his hero's idioms so as to give great effect. And as we have a
brain wave on about Womanhood you may like, as much as I
have, V. Rosen's sketch of English women (to whom he gives
the palm over those of other nations). Speaking of some others
—" very nice to look at perhaps, and very charming in their
ways perhaps, but not sensible, honest, frank like the English
woman, *and not familiar with the seriousness of the world, and
not ready to see the troubles of other people.* But your English-
woman *who is very frank to be amused*, and can enjoy herself
when there is a time for that, who is *generous in time of trouble
and is not afraid*, and can be firm and active and yet very gentle,

and who does not think always of herself, but is ready to help other people, and can look after a house and manage affairs —that is a better kind of woman I think—more to be trusted —more of a companion—oh, there is no comparison ! "

It is very good, isn't it ?—and he is mending the fire during this outburst, and keeps piling coal on coal as he warms with his subject.

I must also just throw you two quotations from Macaulay's most interesting *Life and Letters*. Quotations within quotations, for they are extracts.

> "Antoni Stradivari has an eye
> That winces at false work and loves the true."
>
> (BROWNING.)

> "There is na workeman
> That can both worken wel and hastilie
> This must be done at leisure parfaitlie."
>
> (CHAUCER.)

By the bye, the italics in Black's quotations are *mine*. Good wording I think.

But how one does go back with delight to Scott ! I confess I think to have written the *Heart of Midlothian* is to have put on record the existence of a moral atmosphere in one's own nation as grand as the ozone of mountains. WHAT a contrast to that of French novels (with no disrespect to the brilliant art and refreshing brain quickness of the latter) ; but Ruskin's appeal to the responsibility of those who wield Arts instead of Trades recurs to one as one under which Scott might have laid his hand upon his breast, and looked upwards with a clear conscience. . . .

March 16, 1880.

  *   *   *   *   *   *

I quite agree with you about an artlessness and roughness in Scott's work. I thought what I had dwelt on was the magnificent *tone* of the *H. of Midlothian*. Also he has two

of the first (first in rank and order if not first in degree) quali-
fications for a writer of fiction—Dramatism and individuality
amongst his characters.   He had (rather perhaps one should
say), the quality which is *nascitur non fit*—Imagination.   It is
the great defect, *I think*, of some of our best modern writers.
They are marvellously FIT and terribly little NASCITUR.   It
is why I can never concede the highest palm in her craft to
G. Eliot.   Her writing is glorious—Imagination limited—
Dramatism—nil !

She draws people she has seen (Mrs. Poyser) like a photograph—she imagines a Daniel Deronda, and he is about "as
natural as waxworks."

"I've been reading Jean Ingelow's *Fated to be Free* lately,
and it is a marvellous mixture of beauty and failure.   But *lovely*
passages.   Incisive as G. Eliot, and from the point of view of a
tenderer mind and experience.   This is beautiful, isn't it ?

"Nature before it has been touched by man is almost always
beautiful, strong, and cheerful in man's eyes ; but nature, when
he has once given it his culture and then forsaken it, has usually
an air of sorrow and helplessness.   He has made it live the
more by laying his hand upon it and touching it with his life.
It has come to relish of his humanity, and it is so flavoured
with his thoughts, and ordered and permeated by his spirit,
that if the stimulus of his presence is withdrawn it cannot for a
long while do without him, and live for itself as fully and as
well as it did before."

The double edge of the sentiment is very exquisite, and the
truth of the natural fact very perfect as observation, and the
book is full of such writing.   But oh, dear ! the confusion of
plot is so maddening you have a delirious feeling that everybody is getting engaged to his half-sister or widowed stepmother,
and keep turning back to make sure !   But the dramatism is
very good and leads you on. . . .

March 22, 1880.

. . . . I am getting you a curious little present. It is Thos. À Kempis's *De Imitatione Christi* in Latin *and Arabic.* A scarce edition printed in Rome. I think you will like to have it. That old Thomas was much more than a mere monk. A man for all time, his monasticism being but a fringe upon the robe of his wisdom and *honest* Love of God. It will be curious to see how it lends itself to Arabic. Well, I fancy. Being in very proverb-ial mould. Such verses as this (I quote roughly from memory):

"That which thou dost not understand when thou readest thou shalt understand in the day of thy visitation: for there be secrets of religion which are not known till they be felt—and are not felt but in the Day of a great calamity!" (a piece of wisdom with application to other experiences besides religious ones). I think this will read well in the language of the East. As also " In omnibus rebus Respice Finem," etc. . . .

* * * * * *

Tuesday.

I am quite foolishly disappointed. The À Kempis is gone already! It is a new Catalogue, and I fancied it was an out-o'-way chance. It seems Ridler has no other Arabic books whatever. He may not have known its value. It "went" for six shillings ! ! !

* * * * * *

To the Bishop of Fredericton.

131, *Finborough Road, South Kensington.*
March 23, 1880.

My dear Lord,

I thank you with all my heart for the gift of your book,* and yet more for the kindly inscription, which affected me much.

---

* *The Book of Job,* translated from the Hebrew Text by John, Bishop of Fredericton.

As one gets older one feels distance—or whatever parts one from people one cares for—worse and worse, I think!—However, whatever helps to remedy the separation is all the dearer!

I had devoured enough of your notes, to have laughed more than once and almost to have heard you speak, before I moved from the chair in which the book found me, and had read all the Introduction. I could HEAR you say that "Bildad uttered a few trusims in a pompous tone"!

What I have read of your version seems to me grand, bits here and there I certainly had never felt the poetical power of before. Rex will be delighted with it!

I fully receive all you say about Satan and the Sons of God. But I think a certain painfulness about such portions of Holy Writ—does not come from (1) Unwillingness to lay one's hand upon one's mouth and be silent before God. (2) Or difficulty about the Personality of Satan. I fancy it is because in spite of oneself it is painful that one of the rare liftings of the Great Veil between us and the "ways" of the Majesty of God should disclose a scene of such petty features—a sort of wrangling and experimentalizing, that it would be *pleasanter* to be able to believe was a parable brought home to our vulgar understandings rather than a real vision of the Lord our Strength.

I am, my dear Lord,
Your grateful and ever affectionate old friend,
J. H. E.

To J. H. E.

Fredericton. April 8, 1880.

MY DEAR MRS. EWING,

I will not let the mail go out without proving that I am not a bad correspondent, and without thanking you for your delightful letter. Oh! why don't you squeeze yourself sometimes into that funny little house opposite Miss Bailey's, and let me take a cup of tea off the cushions, or some other place where the books would allow it to be put? And why don't you allow me to stumble over my German? And why doesn't Rex, Esq. (for Rex is too familiar even for a Bishop) correct my musical efforts? How terrible this word *past* is! The past is at all events *real*, but the future is so shadowy, and like the ghosts of Ulysses it entirely eludes one's grasp. I speak of course of things that belong to this life. It was (I assure you) a treat to lay hold of you and your letters, and (a minor consideration) to find that even your handwriting had not degenerated, and had not become like spiders' legs dipped in ink and crawling on the paper, as is the case of some nameless correspondents. There was only one word I could not make out. In personal appearance the letters stood thus, *vs*. It looks like "us," or like the Greek *υν*, which being interpreted is "pig." But M——, who is far cleverer than I am, at once oracularly pronounced it "very," and I believe her and you too. . . .

I was greatly tickled in your getting *amusement* out of "Job," the last book where one would have expected to find it; but stop—I recollect it is out of *me*, not the patriarch, that you find something to smile at, and no doubt you are right, for no doubt I say ridiculous things sometimes. *Au sérieux*, it pleases me much that you enter into my little book, and evidently have *read* it, for I have had complimentary letters from people who plainly had not read a word, and to the best of my belief never will. I wish you had been more critical, and had pointed out the faults and defects of the book, of which there are no doubt some, if not many, to be found. I flatter myself that I have made more clear some passages utterly unintelligible in our A. V., such as, "He shall deliver the island of the innocent, yea," etc., chap. xxii. 30, and chap. xxxvi. 33, and the whole of chap. xxiv. and chap. xx. What a fierce, cruel, hot-headed Arab Zophar is! How the wretch gloats over Job's miseries. Yet one admires his word-painting while one longs to kick him! I am glad to see the *Church Times* agrees with me in the early character of the book. There is not a trace in it of later Jewish history or feeling. The argu-

XVIII. 15

ment on the other side is derived from Aramaic words only, which words are not unsuitable to a writer who either lived, *or had lived* out of Palestine, and scholars agree now that they may belong either to a very late or a very early time, and are used by people familiar with the cognate languages of the East.

A word about your very natural feeling on the subject of Satan. I suppose that Inspiration does not interfere with the character of mind belonging to the inspired person. The writer thinks Orientally, within the range of thought common to the age, and patriarchal knowledge, so that he could neither think nor write as S. Paul or S. John, even though inspired. We criticize his writing (when we do criticize it) from the standpoint of the nineteenth century, *i. e.* from the accumulated knowledge, successive revelations, and refined civilization of several thousand years.

Its extreme simplicity of description may appear to us trivial. But is not the fact indubitable that God tries us as He did Job, though by different methods? And is not our Lord's expression, "whom Satan hath bound, lo! these eighteen years," and S. Paul's, "to deliver such an one to Satan for the destruction of the flesh," analogous to the account in Job? One has only to try to transfer oneself to the patriarchal age, when there was no Bible, no Lord Jesus come in the flesh, but when at intervals divine revelations were given by personal manifestations and then withdrawn, and to take out of oneself all one has known about God from a child, to view the account as an Oriental would look at it, not as a Western Christian. The "experiment" (so to speak) involves one of the grandest questions in the world—Is religion only a refined selfishness, or is there such a thing as real faith and love of God, apart from any temporal reward? The devil asserts the negative and so (observe) do Job's so-called friends; but Job proves the affirmative, and hence amidst certain unadvised expressions he (in the main) speaks of God the thing that is right.

I do not know that there is in the early chapters anything that can be called "petty," more than in the speech of the devils to our Lord, and His suffering them to go into the swine.

We must, however, beware that we do not, when we say "petty," merely mean at bottom what is altogether different from our ordinary notions, formed by daily and general experience of life, as we ourselves find it.

All this long yarn, and not a word about your health, which is shameful. We both do heartily rejoice that you are better, and only hope for everybody's sake and your own, you will nurse and husband your strength. . . .

Your affectionate old friend,
JOHN FREDERICTON.

TO A. E.

April 10, 1880.

   *   *   *   *   *   *

The night before last I dined with Jean Ingelow. I went in to dinner with Alfred Hunt (a water-colour painter to whose work Ruskin is devoted). A *very* unaffected, intelligent, agreeable man; we had a very pleasant chat. On my other side sat a dear old Arctic Explorer, old *Ray*. I fell quite in love with him, and with the nice Scotch accent that overtook him when he got excited. Born and bred in the Orkneys, almost, as he said, *in the sea;* this wild boyhood of familiarity with winds and waves, and storms and sports, was the beginning of the life of adventure and exploration he has led. He told me some very interesting things about Sir John Franklin. He said that great and good as he was there were qualities which he had not, the lack of which he believed cost him his life. He said Sir John went well and gallantly at his end, if he could keep to the lines he had laid down; but he had not "fertility of resource for the unforeseen," and didn't *adapt* himself. As an instance, he said, he always made his carriers *march* along a given line. If stores were at A, and the point to be reached B, by the straight line from A to B he would send the local men he had *hired* through bog and over boulder, whereas if he said to any of

them, "B is the place you must meet me at," with the knowledge of natives and the instinct of savages they would have
gone with half the labour and twice the speed.   He said too
that Franklin's party suffered terribly because none of his officers
were *sportsmen*, which, he said, simply means starvation if your
stores fail you.   We had a long talk about scientific men and
their *deductions*, and he said quaintly, "Ye see, I've just had a
lot of rough expeerience from me childhood ; and things have
happened now and again that make me not just put implicit
faith in all scientific dicta.   I must tell you, Mrs. Ewing, that
when I was a young man, and just back from America and the
Arctic Regions, where I'd lived and hunted from a mere laddie,
I went to a lecture delivered by one of the verra *first* men of
the day (whose name for that reason I won't give to ye) before
some three thousand listeners and the late Prince Consort ; and
there on the table was the head and antlers of a male reindeer—
beasts that, as I'm telling ye, I knew *eentimately*, and had killed
at all seasons.   And this man, who, as I'm telling ye, was one
of the verra furrrst men of the day (which is the reason why I'm
not giving ye his name) spoke on, good and bad, and then he
said, 'Ladies and gentlemen, and your Royal Highness, be
good enough to look at the head of this Reindeer.   Here ye see
the antlers,' and so forth, 'and ye'll obsairve that there's a horn
that has the shape of a shovel and protrudes over the beast's
eyes in a way that must be horribly inconvenient.   But when ye
see its shape, ye'll perceive one of the most beautiful designs of
Providence, a *proveesion* as we may say ; for this inconvenient
horn is so shaped that with it the beast can shovel away the
deep winter snow and find its accustomed food.'

"And when I heard this I just shook with laughing till a
man I knew saw me, and asked what I was laughing at, and I
said, 'Because I happen to know that the male reindeer *sheds
its antlers* every year in the beginning of November, *snow shovel*
and all, and does not resume them till spring.'" ! ! ! ! ! !

         *   *   *   *   *   *

April 26, 1880.

*   *   *   *   *   *

Curious your writing to me about Dante's Hell—and Lethe. Two books in my childhood gave the outward and visible signs of that inward and spiritual interest in Death and the Life to Come which is one of the most vehement ones of childhood (and which breaks out QUITE as strongly in those who have been carefully brought up apart from "religious convictions" as in those whose minds have been soaked in them). One was Flaxman's *Dante*, the other Selous's illustrations in the same style to the *Pilgrim's Progress*. I do not know whether I suffered more in my childhood than other children. Possibly, as my head was a good deal too big for my body! But I remember two troubles that haunted me. One that I should get tired of Eternity. Another that I couldn't be happy in Heaven unless I could *forget*. And in this latter connection I loved indescribably one of Flaxman's best designs. [*Sketch.*] I can't remember it well enough to draw decently, but this was the attitude of Dante whom Beatrice was just laving in the Waters of Forgetfulness before they entered Paradise.

And even more fond was I of the passing of the great river by Christiana and her children, and by that mixed company of the brave and the weak, the young and the old, the gentle and the impatient,—and that grand touch by which the "Mr. Ready-to-Halt" of the long Pilgrimage crossed the waters of Death without fear or fainting.

*   *   *   *   *   *

Why should you think I should differ with Dante in his estimate of sin? I doubt if I could rearrange his Circles, except that "Lust" is a wide word, as = Passion I should probably leave it where it is ; but there are hideous forms of it which are inextricably mingled, if not identical with Cruelty,—and Cruelty I should put at the lowest round of all.

Clyst S. George.   April 30, 1880.

*   *   *   *   *   *

We have had rather a chaff with Mr. Ellacombe (who in his ninety-first year is as keen a gardener as ever!) because he has many strange sorts of *Fritillary*, and when I told him I had seen and gone wild over a sole-coloured pale yellow one which I saw exhibited in the Horticultural Gardens, he simply put me down—"No, my dear, there's no such thing; there's a white Fritillary I can show you outside, and there's *Fritillaria Lutea* which is yellow and spotted, but there's no such plant as you describe." Still it evidently made him restless, and he kept relating anecdotes of how people are always sending him *shaves* about flowers. "I'd a letter the other day, my dear, to describe a white Crown Imperial—a thing that has *never been!*" Later he announced—"I have written to Barr and Sugden—'Gentlemen! Here's another White Elephant. A lady has seen a sole-coloured Yellow Fritillary!'"

This morning B. and S. wrote back, and are obliged to confess that "a yellow Fritillary has been produced," but (not being the producers) they add, "It is not a good yellow." *Pour moi*, I take leave to judge of colours as well as Barr and Sugden, and can assure you it is a very lovely yellow, pale and chrome-y. It has been like a chapter out of Alphonse Karr!

One of the horticultural papers is just about to publish Mr. Ellacombe's old list of the things he has grown in his own garden. Three thousand species!

*   *   *   *   *   *

I hope you liked that *Daily Telegraph* article on the Back Gardener I sent you? It is really fine workmanship in the writing line as well as being amusing. I abuse the Press often enough, but I will say such Essays (for they well deserve the name) are a great credit to the age—in Penny Dailies!!!

"The Nursery Nonsense of the Birds," "A Stratified Chronology of Occupancies," "Waves of Whims," etc., etc., are the work of a man who can use his tools with a master's hand, or at least a *skilled* worker's!

I am reading another French novel, by Daudet, *Jack.* So far (as I have got) it is marvellous *writing.* "Le petit Roi— Dahomey" in the school "des pays chauds" is a Dickenesque character, but quite marvellous—his fate—his "gri-gri"—his final Departure to the land where all things are so "made new" that "the former" do not "come into mind"—having in that supreme hour *forgotten* alike his sufferings, his tormentors, and his friends—and only babbling in Dahomeian in that last dream in which his spirit returned to its first earthly home before "going home" for Good!—is superb ! ! !   The possible meanness and brutality of civilized man in Paris—the possible grandeur and obvious immortality of the smallest, youngest, "gri-gri" worshipping nigger of Dahomey—oh it is wonderful altogether, and I should fancy SUCH a sketch of the *incompris* poet and the rest of the clique ! !   "*C'est* LUI."

  *   *   *   *   *   *

Ecclesfield, Sheffield.   July 23, 1880.

MY DEAR MR. CALDECOTT,
   I am sending you a number of "Jackanapes" in case you have lost your other.

I have made marks against places from some of which I think you could select easy scenes; I mean easy in the sense of being on the lines where your genius has so often worked.

I will put some notes about each at the end of my letter. What I now want to ask you is whether you *could* do me a few illustrations of the vignette kind for "Jackanapes," so that it might come out at Christmas.   Christmas *ought* to mean October ! so it would of course be very delightful if you could have completed them in September—and as soon as might be.   But do not WORRY your brain about dates.   I would rather give it up than let you feel the fetters of Time, which, when they drag one at one's work, makes the labour double.   But if you will begin them, and *see* if they come pretty readily to your fingers, I shall only too well understand it if after all you can't finish in time for this season !

In short I won't press *you* for all my wishes !—but I do feel rather disposed to struggle for a good place amongst the hosts of authors who are besetting you; and as I am not physically or mentally well constituted for surviving amongst the fittest, if there is *much shoving* (!) I want to place my plea on record.

So will you try?—

*   *   *   *   *   *

It was very kind of you and your wife to have us to see your sketches.   I hope you are taking in ozone in the country.

Yours ever,

J. H. E.

[NOTES.]

Respectfully suggested scenes to choose from.

Initial **T** out of the old tree on the green, with perhaps *to secure portrait* the old POSTMAN sitting there with his bag *à la* an old Chelsea Pensioner.

1. A lad carrying his own long-bow (by regulation his own height) and trudging by his pack-horse's side, the horse laden with arrows for Flodden Field (September 9, 1513). Small figures back view (!) going westwards—poetic bit of moorland and sky.

2. If you *like*—a portrait of the little Miss Jessamine in Church.

3 to 5. You may or may not find some bits on page 706, such as the ducking in the pond of the political agitator (very small figures including the old Postman, ex-soldier of Chelsea Pensioner type). Old inn and coach in distance, geese (not the human ones) scattered in the fray.

The Black Captain, with his hand on his horse's mane, bigger—(so as to secure portrait) and vignetted if you like; or *small* on his horse stooping to hold his hand out to a child, Master Johnson, seated in a puddle, and Nurses pointing out the bogy; or standing looking amused behind Master Johnson (page 707).

6. Pretty vignetted portrait of the little Miss J., three-quarter length, about size of page 29 of *Old Christmas*. Scene, girl's bedroom—she with her back to mirror, face buried in her hands, "crying for the Black Captain"; her hair down to just short of her knees, the back of her hair catching light from window and reflected in the glass. Old Miss Jessamine (portrait) talking to her "like a Dutch uncle" about the letter on the dressing-table; aristocratic outline against window, and (as Queen Anne died) "with one finger up"!!!!! (These portraits would make No. 2 needless probably.)

7. Not worth while. I had thought of a very small quay scene with slaves, "black ivory"—and a Quaker's back! (Did you ever read the correspondence between Charles Napier and Mr. Gurney on Trade and War?)

8. A very pretty elopement please! Finger-post pointing to Scotland—Captain *not* in uniform of course.

9 or 10—hardly; too close to the elopement which we *must* have!

11. You are sure to make that pretty.

12. Might be a very small shallow vignette of the field of Waterloo. I will look up the hours, etc., and send you word.

13. As you please—or any part of this chapter.

16. I mean a tombstone like this [*Sketch of flat-topped tombstone*], very common with us.

17, 18. I leave to you.

19 or 20, might suit you.

21. Please let me try and get you a photo of a handsome old general!! I think I will try for General MacMurdo, an old Indian hero of the most slashing description and great good looks.

22. I thought some comic scene of a gentleman in feather-bed and nightcap with a paper—"Rumours of Invasion" conspicuous—might be vignetted into a corner.

23 might be fine, and go down side of page; quite alone as vignette, or distant indication of Jackanapes looking after or up at him.

24. Should you require military information for any scene here?

25—26. I hope you could see your way to 26. Back view of horses—" Lollo the 2nd " and a screw, Tony lying over his holding on by the neck and trying to get at his own reins from Jackanapes' hand. J.'s head turned to him in full glow of the sunset against which they ride; distant line of dust and "retreat " and curls of smoke.

The next chapter requires perhaps a good deal of "war material " to paint with, and strictly soldier-type faces.

27. The cobbler giving his views might be a good study with an advertisement somewhere of the old " souled and healed cheap."

28. This scene I think you might like, and please on the wall have a hatchment with " Dulce et decorum est pro patriâ mori" (excuse my bad Latinity if I have misquoted).

29 would make a pretty scene, I think, and

30 would make me too happy if you scattered pretty groups and back views of the young people, "the Major " and one together, in one of your perfect bits of rural English summer-time.

If there *were* to be a small vignette at the end, I should like a wayside Calvary with a shadowy Knight in armour, lance in rest, approaching it from along a long flat road.

Now please (it is nearly post time !) forgive how very badly I have written these probably confusing suggestions. I am not very well, and my head and *thumb* both fail me.

If you can do it, do it as you like. I will send you a photo of an officer who will do for the Black Captain, and will try and secure a General also. If you could lay your hands on the Illustrated Number that was " extra" for the death of the Prince Imperial—a R.A. officer close by the church door, helping in one end of the coffin, is a very typical military face.

Yours, J. H. E.

To A. E.

July 30, 1880.

*   *   *   *   *   *

Oh, with what sympathy I hear you talk of Shakespeare.
Nay ! not Dante and not Homer—not Chaucer—and not Goethe
—"not Lancelot nor another" are really his peers.

Here blossom sonnets that one puts on a par with his—there,
in another man's work the illimitable panorama of varied and
life-like men and women "merely players," may draw laughter
and tears (Crabbe, and much of Dickens and other men, and
Don Quixote). His coarse wit and satire and shrewdness,
when he is least pure, may I suppose find rivals in some of the
eighteenth or seventeenth century English writers, and in the
marvellous brilliancy of French ones. When he is purest and
highest I cannot think of a Love Poet to touch him. Tennyson
perhaps nearest. But *he* seems quite unable to fathom the heart
of a noble woman with any *strength* of her own, or any knowledge of the world. "Enid" is to me intolerable as well as the
degraded legend it was founded on. Perhaps the brief thing of
Lady Godiva is the nearest approach, and Elaine faultless as the
picture of a maiden-heart brought up in "the innocence of
ignorance." But he can write fairly of "fair women." Scott
runs closer, but his are paintings from without. "Jeanie Deans"
is bad to beat ! !

Shelley comes to his side when *weirdness* is concerned.

"Five fathom deep thy father lies," etc.,

is run hard by—

"Its passions will rock thee
    As the storms rock the ravens on high :
Bright reason will mock thee,
    Like the sun from a wintry sky.

> From thy nest every rafter
> Will rot, and thine eagle home
> *Leave thee naked to laughter,*
> *When leaves fall and cold winds come."*

But I will not bore you with comparisons. My upshot is that no one of the many who may rival him in SOME of his perfections, COMBINE them all in ONE genius. In all these philosophizing days—who touches him in philosophy? From the simplest griefs and pleasures, and humanity at its simplest—Macduff over the massacre of his wife and children—to all that the most delicate brain may search into and suffer, as Hamlet—or the ten thousand exquisite womanish thoughts of Portia, a creature of brain power and feminine fragility—

"By my troth, Nerissa, my little body is a-weary of this great world."

*   *   *   *   *   *

To C. T. G.

Greno House, Grenoside, Sheffield.
Aug. 3, 1880.

*   *   *   *   *   *

A propos of my affairs . . . next year we might do something with some of my "small gems." Don't *you* like "Aldegunda" (Blind Man and Talking Dog)? D. does so much. Do you like the "Kyrkegrim turned Preacher," "Ladders to Heaven," and "Dandelion Clocks"? . . .

. . . As you know, these *little* things are the chief favourites with my more educated friends, whose kindness consoles me for the much labour I spend on so few words (The "Kyrkegrim turned Preacher" was "in hand" two years!!!), and I think their only chance would be to be so dressed and presented as to specially and downrightly appeal to those who would value the Art of the Illustrator, and perhaps recognize the refinement of labour with which the letter-press has been ground down, and clipped, and condensed, and selected—till, as it would appear to the larger buying-public, there is *wonderfully little left you for your money ! !* . . .

Poor old Cruikshank ! How well—and willingly—he would have done "Kyrkegrim turned Preacher." He said, when he read my things, "the Fairies came and danced to him "—which pleased me much.

*　　　*　　　*　　　*　　　*　　　*

Yesterday I pulled myself together and wrote straight to the printers, to the effect that the suffering the erratic and careless printing of " We and the World " cost me was such that I was obliged to protest against X. and Sons economizing by using boys and untrained incapables to print (printing from print being easier, and therefore adapted for teaching the young P. D. how to set up type), pointing out one sentence in which (clear type in *A. J. M.*) the words " insist on guiding my fate by lines of their own ruling " was printed to the effect that they wouldn't insist on *gilding* my *faith*, etc., *their* being changed to *there*. All of which the *reader* had overlooked—to concern himself with my Irish brogue—and certain *reiterations of words* which he mortally hates, and which I regard the chastened use of, as like that of the *plural of excellence* in Hebrew !

(He would have put that demoniacal mark √ against one of the summers in "All the fragrance of summer when summer was gone " ! ! !)

I sent SUCH a polite message PER X. to his reader, thanking him much for trying to mend my brogue (which had already passed through the hands of three or four Irishmen, including Dr. Todhunter and Dr. Littledale), but proposing that for the future we should confine ourselves to our respective trades,— That the printer should print from copy, and not out of his own head—that the reader should read for clerical errors and bad printing, which would leave me some remnant of time and strength to attend to the language and sentiments for which I alone was responsible. My dear love, I must stop.

Ever your devoted,

J. H. E.

To A. E.

Farnham Castle, Surrey.

Oct. 10, 1880.

DIARY OF MRS. PEPYS.

"*Oct.* 9.—Passed an ill night, and did early resolve to send a carrier pigeon unto the Castle to notify that I must lie where I was, being unable to set forward.   But on rising I found myself not so ill that I need put others to inconvenience ; so I did but order a cab and set forth at three in the afternoon, in pouring rain.   My hostess sent with me David her footman, who saved me all trouble with my luggage, and so forth from Frimley to Farnham.   A pause at the South Camp Station, dear familiar spot, a little before which the hut where my good lord lay before we were married loomed somewhat drearily through the mist and rain.   At Farnham the Lord Bishop's servitor was waiting for me, and took all my things, leading me to a comfortable carriage and so forth to the Castle.

Somewhat affrighted at the hill, which is steep, and turns suddenly ; but recovered my steadfastness in thinking that no horses could know the way so well as these.

The Bishopess and her daughter received me on the staircase, and we had tea in the book-gallery, a most pleasing apartment.

Thence to my room to rest till dinner.   It is a mighty fine apartment, vast and high, with long windows having deep embrasures, and looking down upon the cedars and away over the whole town, which is a pretty one.

Methinks if I were a state prisoner, I would fain be imprisoned in an upper chamber, looking level with these same cedar-branches, whereon, mayhap, some bird might build its nest for mine entertainment.

Dinner at 8.15.   Wore my ancient brocade newly furbished with olive-green satin, and tinted lace about my neck, fastened with a brooch made like to a Maltese Cross, green stockings and shoes embroidered with flowers.

Was taken down to dinner by Sir Thos. Gore Browne, an

exceeding pleasant old soldier, elder brother to the Bishop,— having before dinner had much talk with his Lordship, whom I had not remembered to have been the dear friend of our dear friend the Lord Bishop of Fredericton, when both prelates were curates in Exeter."

   *   *   *   *   *   *

I am very much enjoying my visit to this dear old Castle. They are superabundantly kind! After the evening yesterday everybody, visitors and family, all trooped into the dimly-lighted chapel for Evening Prayer. They sang "Jerusalem the Golden," and Gen. Lysons sang away through his glass, in his K.C.B. star, and came up to compliment me about it afterwards. . . .

October 22, 1880.

Yesterday was Trafalgar Day. About half-a-dozen old Admirals of ninety and upwards met and dined together! I don't know what I would not have given to have been present at that most ghostly banquet! How like a dream, a shadow, a bubble, a passing vapour, and all the rest of it, must life not have seemed to these ex-midshipmen of the *Victory* and the *Téméraire!* muffling their poor old throats against this sudden frost, and toddling to table, and hobnobbing their glass in old-fashioned ways to immortal memories,

> "here in London's central roar,
> Where the sound of those he wrought for,
> And the feet of those he fought for,
> Echo round his bones for Evermore!"

The cold is sudden and most severe. I fear it will hustle some of those dear old Admirals to rejoin their ancient comrade —the "Saviour of the silver-coasted isle."

   *   *   *   *   *   *

May 1881.

"The Harbour Bay was clear as glass—
So smooth—ly was it strewn!
And on—the Bây—the moonlight lay
And—the—Shad—ow of—the Moon!"

——thus was it at 11 p.m. on the night of the 4th of May, when I looked out of my bedroom window at Plâce Castle, Fowey, on the coast of Cornwall !!!!—(and we must also remember that Isolde was married to the King of Cornwall, and lived probably in much such a place as Plâce!)

　　*　　　*　　　*　　　*　　　*　　　*

I caught a train on to Fowey, which I reached about 5. There I found a brougham and two fiery chestnuts waiting for me, and after some plunging at the train away went my steeds, and we turned almost at once into the drive. There is no park to Plâce that I could see, but the drive is *sui generis!* You keep going through *cuttings* in the rock, so that it has an odd feeling of a drive *on the stage* in a Fairy Pantomime. On your right hand the cliff is *tapestried*, almost hidden, by wild-flowers and ferns in the wealthiest profusion! Unluckily the wild garlic smells dreadfully, but its exquisite white blossoms have a most aërial effect, with pink campion, Herb Robert, etc., etc. On the left hand you have perpetual glimpses of the harbour as it lies below —oh, *such* a green! I never saw such before—"as green as em-er-âld!"—and the roofs of the ancient borough of Fowey! —I hope by next mail to have photographs to send you of the place. It perpetually reminded me of the Ancient Mariner. As to Plâce (P. Castle they call it now), the photographs will really give you a better idea of it than I can. You must bear in mind that the harbour of Fowey and a castle, carrying artillery, have been in the hands of the Treffrys from time immemorial. . . We went over the Church, a fine old Church with a grand tower, standing just below the Castle. The Castle itself is chiefly Henry VI. and Henry VII. I never saw such elaborate stone carving as decorates the outside. There are beautiful "Rose" windows close to the ground, and the Lilies of France, of course, are everywhere.   The chief drawing-room is a charming room, hung with pale yellow satin damask, and with beautiful Louis Quinze furniture.   The porphyry hall is considered one of *the* sights, the roof, walls, and floor are all of red Cornish porphyry. . . .

Frimhurst, May 10, 1881.

I have been into the poor old Camp.   I will tell thee. Did you ever meet Mr. F., R.E. ? a young engineer of H.'s standing, and his chief friend.   A Lav-engro (Russian is his present study) with a nice taste in old brass pots and Eastern rugs, and a choice little book-case, and a terrier named "Jem"— the exact image of dear old "Rough."   He asked us to go to tea to see the pictures you and I gave to the Mess and so forth. So the General let us have the carriage and pair and away we went.   It *is* the divinest air !   It was like passing quickly through BALM of body and mind.   And you know how the birds sing, and how the young trees look among the pines, and the milkmaids in the meadows, and the kingcups in the ditches, and then the North Camp and the dust, and Sir Evelyn Wood's old quarters with a new gate, and then the racecourse with polo going on and more dust !—and then the R.E. theatre (where nobody has now the spirit to get up any theatricals !), and the "Kennêl" (as Jane Turton called it) where I used to get flags and rushes, and where Trouvé, dear Trouvé ! will never swim again ! And then the Iron Church from which I used to *run* backwards and forwards not to be late for dinner every evening, with the "tin" roof that used to shake to the "Tug of War Hymn,"—and then more dust, and (it must be confessed) dirt and squalor, and *back views* of ashpit and mess-kitchens and wash-houses, and turf wall the grass won't grow on, and rustic work always breaking up ! and so on into the R.E. Lines ! Mr. F. was not quite ready for us, so we drove on a little and looked at No. 3. N. Lines.   T.'s hut is nearly buried in creepers now. An *Isle of Man* (do you remember?) official lives there, they say;

XVIII.   16

but it looked as if only the Sleeping Beauty could.   Our hut
looks just the same.   Cole's greenhouse in good repair.   But
through all the glamour of love one could see that there *is* a
good deal of dirt and dust, and refuse and coal-boxes ! ! !
    Then a bugle played !—

> "The trumpet blew ! "

    I *think* it was "Oh come tŏ the Orderlў Room ! " *We* went
to the Mess.   The Dining-Room is much improved by a big window, high pitched, opposite the conservatory.   It is new papered,
prettily, and our pictures hang on each side of the fireplace.   Mr.
G. joined us and we went into the Ante-Room.   Then to the
inevitable photo books, in the window where poor old Y. used
to sit in his spotless mufti.   When G. (who is not *spirituel*)
said, turning over leaves for the young ladies, "that and that are
killed" I turned so sick ! Mac G. and Mac D. ! Oh dear ! There
be many ghosts in "old familiar places."   But I have no devouter
superstition than that the souls of women who die in childbed and
men who fall in battle go straight to Paradise ! ! ! Requiescant
in Pace.
    Then to tea in Mr. F.'s quarters next to the men.   Then—
now mark you, how the fates managed so happy a coincidence—
G. said casually, "I saw Mrs. Jelf in the Lines just now ! " I
nearly jumped out of my boots, for I did not know she had got to
England.   Then F. had helped to nurse Jelf in Cyprus and was
of course interested to see her, so out went G. for Mrs. J., and
anon, through the hut porch in she came——Tableau——!
    Then I sent the girls with Messrs F. and G. to "go round
the stables," and M. and *Jem* and I remained together.   Jem
went to sleep (with one eye open) under the table, and the sun
shone and made the roof very hot, and outside—" The trumpets
blew ! "
    It was an afternoon wonderfully like a Wagner opera, thick-
set with recurring *motifs*. . . .

Frimhurst. June 15, 1891.

      *   *   *   *   *   *

The old editions of Dickens are here, and I have been re-reading *Little Dorrit* with keen enjoyment. There is a great deal of poor stuff in it, but there is more that is first-rate than I thought. I had quite forgotten Flora's enumeration of the number of times Mr. F. proposed to her—"seven times, once in a hackney coach, once in a boat, once in a pew, once on a donkey at Tunbridge Wells, and the rest on his knees." But she is very admirable throughout.

I've also been reading some more of that American novelist's work, Henry James, junior,—*The Madonna of the Future*, etc. He is not *great*, but very clever.

Used you not to like the first-class Americans you met in China very much? It is with great reluctance—believing Great Britons to be the salt of the earth ! !—but a lot of evidence of sorts is gradually drawing me towards a notion that the best type of American Gentleman is something like a generation ahead of our gentlemen in his attitude towards women and all that concerns them. There are certain points of view commonly taken up by Englishmen, even superior ones, which always exasperate women, and which seem equally incomprehensible by American men. You will guess the sort of things I mean. I do not know whether it is more really than the *élite* of Yankees (in which case we also have our *âmes d'élite* in chivalry)—but I fancy as a race they seem to be shaking off the ground-work idea of woman as the lawful PREY of man, who must keep Mrs. Grundy at her elbow, and *show cause why she shouldn't be insulted.* (An almost exclusively *English* feeling even in Great Britain, I fancy. By the bye, what odd flash of self-knowledge of John Bull made Byron say in his will that his daughter was not to marry an Englishman, as either Scotch or Irishmen made better husbands?) . . .

July 6, 1881.

*   *   *   *   *   *

The Academy this year is very fine. Some truly beautiful things. But before one picture I stood and simply laughed and shook with laughing aloud. It is by an Italian, and called "A frightful state of things." It is a baby left in a high chair in a sort of Highland cottage, with his plate of "parritch" on his lap—and every beastie about the place, geese, cocks, hens, chicks, dogs, cats, etc., etc., have invaded him, and are trying to get some of his food. The painting is exquisite, and it is the most indescribably funny thing you can picture: and so like dear Hector, with one paw on little Mistress's eye eating her breakfast ! ! ! . . .

*   *   *   *   *   *

Ecclesfield.   August 24, 1881.

. . . André has made the "rough-book" (water colours) of " A week spent in a Glass Pond, By the Great Water Beetle." I only had it a few hours, but I scrambled a bit of the title-page on to the enclosed sheet of green paper for you to see. It is entirely in colours. The name of the tale is beautifully done in letters, the initials of which *bud and blossom* into the Frogbit (which shines in white masses on the Aldershot Canal !) [*Sketch.*] To the left the "Water Soldier" (*Stratiotes Aloides*) with its white blossoms. At the foot of the page "the Great Water Beetle" himself, writing his name in the book—*Dyticus Marginalis*. There is another blank page at the beginning of the book, where the beetle is standing blacking himself in a penny ink-pot ! ! ! ! and another where he is just turning the leaves of a book with his antennæ—the book containing the name of the chromolithographers. He has adopted almost all my ideas, and I told him (though it is not in the tale) "I should like a *dog* to be with the children in all the pictures, and a cat to be with the old naturalist,"—and he has such a dog (a white bull terrier) [*sketch*], who waits on the woodland path for them in one picture, *noofles* in the colander at the water-beasts in another, examines the beetle in a third, stands on his hind legs to peep into the aquarium in a fourth, etc. But I cannot describe it all to you. I have asked to have it again by and by, and will send you a coloured sketch or two from it. I am so much pleased! . . . Perhaps the best part of the book is *the cover.* It is very beautiful. The Bell Glass Aquarium (lights in the water beautifully done) carries the title, and reeds, flowers, newts, beetles, dragon-flies, etc., etc., are grouped with wondrous fancy! This entirely his own design. . . .

Jesmond Dene, Newcastle-on-Tyne.
August 30, 1881.

*　　*　　*　　*　　*

The four Jones children and their nurse are in lodgings at a place ealled Whitley on the coast, not far from here. Somebody from here goes to see them most days. To-day Mrs. J. and I went. As we were starting dear " Bob " (the collie who used to belong to the Younghusbands) was determined to go. Mrs. Jones said No. He bolted into the cab and crouched among my petticoats; I begged for him, and he was allowed. At the station he was in such haste he *would* jump into a 2nd class carriage, and we had hard work to get him out. (This *is* rather funny, because she usually goes there 2nd class with the children : and he looked at the 1st and would hardly be persuaded to get in.) Well, the coast is rather like Filey, and such a wind was blowing, and *such* white horses foamed and fretted, and sent up wildly tossed fountains of foam against the rocks, and such grey and white waves swallowed up the sands! I ran and played with the children and the dog—and built a big sand castle ("Early English if not Della Cruscan "!!), and by good-luck and much sharp hunting among the storm-wrack flung ashore among the foam, found four cork floats, and made the children four ships with paper sails, and had a glorious dose of oxygen and iodine. How strange are the properties of the invisible air! The air from an open window at Ecclesfield gives me neuralgia, and doubly so at Exeter. To-day the wild wind was driving huge tracts of foam across the sands in masses that broke up as they flew, and driving the sand itself after them like a dust-storm. I could barely stand on the slippery rocks, and yet my teeth seemed to *settle in my jaws* and my face to get PICKLED (!) and comforted by the wild (and very cold) blast. . . . Now to sweet repose, but I was obliged to tell you I had been within sound of the sea, aye! and run into and away from the waves, with children and a dog. This is better than a Bath Chair in Brompton Cemetery! . . .

Thornliebank, Glasgow.   September 8, 1881.

. . . "It is good to be sib to" kindly Scots! and I am having a very pleasant visit. You know the place and its luxuries and hospitalities well.

I came from Newcastle last Friday, and (in a good hour, etc.) bore more in the travelling way than I have managed with impunity since I broke down. I came by the late express, got to Glasgow between 8 and 9 p.m., and had rather a hustle to to get a cab, etc. A nice old porter (as dirty and hairy as a Simian!) secured one at last with a cabby who jabbered in a tongue that at last I utterly lost the running of, and when he suddenly (and as it appeared indignantly!) remounted his box, whipped up, and drove off, leaving me and my boxes, I felt inclined to cry (!), and said piteously to the porter, "What *does* he say? I *cannot* understand him!" On which the old Ourang-Outang began to pat me on the shoulder with his paw, and explain loudly and slowly to my Sassenach ears, "He's jest telling ye—that 't'll be the better forrr ye—y'unnerstan'—to hev a cāāāāb that's got an i(ro)n railing on the tôp of it—for the sake of yourrr bōxes." And in due time I was handed over to a cab with an iron railing, the Simian left me, and so friendly a young cabby (also dirty) took me in hand that I began to think he was drunk, but soon found that he was only exceedingly kind and lengthily conversational ! When he had settled the boxes, put on his coat, argued out the Crums' family and their residences, first with me and then with his friends on the platform, we were just off when a thought seemed to strike him, and back he came to the open window, and saying "Ye'll be the better of havin' this ap"—scratched it up from the outside with nails like Nebuchadnezzar's. Whether my face looked as if I did not like it or what, I don't know, but down came the window again with a rattle, and he wagged the leather strap almost in my face and said, "there's hôals in't, an' ye can jest let it down to yer own satisfaction if ye fin' it gets clōs." Then he rattled it up again, mounted the box, and off we went. Oh, *such* a jolting drive of six miles ! Such wrenching over tramway lines ! But I had my fine air-cushions, and my spine must simply be another thing to what it was six months back. Oh, he was funny ! I found that he did NOT know the way to Thornliebank, but having a general idea, and a (no doubt just) faith in his own powers, he swore he did know, and utterly resented asking bystanders. After we got far away from houses, on the bleak roads in the dark night, I merely felt one must take what came. By and by he turned round and began to retrace his steps. I put out my head (as I did at intervals to his great disgust ; he always pitched well into me—"We're āāl right—just com—pôse yeself," etc.), but he assured me he'd only just gone by the gate. So by and by we drew up, no lights in the lodge, no answer to shouts—then he got down, and in the darkness I heard the gates grating as if they had not been opened for a century. Then under overhanging trees, and at last in the dim light I saw that the walls were broken down and weeds were thick round our wheels. I could bear it no longer, and put out my head again, and I shall never forget the sight. The moon was coming a little bit from behind the clouds, and showed a court-yard in which we had pulled up, surrounded with buildings in ruins, and overgrown with nettles and rank grass. We had not seen a human being since we left Glasgow, at least an hour before,—and of all the places to have one's throat cut in ! !——

The situation was so tight a place, it really gave one the courage of desperation, and I ordered him to drive away at once. I believe he was half frightened himself, and the horse ditto, and never, never was I in anything so nearly turned over as that cab! for the horse got it up a bank. At last it was righted, but not an inch would my Scotchman budge till he'd put himself through the window and confounded himself in apologies, and in explanations calculated to convince me that, in spite of appearances, he knew the way to Thornliebank "pairfeckly well." "Noo, I do beg of ye not to be nārrrr-vous. Do NOT give way to't. Ye may trust me entirely. Don't be discommodded in the least. I'm just pairfectly acquainted with the road. But it'll be havin' been there in the winter that's just misled me. But we're aal right." And all right he did eventually land me here! so late J. had nearly given me up.

*   *   *   *   *   *

To Mrs. Elder.

Greno House, Grenoside, Sheffield.
October 26, 1881.

Dearest Aunt Horatia,

*   *   *   *   *   *

D. says you would like some of the excellent Scotch stories I heard from Mr. Donald Campbell. I wish I could take the wings of a swallow and tell you them. You must supply gaps from your imagination.

They were as odd a lot of tales as I ever heard—*drawled* (oh so admirably drawled, without the flutter of an eyelid, or the quiver of a muscle) by a Lowland Scotchman, and queerly characteristic of the Lowland Scotch race!!!! Picture this slow phlegmatic rendering to your "mind's eye, Horatia!"

A certain excellent woman after a long illness—departed this life, and the Minister went to condole with the Widower. "The Hand of affliction has been heavy on yŭ, Donald. Ye've had a sair loss in your Jessie."

"Aye—aye—I've had a sair loss in my Jessie—an' a heavy ex-pense."

A good woman lost her husband, and the Minister made his way to the court where she lived. He found her playing cards with a friend. But she was *æquus ad occasionem*—as Charlie says!—

"Come awa', Minister! Come awa' in wi' ye. Ye'll see *I'm just hae-ing a trick with the cairds to ding puir Davie oot o' my heid.*"

I don't know if the following will *read* comprehensibly. *Told* it was overwhelming, and was a prime favourite with the Scotch audience.

Hoo oor Baby was *burrrned.*
(How our Baby was burnt.)

(You must realize a kind of amiable bland *whine* in the way of telling this. A caressing tone in the Scotch drawl, as the good lady speaks of *oor wee Wullie,* etc. Also a roll of the r's on the word burned.)

"Did ye never hear hoo oor wee Baby was burrrned? Well ye see—it was *this* way. The Minister and me had been to *Peebles*—and we were awfu' tired, and we were just haeing oor bit suppers—when oor wêê Wullie cam doon-stairs and he says—'Mither, Baby's *burrrning.*'

"—Y'unerstan it was the day that the Minister and me were at Peebles. We were *awful* tired, and we were just at oor suppers, and the Minister says (very loud and nasal), '*Ca'll Nurrse!*'—but as it rarely and unfortunitly happened—Nurrse was washing and she couldna be fashed.

"And in a while our WEE Wullie cam down the stairs again, and he says—'Mither! Baby's burning.'

"—as I was saying the Minister and me had been away over at Peebles, and we were in the verra midst of oor suppers, and I said to him—'Why didna ye call Nurse?'—and off he ran.

"—and there was the misfirtune of it—Nurrse was washing, and she wouldn't be fashed.

" And—in—a while—oor weee Wullie—came doon the stairs again—and he says ' Mither ! Baby's burrrned.'   And that was the way oor poor wee baby was burnt ! "

Now for one English one and then I must stop to-day.   I flatter myself I can tell this with a nice mincing and yet vinegar-ish voice.

" When I married my 'Usbin I had no expectation that he would live three week.

" But Providence—for wise purposes no doubt !—has seen fit to spare him three years.

" And there he sits, all day long, a-reading the *Illustrious News.*"

Now I must stop. . . .

Your loving niece,

JULIANA HORATIA EWING.

To A. E.

Grenoside.   Advent Sunday, 1881.

*   *   *   *   *

On one point I think I have improved in my sketching.   I have been long wanting to get a *quick style*, sketching not paint- ing.   Because I shall never have the time, or the time and strength to pursue a more finished style with success.   Now I have got paper on which I can make no corrections (so it forces me to be "to the point "), and which takes colour softly and nicely.   I have to aim at very correct drawing *at once*, and I lay in a good deal both of form and shade with a very soft pencil and then wash colour over ; and with the colour I aim at blend- ing tints as I go on, putting one into the other whilst it is wet, instead of washing off, and laying tint over tint, which the paper won't bear.   I am doing both figures and landscape, and in the same style.   I think the nerve-vigour I get from the fresh air helps me to decision and choice of colours.   But I shall bore you with this gallop on my little hobby horse !   .   .   .   .

November 30.

. . . I have sketched up to to-day, but it was cold and sunless, so I did some village visiting. I am known here, by the bye, as " *Miss Gatty as was* " ! I generally go about with a tribe of children after me, like the Pied Piper of Hamelin ! They are now fairly trained to keeping behind me, and are curiously civil in taking care of my traps, pouring out water for me, and keeping each other in a kind of rough order by rougher adjurations !

" Keep out o' t' *leet* can't ye ? "

" Na then ! How's shoo to see through thee ? "

" Shoo's gotten t' Dovecot in yon book, and shoo's got little Liddy Kirk—and thy moother wi' her apron over her heead, and Eliza Flowers sitting upo' t' doorstep wi' her sewing—and shoo's got t' woodyard—and Maester D. smooking his pipe—and shoo's gotten *Jack*."

"Nây ! Has shoo gotten Jack ? "

" Shoo 'as. And shoo's gotten ould K. sitting up i' t' shed corner chopping wood, and shoo's bound to draw him and Dronfield's lad criss-cross sawing."

"Aye. Shoo did all Greno Wood last week, they tell me."

" Aye. And shoo's done most o' t' village this week. What's shoo bound to do wi' 'em all ? "

" *Shoo'll piece 'em all together and mak a big picter of t' whole place.*" (These are true bills !)

Mr. S—— brings in some amusing *ana* of the village on this subject.

A.W., a nice lad training for school-master, was walking to Chapeltown with several *rolls of wall paper* and a big wall pastebrush, when he was met by " Ould K." (a cynical old beggar, and vainer than any girl, who has been affronted because I put Master D. into my foreground, and not him), who said to him— "Well, lad ! I see thou's *going out mapping*, like t' rest on 'em." This evening Mr. S—— tells me his landlord told him that some men who work for a very clever file-cutter here, who is *facile princeps* at his trade, but *mean*, and keeps ¡" the shop "

cold and uncomfortable for his workmen—devised yesterday the
happy thought of going to their Gaffer and telling him that I had
been sketching down below (true) and was coming up their way,
and that I was sure to expect a glint of fire in the shop, which
ought to look its best. According to N. he took the bait completely, piled a roaring fire, and as the day wore on kept
wandering restlessly out and peering about for me ! When they
closed for the night he said it was strange I hadn't been, but he
reckoned I was sure to be there next day, and he could wish I
would "tak him wi' his arm uplifted to strike." (He is a very
powerful smith.) I think I *must* go if the shop is at all picturesque. . . . .

Nov. 25, 1881.

*   *   *   *   *   *

Be happy in a small round. But, none the less, all the more
does it refresh me to get the wave of all your wider experience
to flood my narrow ones—and to enjoy all the *calm* bits
of your language study and the like. And oh, I am *very*
glad about the Musical Society ! Though I dare say you'll
have some *mauvais quarts d'heure* with the strings in damp
weather ! . . .

I have really got some pretty sketches done the last few days.
Not *finished* ones, the weather is not fit for long sitting ; but
H. H. has given me some " Cox " paper, a rough kind of stuff
something like what *sugar* is wrapped up in, and with a very
soft black pencil I have been getting in quick outlines—and
then tinting them with thin pure washes of colour. I have been
doing one of the Clog-shop. This quaint yard has doors—old
doors—which long since have been painted a most charming
red. Then the old shop is red-tiled, and an old stone-chimney
from which the pale blue smoke of the wood-fire floats softly
off against the tender tints of the wood, on the edge of which
lie fallen logs with yellow ends, ready for the clog-making, and
all the bare brown trees, and the green and yellow sandstone
walls, and Jack the Daw hopping about. The old man at the

clog-yard was very polite to me to-day. He said, "It's a pratty bit of colour," and "It makes a nicet sketch now you're getting in the *dit*tails." He went some distance yesterday to get me some india-rubber, and then wanted me to keep it! He's a perfect "picter card" himself. I must try and get *his* portrait.

* * * * * *

Ecclesfield. Dec. 23, 1881.

. . . I cannot tell you the pleasure it gives me that you say what you do of "Daddy Darwin." No; it will not make me overwork. I think, I hope, nothing ever will again. Rather make me doubly careful that I may not lose the gift you help me to believe I have. I have had very kind letters about it, and Mrs. L. sent me a sweet little girl dressed in pink—a bit of Worcester China!—as " Phœbe Shaw." . . .

Aunt M. sent "Daddy Darwin" to T. Kingdon (he is now Suffragan Bishop to Bishop Medley), and she sent us his letter. I will copy what he says: " 'Daddy Darwin' is very charming —directly I read it I took it off to the Bishop—and he read it and cried over it with joy, and then read it again, and it has gone round Fredericton by this time. The story is beautifully told, and the picture is quite what it should be. When I look at the picture I think nothing could beat it, and then when I read the story I think the story is best—till I look again at the picture, and I can only say that *together* I don't think they could be beaten at all in their line. I have enjoyed them much. There is such a wonderful fragrance of the Old Country about them."

I thought you would like to realize the picture of our own dear old Bishop crying with joy over it! What a young heart! tenderer than many in their teens; and what unfailing affection and sympathy. . .

January 17, 1882.

*   *   *   *   *   *

Mrs. O'M. is delighted. with "Daddy Darwin." I had a most curious letter about it from Mrs. S., a very clever one and very flattering ! F. S. too wrote to D., and said things almost exactly similar. It seems odd that people should express such a sense of "purity" with the "wit and wisdom" of one's writing ! It seems such an odd reflection on the tone of other people's writings ! ! ! But the minor writers of the "Fleshly school" are perhaps producing a reaction ! Though it's *marvellous* what people will read, and think "so clever ! " Some novels lately —*Sophy* and *Mehalah*, deeply recommended to me, have made me aghast. I'm not very young, nor I think very priggish ; but I do decline to look at life and its complexities solely and entirely from a point of view that (bar Christian names and the English language) would do equally well for a pig or a monkey. If I *am* no more than a Pig, I'm a fairly "learned" pig, and will back myself to get some small piggish pleasures out of this mortal stye, before I go to the Butcher ! ! But—IF—I am something very different, and very much higher, I won't ignore my birthright, or sell it for Hog'swash, because it involves the endurance of some pain, and the exercise of some faith and hope and charity ! *Mehalah* is a well-written book, with a delicious sense of local colour in nature. And it is (pardon the sacrilege !) a LOVE *story !* The focus point of the hero's (!) desire would at quarter sessions, or assizes, go by the plain names of outrage and murder, and he succeeds in drowning himself with the girl who hates him lashed to him by a chain. In not one other character of the book is there an indication that life has an aim beyond the lusts of the flesh, and the most respectable characters are the tenants whose desires are summed up in the desire of more suet pudding and gravy ! ! ! To any one who KNOWS the poor ! who knows what faiths and hopes (true or untrue) support them in consumption and cancer, in hard lives and dreary deaths, the picture is as untrue as it is (to me !) disgusting.

*   *   *   *   *   *

March 22, 1882.

*   *   *   *   *   *

On Saturday night I went down with A. and L. to Battersea, to one of the People's Concerts. I enclose the programme. It is years since I have enjoyed. anything so much as *Thomas's* Harp-playing. (He is not Ap-Thomas, but he *is* the Queen's Harper.) His hands on those strings were the hands of a *Wizard*, and form and features nearly as quaint as those of Mawns seemed to dilate into those of a poet. It was very marvellous.

Did I tell you that Lady L. has sent *me* a ticket this year for her Sunday afternoons at the Grosvenor? We went on Sunday. The paintings there just now are Watts's. Our old blind friend at Manchester has sent a lot. It is a very fine collection. I think few paintings do beat Watts's 'Love and Death'—Death, great and irresistible, wrapped in shrowd-like drapery, is pushing relentlessly over the threshold of a home, where the portal is climbed over by roses and a dove plays about the lintel. You only see his back. But, facing you, Love, as a young boy, torn and flushed with passion and grief, is madly striving to keep Death back, his arms strained, his wings crushed and broken in the unequal struggle.

Beside the paintings it was great fun seeing the company! Princess Louise was there, and lots of minor stars. And—my Welsh Harper was there! I had a long chat with him. He talks like a true artist, and WE must know him hereafter. When I said that when I heard him play the 'Men of Harlech,' I understood how Welshmen fought in the valleys if their harpers played upon the hills (*most true !*), he seized my hand in both his, and thanked me so excitedly I was quite alarmed for fear Mrs. Grundy had an eye round the corner ! ! !

*   *   *   *   *   *

Amesbury, May 28, 1182.

. . . 'Tis a sweet, sweet spot ! Not one jot or one tittle of the old charm has forsaken it. Clean, clean shining streets and

little houses, pure, pure air!—a changeful and lovely sky—the
green watermeads and silvery willows—the old patriarch in his
smock—the rushing of the white weir among the meadows, the
grey bridge, the big, peaceful, shading trees, the rust-coloured
lichen on the graves where the forefathers of the hamlet sleep
(oh what a place for sleep!), the sublime serenity of that in-
comparable church tower, about which the starlings wheel,
some of them speaking words outside, and others replying from
the inside (where they have no business to be!) through the
belfry windows in a strange chirruping antiphon, as if outside
they sang:

"Have you found a house, and a nest where you may lay
your young?

(and from within):

Even Thy altars, O Lord of Hosts! my King and my God!"

D. and I wandered (how one *wanders* here) a long time
there yesterday evening. Then we went up to the cemetery on
the hill, with that beautiful lych-gate you were so fond of. I
picked you a forget-me-not from the old Rector's grave, for he
has gone home, after fifty-nine years' pastorship of Amesbury.
His wife died the year before. Their graves are beautifully
kept with flowers.

Whit-Monday, 9.30 p.m. We are in the upper sitting-room
to-day, the lower one having been reserved for "trippers." It
is a glorious night—beyond the open window one of several
Union Jacks waves in the evening breeze, and one of several
brass bands has just played its way up the street. How these
admirable musicians have found the lungs to keep it up as they
have done since an early hour this morning they best know!
Oh, how we have laughed! How *you* would have laughed!!
It has been the most good-humoured, civil crowd you can
imagine! Such banners! such a "gitting of them" up and
down the street by ardent "Foresters" and other clubs in huge
green sashes and flowers everywhere! Before we were up this
morning they were hanging flags across the street, and seriously
threatening the stability of that fine old window!

When I was dressed enough to pull up the blind and open the window some green leaves fluttered in in the delicious breeze. I went off into raptures, thinking it was a big *Vine* I had not noticed before, creeping outside ! !

It was a maypole of sycamore branches, placed there by the Foresters ! ! !

Frances Peard laughed at me much for something like to this I said at Torquay ! She said, " You are just like my old mother. Whenever we pass a man who has used a fusee, she always becomes knowing about tobacco, and says, ' *There*, Frances, my dear—there IS a fine cigar.' "

*   *   *   *   *   *

. . . We came here last Thursday. When I got to Porton D. had sent an air-cushion in the fly, and though I had a five miles drive it was through this exquisite air on a calm, lovely evening, and by the time we got to a spot on the Downs where a little Pinewood breaks the expanse of the plains, the good-humoured driver and I were both on our knees on the grass digging up plots of the exquisite Shepherd's Thyme, which carpets the place with blue !

Yesterday we drove by Stonehenge to Winterbourne Stoke. It was glaring, and I could not do much sketching, but the drive over the downs was like drinking in life at some primeval spring. (And this though the wind did give me acute neuralgia in my right eye, but yet the air was so exquisitely refreshing that I could cover my eye with a handkerchief and still enjoy !) The charm of these unhedged, unbounded, un-"cabined, cribbed, confined "*prairies* is all their own, and very perfect! And *such* flowers *enamel* (it *is* a good simile in spite of Alphonse Karr !) the close fine grass ! The pale-yellow rock cistus in clumps, the blue " shepherd's thyme " in tracts of colour, sweet little purple-capped orchids, spireas and burnets, and everywhere "the golden buttercup" in sheets of gleaming yellow, and the soft wind blows and blows, and the black-nosed sheep come up the leas, and I drink in the breeze ! Oh, those flocks of black-faced lambs and sheep are TOO-TOO ! and I must tell you that

XVIII.   I 7

the old Wiltshire "ship-dog" is nearly extinct. I regret to say that he is not found equal to "the Scotch" in business habits, and one see Collies everywhere now. . .

London. June 29, 1882.

* * * * * *

I had a great treat last Sunday. One you and I will share when you come home. D., U., and I took Jack to church at the Chelsea Hospital, and we went round the Pensioners' Rooms, kitchen, sick-wards, etc. afterwards, with old Sir Patrick Grant and Col. Wadeson, V.C. (Govr. and Lieut.-Govr.), and a lot of other people.

It is an odd, perhaps a savage, mixture of emotions, to kneel at one's prayers with some *pride* under fourteen French flags—*captured* (including one of Napoleon's while he was still Consul, with a red cap of Liberty as big as your hat!), and hard by the FIVE bare staves from which the FIVE standards taken at Blenheim have rotted to dust!—and then to pass under the great Russian standard (twenty feet square, I should say!) that is festooned above the door of the big hall. If Rule Britannia IS humbug—and we are mere Philistine Braggarts— why doesn't Cook organize a tour to some German or other city, where we can sit under fourteen captured British Colours, and be disillusioned once for all ! ! ! Where is the Hospital whose walls are simply decorated like some Lord Mayor's show with trophies taken from us and from every corner of the world ? (You know Lady Grant was in the action at Chillianwallah and has the medal ?) We saw two Waterloo men, and Jack was handed about from one old veteran to another like a toy. "Grow up a brave man," they said, over and over again. But "The Officer," as he called Colonel Wadeson, was his chief pride, he being in full uniform and cocked hat ! !

And I must tell you—in the sick ward I saw a young man, fair-curled, broad-chested, whose face seemed familiar. He was with Captain Cleather at the Aldershot Gym., fell, and is "going home"—slowly, and with every comfort and kindness about him, but of spinal paralysis. It *did* seem hard lines! He was at the Amesbury March Past, and we had a long chat about it.

*   *   *   *   *   *

July 21, 1882.

*   *   *   *   *   *

I cannot tell you how it pleases me that you liked the bit about Aldershot in "Lætus." I hope that it must have *grated* very much if I had done it badly or out of taste, on any one who knows it as well as you do; and that its moving your sympathies does mean that I have done it pretty well. I cannot tell you the pains I expended on it! All those sentences about the Camp were written in scraps and corrected for sense and euphony, etc., etc., bit by bit, like "Jackanapes"!!! Did I tell you about "Tuck of Drum"? Several people who saw the proof, pitched into me, "Never heard of such an expression." I was convinced I knew it, and as I said, as a *poetical* phrase; but I could not charge my memory with the quotation: and people exasperated me by regarding it as "camp slang." I got Miss S. to look in her *Shakespeare's Concordance*, but in vain, and she wrote severely, "My Major lifts his eyebrows at the term." I was in despair, but I sent the proof back, trusting to my instincts, and sent a postcard to Dr. Littledale, and got a post-card back by return—"Scott"—"Rokeby."

> "With burnished brand and musketoon,
>   So gallantly you come,
> I rede you for a bold dragoon,
>   That lists the tuck of drum."—
> "I list no more the tuck of drum,
>   No more the trumpet hear;
> But when the beetle sounds his hum,
>   My comrades take the spear."

And I copied this on to another postcard and added, *Tell your Major!* and despatched it to Miss S.! She said, "You *did* Cockadoodle!"—

But isn't it *exquisite?* *What* a creature Scott was! Could words, could a long romance, give one a finer picture of the ex-soldier turned "Gentleman of the Road"? The touch of regret—"I list no more the tuck of drum," and the soldierly necessity for a "call"—and then *such* a call!

When the Beetle *sounds his hum*—

The Dor Beetle!—

I hope you will like the tale as a whole. It has been long in my head.

*   *   *   *   *   *

Oh! how funny Grossmith was! Yesterday I was at the Matinée for the Dramatic School, and he did a "Humorous Sketch" about Music, when he said with care-carked brows that there was only one man's music that *thoroughly* satisfied him (after touching on the various schools!)—and added—"my own." It was inexpressibly funny. His "Amateur Composer" would have made you die!

Ah, but THE treat, such a treat as I have not heard for years—was that old Ristori RECITED the 5th Canto of the *Inferno*. I did not remember which it was, and feared I should not be able to follow, but it proved to be "Francesca." Never could I have believed it possible that reciting could be like that. I could have gone into a corner and cried my heart out afterwards, the tension was so extreme. And oh what power and WHAT refinement!

*   *   *   *   *   *

July 28, 1882.

*   *   *   *   *   *

Last Saturday D. and I went down to Aldershot to the Flat Races!!! As we went along, tightly packed in a carriage full of ladies in what may be termed "dazzling toilettes," pretty girls and Dowager Mammas everywhere!—and as we ran past the familiar "Brookwood North Camp," where white "canvas" shone among the heather (and the heather, the cat heather, oh so bonny! with here and there a network of the red threads of the dodder, so thick that it looked like red flowers), and all the ladies, young and old, craned forward to see the tents, etc., I really laughed at myself for the accuracy of my own descriptions in "Lætus"! P. met us at the R. E. Mess, where we had luncheon. After lunch we went to the familiar stables, and inspected the kit for Egypt. Then P. drove us to the Race Course. I met a lot of old friends. The Duke and Duchess of Connaught were there. It all looked very pretty, the camp is so much grown up with plantations now. The air was wondrous sweet. P. drove us back to the Mess for tea, and then down to the station. It was a great pleasure, though rather a sad one. Everybody was very grave. A sort of feeling, "What will be the end?" . . .

The Castle, Farnham.
Aug. 17, 1882.

*   *   *   *   *   *

It is one of the sides of X.'s mind which makes me feel her so *limited* an artist that she seems almost to take up a school as she takes up a lady-friend—"one down another come on." I think her abuse of Wagner now curiously *narrow.* I can't see why one should not feel the full spell and greater purity of Brahms without dancing in his honour on Wagner's bones ! ! It seems like her refusing to see any merit in, or derive any enjoyment from modern pictures because she has been "posted" in the Early Italian School. So from year to year these good people who have been to Florence will not even look at a painting by Brett or Peter Graham, though by the very qualities and senses through which one feels the sincerity, the purity, the nobleness, and the fine colour of those great painters, the photographs of whose pictures even stir one's heart,—one surely ought also to take delight in a landscape school which simply did not exist among the ancients. If sea and sky as GOD spreads them

before our eyes are admirable, I can't think how one can be
blind to delight in such pictures as 'The Fall of the Barometer,'
'The Incoming Tide,' or Leader's 'February Fill-dyke.'
Things which no Florentine ever approached, as transcripts of
Nature's mood apart from man. . . .

Yesterday we had a most delicious drive through the heather
and pines to Crookham. Ah, 'tis a bonny country, and I *did*
laugh when I said to Mr. Walkinshaw, "How glorious the
heather is this year!" and he said, "Yes. If only it was growing on its native heath." For a minute I couldn't tell what he
meant. Then I discovered that he regards heather as the
exclusive property of bonnie Scotland!!!

I think you will be pleased to hear that I did, what I have
long wanted, yesterday. Thoroughly made Mrs. Walkinshaw's
acquaintance, and thanked her for that old invitation we never
accepted to go there to see the Chinnerys' sketches. How
Scotch and *kindly* she is! She insisted on bringing her
husband and daughters to be introduced, and sent *warmest*
messages to you. She said she feared you must have quite
forgotten her; but I told her she was quite wrong there! She
says she has a little Chinnery she meant to give me long ago,
and she insists on sending it. . . .

Sept. 1, 1882.

*   *   *   *   *   *

I must tell you that I had such a mixture of pain and pleasure
at Britwell in the nearest approach to Trouvé I have ever
known. A larger dog, and not quite so "Möcent," but in
character and ways his living image. The same place on his
elbow (which his Aunt was always wanting to gum a bit of astra-
chan on to); he "took" to his Aunt at once! *Nero* by name.
The sweetest temper. I have kissed the nice soft places on his
black lips and shaken hands by the hour!!! Yesterday the
others went to a garden-party, so I went on to the Downs to
sketch, and when the dogs saw me, off they came, Nero
delighted, and little Punch the Pug. They came with me all

the way, and lay on the grass while I was sketching, and Nero kept sitting down to save a corner, and watch which way I meant to go, just like dear True! [*Sketch.*] They were very good, sitting with me on the downs, but they roamed away into the woods after game a good deal on the road home! . . .

Grenoside. Oct. 5, 1882.

* * * * * *

I do so long to hear how you like the end of "Lætus." As F. S.'s tale turned out seven pages longer than was accounted for, I had to cut out some of *my* story, and so have missed the point of its being S. Martin's Day on which Leonard died. S. Martin was a soldier-saint, and the Tug-of-War Hymn is only sung on Saints' Days.

I have completed a tale* for the November No., and gave a rough design to André for the illustration, which will be in colours. I hope you will like *that*. There is not a tear in it this time! "Lætus" was too tragic!

* * * * * *

Will we or will we not have a Persian Puss in our new home by the name of —Mārjāra?—It is quite perfect! Do Brahmans like cats? I must have a tale about Mārjāra ! ! !— Kārāva is grand too!

Oh Karava !
Oh the Crier !
Oh Karava !
Oh the Shouter !
Oh Karava, oh the Caller !
Very glossy are your feathers,
Very thievish are your habits,
Black and green and purple feathers,
Bold and bad your depredations ! ! !

---

* " Sunflowers and a Rushlight," vol. xvi.

Doesn't he sound like a fellow in *Hiawatha ?*
Oh, it's a fine language, and must have fine *lils* in it !

*　　　*　　　*　　　*　　　*　　　*

To Mrs. Jelf.

Ecclesfield. Oct. 10, 1882.

My Dearest Marny,

Your dear, kind letter was very pleasant sweetmeat
and encouragement. I am deeply pleased you like the end of
"Lætus"—and feel it to the point—and that my polishings were
not in vain ! I polished that last scene to distraction in "the
oak room " at Offcote !

I should *very* much like to hear how it hits the General. I
think "*Pav*ilions" (as my Yorkshire Jane used to call civilians !)
may get a little mixed, and not care so much for the points.
Some who have been rather extra kind about it are—Lady
W—— (but yesterday she amusingly insisted that she *had* lived
in camp —— at Wimbledon ! !)—the Fursdons and "Stella
Austin," author of *Stumps,* etc.—(literary "civilians" who
think it the best thing I have ever done), and two young bar-
risters who have been reading it aloud to each other in the
Temple—with tears. And yet I fancy many non-military
readers may get mixed. P. vouchsafes no word of it to *me,*
but I hear from D. (under the veil of secrecy !) that he and Mr.
Anstruther read it together in Egypt with much approval. I
am more pleased by military than non-military approval. Old
Aldershottians would so easily spot blunders and bad taste ! ! !
Mrs. Murray wrote to me this morning about it—and of course
wished they were back in dear old Aldershot !

You make me very egotistical, but I do wish you to tell me
what you, *and* Aunty, *and* Madre think of "Sunflowers and a
Rushlight," when you read it. I fear it has rather scandalized
my Aunt, who is staying with us. She is obviously shocked at
the plain-speaking about drains and doctors, and thinks that
part ought to have been in an essay—not in a child's tale. I am

a little troubled, and should *really* like (what is seldom soothing !) a candid opinion from *each of you.* You know how I think the riding *some* hobbies takes the *fine edge* off the mind, and if you think I am growing coarse in the cause of sanitation—I beseech you to tell me ! As to putting *the teaching* into an essay—the crux there is that the people one wants to stir up about sanitation are just good family folk with no special literary bias ; and they will read a tale when they won't read an essay ! But do tell me if any one of you feel that the subject *grates*, or my way of putting it.

Now, my darling, I must tell you that I have got a telegram from my goodman—the Kapellmeister !—to say he IS to be sent home in "early spring." This is a great comfort. I would willingly have let him stay two months longer to escape spring cold ; but he has got to *hate* the place so fiercely, that I now long for him to get away at any cost. It must be most depressing ! The last *letter* I got, he had had a trip by sea, and said he felt perfectly different till he got back to Colombo, when the oppression seized him again. He has been to Trincomalee, and is charmed with it, and said he could read small print when he got there, but his eyes quite fail in the muggyness of Colombo. However he will cheer up now, I hope ! and Nov. and Dec. and Jan. are good months.

Now good-bye, dear. My best love to Aunty and Madre.

Your loving,

J. H. E.

To A. E.

Ecclesfield. October 24, 1882.

. . . It was very vexatious that the Megha Duta came just too late for last mail. It is a beautiful poem. Every now and then the local colour has a weird charm all its own. It lifts one into another land (without any jarring of railway or steamship !) to realize the *locale* in which rearing masses of grey cumuli suggest elephants rushing into combat ! And the husband's picture of his wife in his absence is as noble, as sympathetic, and as perceptive as anything of the kind I ever read. So full of human feeling and so refined. I enjoyed it very much. It reminded me, oddly enough, more than once of Young's *Night Thoughts*. I think perhaps (if the charm of another tongue, and the wonder of its antiquity did not lead one to give both more *attention* and more *sympathy* than one would perhaps bestow on an English poem) that the poem does not rank much higher than a degree short of the first rank of our poets. But it is very charming. And oh, what a lovely text! It is a *most beautiful* character. . . .

To MRS. MEDLEY.

Ecclesfield, Sheffield.
November 17, 1822.

MY VERY DEAR MRS. MEDLEY,
There has been long word silence between us! I made a break in it the other day by sending you my new "Picture Poem"—"A Week Spent in a Glass Pond."

It was a sort of repayment of a tender chromolithographic (!) debt.

Do you remember, when Fredericton was our home, and when everything pretty from Old England did look so very pretty—how on one of those home visits from which he brought back bits of civilization—the Bishop brought *me* a "chromo" of dogs and a fox which has hung in every station we've had since?

Now—as a friend's privilege is—I will talk without fear or favour of myself! The last real contact with you was the Bishop's too brief peep at us in Bowdon—a shadowy time out of which his Amethyst ring flashes on my mind's eye. No! Not Amethyst—what IS the name? Sapphire!—(I have a little mental confusion on the subject. I have a weak—a very weak corner—in my heart for another Bishop, an old friend of your Bishop's—Bishop Harold Browne; and have had the honour now and again of wearing his rings on my thumb—a momentary relaxation of discipline and due respect, which I doubt if your Bishop would admit !!! though I hope he has a little love for me, frightened as I now and then am of him !!!! The last time but one I was at Farnham, I was asked to stay on another two days to catch the Brownes' fortieth wedding-day. Just as we were going down to dinner I reproached the Bishop for not having on his "best" ring! Very luckily—for he said he always made a point of it on his wedding-day—left me like a hot potato in the middle of the stairs and flew off to his room, and returned with *the* grand sapphire !)

Well, dear—that's a parenthesis—to go back to Bowdon. I was not to boast of there, and after the move to York, and I had fitted up my house and made up for lost time in writing work, I was a very much broken creature, keeping going to Jenner and getting orders to rest !—and then came the order to Malta, not six months after we were sent to York, and I stayed to pack up and sent out all our worldly goods and chattels, and then started myself, and was taken ill in Paris and had to come back, and have been "of no account" for three years.

Well. My news is now far better than once I hoped it ever could be. I'm not strong, but I can work in moderation, though I can't "rackett" the least bit. And—Rex is to come home in Spring!—the season of hope and *nest-building*—and I am trying not to wonder my wits away as to what part of the British Isles it will be in which I shall lay the cross-sticks and put in the moss and wool of our next nest !! There is every reason to suppose we shall be "at home" for five years, I am thankful to say. . . .

Rex loved Malta, and *hates* Ceylon. But he has been *very* good and patient about it.

Latterly he has consoled himself a good deal with the study of Sanscrit, which he means me also to acquire, though I have not got far yet ! It is a beautiful character. He says, "Of all the things I have tried Sanscrit is the most utterly delicious ! Of the alphabet alone there are (besides the ten vowels and thirty-three simple consonants) rather more than two hundred compound consonants," etc., etc. ! He adds, "स्र ट are my detached initials, but I could write my whole name in 'Devanagiri,' or ' Writing of the Gods.'"

To A. E.

Ecclesfield. December 8, 1882.

. . . I got back from Liverpool on Monday. When I called at the Museum on that morning a Dr. Palmer was there, who said, " I was in Taku Forts with your husband," and was very friendly. He gave me a prescription for neuralgia ! and sent you his best remembrances.

First and last I have annexed one or two nice "bits of wool for our nest." For 8*s.* (a price for which I could not have bought *the frame*, a black one with charming old-fashioned gold-beading of this pattern) [*sketch*] I bought a real fine old soft mezzotint, after Sir Joshua Reynolds' portrait of Richard Burke. Oh, such a lovely face ! Looking lovelier in powder and lace frill. But a charming thing, with an old-fashioned stanza in English deploring his early death, and a motto in Latin. It was a great find, and I carried it home from the Pawnbroker's in triumph !—

I have got a very nice Irish anecdote for you from Mr. Shee :

Two Irishmen (not much accustomed to fashionable circles) at a big party, standing near the door. After a long silence :

Paddy I.—" D'ye mix much in society ? "

P. II.—" Not more than six tumblers in the evening."

*   *   *   *   *   *

S. John Evangelist, 1882.

*   *   *   *   *   *

C. "dealt" for me for the old Japanese Gentleman (pottery) on whom I turned my back at £1. He has got him for 15*s.* You will be delighted with him, and I have just packed him (and a green pot lobster !) in a box with sawdust.

Do you remember how your 'genteel' clerk's wife came (starving) from Islington, or some such place, to us at Aldershot, and told me she had *sold* all her furniture (as a nice preparation to coming to free but empty quarters) EXCEPT *her parlour pier-glass and fire-irons ?*

I sometimes feel as if I bought house plenishing that packed together about as nicely as that ! ! !   Witness my pottery old gentleman, and my bronze Crayfish. . . .

December 20, 1882.

*   *   *   *   *   *

I am so glad you like " Sunflowers and a Rushlight." It was very pleasurable work, though hard work as usual, writing it.   It was written at Grenoside, among the Sunflowers, and generally with dear old Wentworth, the big dog, walking after me or lying at my feet.

You may, or may not, have observed, that the *Times* critic says, that " of one thing there can be no doubt "—and that is— " *Miss* Ewing's nationality.   No one but a Scotchwoman bred and born *could* have written the ' Laird and the Man of Peace.' "

It is " rich in pawky humour."   But if I can get a copy I'll send it to you.   It is complimentary if not true !

I am putting a very simple inscription over our dear Brother. Do you like it ?

TROUVÉ,
commonly and justly called
TRUE.
FOUND 1869; LOST 1881,
by A. E. and J. H. E.

To H. K. F. G.

Ecclesfield. December, 1882.

. . . I rather HOPE to have a story for you for March, which will be laid in France.   Will it do if you have it by February 8 ? . . .

It is a terribly close subject, and I shall either fail at it, or make it I hope not inferior to "Jackanapes." I don't *think* it will be long. The characters are so few. I have only plotted it. It will be called—

"THE THINGS THAT ARE SEEN": AN OLD SOLDIER'S STORY.

DRAM. PERS.

MADAME.
HER MAID.
THE FATHER OF MADAME.
THE FATHER OF THE SERGEANT.
THE MOTHER OF THE SERGEANT.
THE SERGEANT.
THE PRIEST.
THE MURDERER.
A POODLE.

Soldiers, Peasants, Priests, Gendarmes, a Rabble, Reapers— but you know I generally overflow my limits. I hope I can do it, but it tears me to bits! and I've walked myself to bits nearly in plotting it this morning,—a very little written, but I believe I could be *ready* by February 8. I don't think it will be as long as "Daddy Darwin," not nearly.

Please settle with Mr. B. what you will do about an illustration. The first scene is that of the death-bed of the sergeant's father. I think it would be quite as good a scene for illustration as any, and will, I trust, be ready in a day or two. Is it worth Mr. B.'s while to see if R. C. would do it in shades of brown or grey? (a very chiaroscuro scene in a tumble-down cottage, light from above). All *I* must have is a good illustration or none at all. (I would send copy of scene to R. C. and ask him.) I think it might pay, because I am certain to want to *re*publish it, and whoever I publish it with will pay half-price for the old illustration. I do myself believe that it might be *colour-printed* in (say seven instead of seventeen) shades of colour (blues, and browns, and black, and yellow, and white) at much less cost than a full-coloured one, but that I leave to Mr. B. : only I have some strong theories about it, and when I come to town I mean to make Edmund Evans's acquaintance.

Strange to say, I believe I *could* make the tale illustrate the " Portrait of a Sergeant " if it were possible to get permission to have a thing photoed and reduced from *that ! ! !*—Goupil would be the channel in which to inquire—but the artist would not be a leading character, as far as I can see, so it might not be all one could wish. But it is worth investigating. . . .

Or again, I wonder what Herkomer would charge for an *etching* of the dying old Woodcutter, and his kneeling son? I believe THAT would be the thing !—But the plate must be surfaced so that *A. J. M.* mayn't exhaust all the good impressions. If Herkomer would etch that, and add a vignette of a scene I could give him with a beautiful peasant girl—or of the old sergeant and the portly and worldly " Madame," we SHOULD " do lovely !" Will you try for that, please?

No more to-day for

" I am exhaust
I can not ! "

Your devoted, J. H. E.

Remember *I* wish for Herkomer. He will be the right man in the right place. R. C. is for dear old England, and this is French and Roman Catholic—and Keltic peasant life.

To A. E.

January 4, 1883.

* * * * * *

Caldecott says his difficulty over my writing is that "the force and finish " of it frightens him. It is painted already and does not need illustration ; and he has lingered over " Jackanapes " from the conviction that he could " never satisfy me "!! This difficulty is, I hope, now vanquished. He is hard at work on a full and complete edition of "Jackanapes," of which he has now begged to take the entire control, will "submit" paper and type, etc. to me, and hopes to please. "But you are *so* particular!"

I need hardly say I have written to place everything in his hands. I am "not such a fool as" to think I can teach *him!* (though I am insisting upon certain arrangements of types, etc., etc., to give a *literary*—not Toy Book—aspect to the volume).

André I *know I help*. But then only a man of real talent and mind would accept the help and be willing to be taught. The last batch of *A Soldier's Children* that came had three pages that grated on me.

1. "They mayn't have much time for their prayers on active service, *and we ought to say them instead*." The first part of this line is splendidly done by a brush with Zulus among mealies, but the second part (as underlined) was thus. Nice old church (good idea) and the officer's wife and children at prayer. BUT— the lady was like a shop-girl, in a hat and feathers, tight-fitting jacket with skimpy fur edge (inexpressibly vulgar cheap finery style!), kneeling with a highly-developed figure backwards on to the spectator! and with her eyes up in a theatrical gaze heavenwards. Little boy *sitting* on seat, with his hat on.

2. For "GOD bless the good soldiers like old father and Captain Powder and the men with good conduct medals, and please let the naughty ones be forgiven,"—he had got some men being released out of prison cells.

3. For "There are eight verses and eight Alleluias, and we can't sing very well, but we did our best.

"Only Mary would cry in the verse about 'Soon, soon to faithful warriors comes their rest'!"— —he had got a very poor thing of three children singing.

Now these were all highly-finished drawings. Quite complete, and I know the man is *driven* with work (for cheap pay!). So I hesitated, and worried myself. At last I took courage and sent them back, having faith in the "thoroughness" which he so eminently works with.

For 1, I sent him a sketch! said the lady must wear a bonnet in church, and her boys must take off their hats! That she must kneel *forwards*, be dressed in a deep sealskin with heavy fox edge, and have her eyes *down*, and the children must kneel *imitating her*, and I should like an old *brass* on the wall above them with one of those queer old kneeling families in ruffs.

For 2, I said I could not introduce child readers to the cells, and I begged for an old Chelsea Pensioner showing his good conduct medal to a little boy.

3. I suggested the tomb of a Knight Crusader, above which should fall a torn banner with the words, " In Cœlo Quies."

Now if he had kicked at having three pictures to do utterly over again, one could hardly have wondered, pressed as he is. But, back they came! "I am indeed much indebted to you," the worst he had to say! The lady in No. 1 now *is* a lady ; and as to the other two, they will be two of the best pages of the book. Old Pensioner first-rate, and Crusader under torn banner just leaving "Cœlo Quies," a tomb behind "of S. Ambrose of Milan" with a little dog—and a snowy-moustached old General, with bending shoulders and holding a little girl by the hand, paying *devoir* at the Departed Warrior's tomb in a ray of rosy sunlight!!

This is the sort of way we are fighting through the Ewing-André books.

*　　　*　　　*　　　*　　　*　　　*

Ecclesfield. January 10, 1883.

*　　　*　　　*　　　*　　　*　　　*

Fancy me "learning a part" again! *That* has a sort of sound like old times, hasn't it?

I feel half as if I were a fool, and half as if it would be very good fun ! R.A. theatricals at Shoeburyness. The Fox-

XVIII. 18

Strangways have asked me. Major O'Callaghan is Stage
Manager I believe. Then there is a Major Newall, said to be
very good. He says he "has a fancy to play 'A Happy Pair'
with me !" It is his *cheval de bataille* I believe.

I think it is best to try and do what one is *asked* over parts
(though they were very polite in offering me a choice), so I said
I would try, and am learning it. I think I shall manage it.
They now want me to take "A Rough Diamond" as well,
Margery. I doubt its being wise to attempt both. It will be
rather a strain, I think. .

* * * * * *

Shoeburyness. January 25, 1883.

* * * * * *

I am playing Mrs. Honeyton in "A Happy Pair" with
Major Newall. He knows his work well, is a good coach, and
very considerate and kind.

In my soul I wish that were all, but they have persuaded me
also to take Margery in "A Rough Diamond," and getting THAT
up in a week is "rough on" a mediocre amateur like myself !

This is a *curious* place. Very nice, bar the east winds. I
have been down on the shore this morning. The water sobs at
your feet, and the ships and the gulls go up and down. Above,
a compact little military station clusters together, and everywhere are Guns, Guns, Guns; old guns lying in the grass, new
guns shattering the windows, and only *not* bringing down the
plaster because the rooms are ceiled with wood "for the same
purpose." . . .

To MRS. JELF.

Sunday, April 1883.

MY DEAREST MARNY,

I must write a line to you about your poor friends ! It
is THE tragedy of this war ! Very terrible. I hope the bitterness of death was *short*, and to gallant spirits like theirs hope

and courage probably supported them till the very last, when higher hopes helped them to undo their grasp on this life.

In the dying—they suffered far less than most of us will probably suffer in our beds—but to be at the fullest stretch of manly powers in the service of their country among the world's hopes and fears and turmoils, and to be suddenly called upon to "leave all and follow Christ"—when the "all" for them had most righteously got every force of mind and body devoted to it—must be at least one hard struggle. And death away from home does seem so terrible!

Richard will feel it very much. That Nottingham election seems so short a time ago.

*   *   *   *   *   *

Back from Church! Great haste. We have had that grand hymn with—

"Soon, soon to faithful warriors comes their rest."

I did not forget the poor souls.

Prayers for the dead is one of those things which always seems to me the most curiously obvious and simple of duties!

Your most loving, J. H. E.

71, *Warwick Road.* April 9, 1883.

DEAREST MARNY,

I write a line to tell you that D. was at S. Paul's yesterday afternoon to Evensong, and to hear Liddon preach.

I know you will like to hear how very gracefully he alluded to your poor friend as "the accomplished Engineer," and to Charrington and Palmer. Of the last—he spoke very feelingly —as to his great loss from the learning point of view. He said —or to this effect—"We laid them here last Friday in the faith of Him who died for their sins and ours, and this is the first Sunday when above their ashes we commemorate that Resurrection through which we hope that they and we shall rise again."

The "Drum Band" was duly played after the service, and D. says that crowds remained to listen.

I know you will like to hear this, though I have given a bad second-hand account.

I hope my Goodman gets to Malta to-day or to-morrow !

*　　　*　　　*　　　*　　　*　　　*

Ever, dearest Marny,
Your loving J. H. E.

To A. E.

April 24, 1883.

. . . I sent you a telegram this morning to make you feel quite happy in your holiday. "Real good times" (a Yankeeism I hate, but it is difficult to find its brief equivalent !) are not so common in "this wale" that you should cut yours short. I rather hope this may be in time to catch you (it is not *my* fault that you will be without letters). If you would like to linger longer—Do. You are not likely to find "the like of" your present surroundings on leave in Scotland, least of all as to sunshine and flowers. One doesn't go to Malta every day. I wish I was there ! But I can't be, and ten to one should catch typhoid where you only smell orange-blossoms, and I don't think my sins run in the Dog-in-the-manger line, and I hope you'll quaff your cup of content as deeply as you can.

For one thing winter has returned. We had snow yesterday, and the east wind, the Beast Wind ! through which I went this morning to send your telegram was simply killing; dust like steel filings driving into your skin, waves of hard dust with dirty paper foam.—Ugh ! !—Spend as much of your leave as you and your friends think well where you are. I've waited three years. I can wait an odd three weeks and welcome ! Especially as I am up to my eyes in packing and arranging matters for our new home. What I do hope is you will be happy *there !* But I believe in laying in happiness like caloric. A good roast keeps one warm a long time !

How often I have thought that philosophers who argue from the premiss of the fleeting nature of pleasure, might give pause if they had had my experience. A body so frail that *nearly* every pleasure of the senses has had to be enjoyed chiefly after it had "fleeted"—by the memory. Pictures (one of my chiefest pleasures), the theatre, any great sight, sound, or event, being a pleasure after they (and the *headache!*) have passed away. The "passing pleasures" of life are just those which this world gives very capriciously, but cannot take away! They are possessions as real as . . . . . . marqueterie chairs! Of which —more anon,—when you return to the domestic hearth.

*   *   *   *   *   *

I had such a round in Wardour Street the other day! I do wish for a Dutch marqueterie chest of drawers with toilet glass attached, but he is £8! Too much. But (I *must* let it out!) I got two charming Dutch marqueterie chairs for my drawing-room for 35/- each. You will be surprised to find what nice things we have! . . .

TO MRS. JELF.

7, Mount Street, Taunton.
June 3, 1883.

DEAREST MARNY,

I know you forgive a long silence—especially as I have "packed in spite of you"!

*   *   *   *   *

I took lots of time over it all. All my "remains" are piled in cases in the attics, and I have arranged "terms" with the Great Western, and hope to do my moving very cheaply.

We had need economize somewhere, for, my dear! we have been VERY extravagant over our house!!! I should like to hear if you and your dear ladies (I know Auntie would be candid!) think we have been wisely so!—Our predecessor had a cottage and garden for £35—the Col. Commanding only paid £55—and we are paying £70!!!

It is a question of *three things:* 1st, higher and healthier situation—2nd, modern appliances and drains unconnected with the old town sewers—3rd, my Goodman took a wild fancy to the house—and picked his own den—and said he could "live and be at peace" there : and this means life and death to *me!*

So we have boldly taken this other house ! A mile *above* the town—on high ground, built by one of the sanitary commission (!), brand new—and with a glorious view. Not a stick in the garden ! but things grow fast here. I shall have a charming drawing room 24 feet long (so it will hold me ! ! !), with two quaint little fire-places with blue tiles. Rex has a very nice den with French doors into the garden, where he seems to hope to "attain Nirwana"—and live apart from the world. Small as I am, I have an odd liking for large rooms (the oxygen partly—and partly that I "quarterdeck" so when I am working—and suffer so in my spine and head from close heat). Now it is *very* hot here. There's no doubt about it ! So, on the whole, I hope we've done well to house ourselves as we have. And we *can* give a comfortable bedroom to a friend ! My dear Marny—you *must* come and see me ! It's really a quaint old town—with a rather foreign-looking cloistered " Place "—and a curious Saturday Market—with such nice red pottery on sale ! !

Now to go back—and tell you about my Goodman. He had three weeks of "real high time" in Malta. Then he came home—to Warwick Road. At first I thought him much *hot-climatized,* and was worried. But he is now looking as well as can be. We had a few very happy days at Ecclesfield. It is a most tender spot with me that he is so fond of my old home ! They know his ways—he says he is at peace—and he rambles about among the old books—and the people in the village are so glad to see him—and it is very nice.

He took up his duties here on our 16th wedding day !

The place suits him admirably. I felt sure it would. But I did not hope *I* should feel as well in it as I do. It is hot—and not VERY dry—but it is *much* less relaxing than I thought, and where we have got our house it is high and breezy—and very,

very nice. I am most thankful, and only long to get settled and be able to work !

We are in lodgings close to—next door to—the very fine barracks. Our room looks into the barrack-yard, and the dear bugles wake and send us to sleep !

Your loving
J. H. E.

Caldecott has done *seventeen* illustrations to "Jackanapes."

To Mrs. A. P. Graves.

June 15, 1883.

My Dear Mrs. Graves,

Once more I thank you for lovely flowers ! including one of my chief favourites—a white Iris. It is very good of you. You do not know what pleasure they give me ! If you continue to bless me with an occasional nosegay when I move into my house, I shall not so bitterly suffer from the barrenness of the garden.

This is suggestive of the nasty definition of gratitude that it is a keen sense of favours to come !

I have been meaning to write to you to express something of our delight with the "Songs of Old Ireland."

Major Ewing is charmed by the melodies, on which his opinion is worth something and mine is not ! and *I* can't "read them out of a printed book" without an instrument. But—we are equally charmed by the words ! !

It is a very rare pleasure to be able to give way to unmitigated enjoyment of modern verse by one's friends. Don't you know ? But we have fairly raved over one after the other of these charming songs !

I do hope Mr. Graves does not consider that friendly criticisms come under the head of "personal remarks" and are offensive !

I cannot say how truly I appreciate them. Anything absolutely first-rately done of its kind is always very refreshing, and I do not see how such national songs could be done much better. They are Irish to the core !

Irish in local colour—in wealth of word variety—in poetry of the earliest and freshest type—in shallow passion like a pebbly brook !—and in a certain comicality and shrewdness.   Irish—I was going to say in refinement, but that is not the word— modern literature is full of refinements—but Irish in the sur- passingly Irish grace of purity, so rare a quality in modern verse !

How we have laughed over Father O'Flynn ! Kitty Bawn is perfect of its kind—and No. 1 and No. 2.

It is a most graceful collection.   Will it be published soon ? My husband says this copy is only a proof.

I am unjustifiably curious to know if Mr. Graves has given much labour and polishing to these fresh impetuous things.   It is against all my experiences if he has *not !*—but then it would be an addition to my experiences to find they were "tossed off" !

They have been a pleasant interlude amid the sordid cares of driving the workmen along !   I am getting terribly tired of it !

Yours very sincerely,
JULIANA HORATIA EWING.

TO MRS. GOING.

Villa Ponente, Taunton.   July 11, 1883.

DEAR MADAM,

Your letter was forwarded to me last month, when I was (and to some extent am still) very very busy in the details of setting up a new home—of the temporary nature of military homes !—as Major Ewing has been posted to Taunton.

As yet there are many things on which I cannot "lay my hand," and a copy of the Tug of War Hymn is among them !

When I can find it—I will lend it to you.   Should I omit to do so—please be good enough to jog my memory !

It is a rather "ranting" tune—but has tender associations for my ears.

The soldiers of the Iron Church, South Camp, Aldershot, used to "bolt" with it in the manner described, and some dear little sons of an R.E. officer always called it the "Tug of War Hymn."

With many thanks for your kind sayings, I am, dear Madam,

Yours very truly,

JULIANA HORATIA EWING.

TO THE REV. J. GOING.

October 11, 1883.

DEAR MR. GOING,

I append a rough plan of my small garden. We do not stand dead E. and W., but perhaps a little more so than the arrows show. We are very high and the winds are often high too! The walls are brick—and that south bed is very warm. I mean to put bush roses down what is marked the Potato Patch—it is the original soil with one year's potato crop where I am mixing vegetables and flowers. The borders are given up to flowers—mixed herbaceous ones. And on my south wall I have already planted a Wistaria, a blue Passion-flower—and a Rose of Sharon! I am keeping a warm corner for "Fortune's Yellow"—and now looking forward with more delight and gratitude than I can express to "Cloth of Gold"!

I have sent to order the "well-rotted"—and the Gardener for Saturday morning!

Now will you present my grateful acknowledgments to Mrs. Going, and say that with some decent qualms at my own greediness—I "too-too" gratefully accept her further kind offers. I deeply desire some "Ladders to Heaven"—(does she know that old name for Lilies of the Valley?)—and I am devoted to pansies and have only a scrap or two. A neighbour *has* given me a few Myosotis—but I am a daughter of the horse-leech I fear where flowers are concerned, and if you really have one or two TO SPARE I thankfully accept. The truly Irish

liberality of Mrs. Going's suggestions—emboldens me to ask
if you happen to have in your garden any of the Hellebores? I
have one good clump of Xmas Rose—but I have none of those
green-faced varieties for which I have a peculiar predilection.

(I do not expect much sympathy from you! In fact I fear
you will think that any one whose taste is so grotesque as to
have a devotion for Polyanthuses—Oxlips—Green Hellebores—
every variety of Arum (including the "stinking" one !)—Dog's-
tooth violets—Irises—Auriculas—coloured primroses—and such
dingy and undeveloped denizens of the flower garden—is hardly
worthy to possess the glowing colours and last results of
development in the Queen of flowers !)

But I DO appreciate roses I assure you.

And I am most deeply grateful to you for letting me benefit
by—what is in itself such a treat ! your—enthusiasm.

Mrs. Going seems to think that my soil and situation are
better than yours.

Could it be possible that you might have any rose under
development that you would care to deposit here for the winter
and fetch away in the spring? I don't know if change of air
and soil is ever good for them ?

I fear you'll think mine a barren little patch on which to
expend your kindness ! But you are a true *Ama*—teur—and
will look at my Villa Garden through *rose*-coloured spectacles !

Yours gratefully, J. H. E.

To Mrs. Jelf.

October 19, 1883.

Dearest Marny,

*   *   *   *   *   *

One bit more of egotism before I stop !

You know how I love my bit of garden !—An admirer—
specially of "Laetus"—whom I had never seen—an Irishman
—and a Dorsetshire Parson. (But who had worked for over
twenty years in the slums of London—which it is supposed only
the Salvation Army venture to touch !)—

——arrived here last Saturday with nineteen magnificent climbing roses, and has covered two sides of my house and the south wall of my garden !—but one sunny corner has been kept sacred to Aunty's Passion-flower, which is doing well—and one for a rose Mrs. Walkinshaw has promised me. He is a very silent Irishman—a little alarming—possibly from the rather brief, authoritative ways which men who have worked big parishes in big towns often get. When Rex said to him, at luncheon—" How did you who are a Rose Fancier and such a flower maniac—LIVE all those years in such a part of London ? " in rather a muttered sort of way he explained,

" Well, I had a friend a little out of town who had a garden, and his wife wanted flowers, and they knew nothing about it : so I made a compact. I provided the roses—I made the soil— I planted them—and I used to go and prune them and look after them. They were *magnificent*."

"Oh, then you *had* flowers ? "

"Well, I made a compact. They never picked a rose on Saturday. On Saturday night I used to go and clear the place. I had roses over my church on Sundays—and all Festivals. The rest of the year his wife had them."

It struck me as a most touching story—for the man is Rose Maniac. What a sight those roses must have been to the eyes of such a congregation ! The Church should have been dedicated to S. Dorothea ! He is of the most modest order of Paddies—and as I say a little alarming. I was *appalled* when I saw the *hedge* of the "finest-named" roses he brought, and it was very difficult to "give thanks" adequately !— I said once—" I really simply cannot tell you the pleasure you have given me." He said rather grumpily—" You've given me pleasure enough—and to lots of others." Then he suddenly *chirped* up and said—" Laetus cost me 2*s*. 6*d*. though. My wife bet me 2*s*. 6*d*. I couldn't read it aloud without crying. I thought I could. But after a page or two—I put my hand in my pocket—I said—There ! take your half-crown, and let me cry comfortably when I want to ! ! ! "

My dear, what a screed I have written to you ! !

But your letter this morning *was* a pleasure.   There is something so nice in your getting the very hut where—as I think—"Old Father" first began to recover after Cyprus-fever.   I wish you had had F. to stride about the old lines also—and knock his head against your door-tops !—Best love to R., F., and the Queers—

Your loving, J. H. E.

Dec. 3, 1883.

My Dearest Marny,

You are always so forbearing !—and I have been driven to a degree by work which I had promised, and have just despatched ! Some day it may appeal to "the Queers." For it is a collated (and Bowdlerized !) version of the old Peace Egg Mumming Play for Christmas.   I have been often asked about it : and the other day a Canon Portal wrote to me, and he urged me to try and do it, and it is done !

But it was a much larger matter than I had thought.   The version I have made up is made up from five different versions, and I hope I have got the cream of them.   It will be in the January number, which will be out before Xmas.

I have also been trying to see my way—I SHOULD so like to go to you—and if I can't yet awhile I hope you'll give me another chance.

This week I certainly cannot—thank you, dear ! And I *don't* see my way in December at all.   I will *post-card* you in a day or two again.

I am yours always lovingly,
J. H. E.

My garden is great joy to me.   Even you, I think, would allow me a moderate amount of "grubbing" in between brain work.

To Mrs. Going.

Thursday (December 1883).

My Dear Mrs. Going,

You are too profusely good to me. Have you really *given me* Quarles? I have never even seen his *School of the Heart*, and am charmed with it. The Hieroglyphics of the life of Man were in the very old copy of *Emblems* belonging to my Mother which I have known all my life.

Thank you a thousand times.

I write for a seemingly ungracious purpose, but I know you will comprehend my infirmities! I am not at all well. I had hoped to be better by the time your young ladies came—but luck (and I fear a little chill in the garden!) have been against me. I tried to get *Macbeth* deferred but it could not be—and I think my only hope of enduring a long drive, and appearing as Lady Macbeth on Saturday evening with any approach to "undaunted mettle"—is to shut myself up in absolute silence and rest for several hours before we start. This, alas! means that it would be better for your young ladies (what is left of them, after brain fag and fish dinners!) to return to you by an earlier train, as I could be "no account" to them on Saturday afternoon.

* * * * * *

I'll take care of *the poor students* though I *am* not at my best! Their fish is ordered. We will spend a soothing evening on sofas and easy chairs—and go early to bed! They shall have breakfast in bed if they like. This does not sound amusing but I think it will be wholesome for their relics!

Again thanking you for the dear little book—which comes in so nicely for Advent!

To Mrs. R. H. Jelf.

Dearest Marny,

The Queers' letters are VERY nice. Thank them with my love.

* * * * * *

Forgive pencil, dear—I'm in bed.   Got rid of my throat—
and now all my "body and bones" seem to have given way.
I thought it was lumbago or sciatica—but Rex said—"Simply
nerve exhaustion from over-writing"—so I took to bed (for I
couldn't walk !), high living and quinine !   I hope I'll soon be
round again.   The vile body is a nuisance.   I've got a story
in my head—and that seems to take the vital force out of my
legs ! ! !

Apropos to Richard's *Churchwarden's* conscience, does he
remember the (possibly churchwarden !) "soul long hovering in
fear and doubt"—in À Kempis, who prostrated himself in prayer
and groaned—"Oh if I only *knew that I should persevere !*"
To whom came the answer of God—"If thou *didst* know it,
what wouldst thou do then ?   Continue to *do that* and thou shalt
be safe."

His letter and yours were *very* comforting.   I was just
feeling very low about my writing.   I always do when I have
to re-read for new editions !   It does seem such twaddle—and
so unlike what I want to say !

Thank you greatly for believing in me !

*   *   *   *   *   *

Your loving, J. H. E.

To Mrs. Howard.

Villa Ponente, Taunton.
Jan. 18, 1884.

My Dear Mrs. Howard,

In this Green Winter (and *you* know how I love a
Green Winter !) you and all your kindness comes back so often
to my mind.   "Grenoside" is a closed leaf in my life as well as
in yours, but it is one that I shall never forget so long as I can
remember any of the things that have mitigated the pains of life
for me, or added to its pleasures !—The bits of Green Winter I
enjoyed with you did both—I hardly know which the most !
For the pleasure was very great, and the benefit immeasurable—

though now a fair amount of strength and " all my faculties "
have come back to me, I feel what a very tedious companion I
must have been when *vegetating* was all I was fit for, and I
did such delightful vegetating between your sofa—and Greno
wood.

I want to tell you that I have some bits of you in what does
the work of Greno Wood for me here—namely, my little patch
of garden, looking out upon, what I call *my* big fields. For
some time I feared the said bits were not going to live, but they
have now, I really think, got grip of the ground. They are
those offshoots of your American Bramble which you gave to me.
And, ere long, I hope to sow a little paper of your poppy seed,
and—if two years' keeping has not destroyed its vitality—I may,
perchance, send you some of your own poppies to deck your
London rooms. You cannot think—or rather I have no doubt
that you can !—the refreshment my bit of garden is to me. It
has become so dear, that (like an ugly face one loves and ceases
to see plain !)—I find it so charming that it is *with a start* that I
recognize that new friends see no beauty in—

[Sketch.]

This four-square patch ! !

But A and B are " beds," and there are borders under the brick
walls, and a rose-growing admirer of " Laetus " made a pilgrimage to see me !—and brought me nineteen grand climbing roses—
and wall S faces *nearly quite* south, and on it grow Maréchal
Niel, and Cloth of Gold, and Charles Lefebvre, and Triomphe
de Rennes, and a Banksia and Souvenir de la Malmaison, and
Cheshunt Hybrid, and a bit of the old Ecclesfield summer white
rose—sent by Undine—and some Passion Flowers from dear old
Miss Child in Derbyshire—and a *Wistaria* which the old lady of
the lodgings we were in when we first came, tore up, and gave to
me, with various other *oddments* from her. garden ! and—the
American Bramble ! And also, by the bye, a very lovely rose,
" Fortune's Yellow,"—given to me by a friend in Hampshire.

Major Ewing declares my borders are " so full *there is no*

room for more," which is very nasty of him !—but I have been very lucky in preserving, and even multiplying, the various contributions my bare patch has been blessed with ! D. sent me a *barrel* of bits last autumn from the Vicarage, and Reginald sent me an excellent hamper from Bradfield, and Col. Yeatman sent me a hamper from Wiltshire, and several friends here have given me odds and ends, and our old friend Miss Sulivan, before she went abroad, sent me a farewell memorial of sweet things— Lavender, Rosemary, Cabbage Rose, Moss Rose, and Jessamine ! ! !—Oh ! talking of sweet things, I must tell you—I went into the market here one day this last autumn, and of a man standing there—I bought a dug-up clump of BAY *tree*— for 2/6.

You know how you indulged my senses with bay leaves when I was far from them ? Well, I put my clump and myself into a cab and went home—where I pulled my clump to pieces and made eight nice plants of him—and set me a bay hedge, which has thriven so far very well ! ! ! But then—'tis a Green Winter !

Now I want to know if there is a chance of tempting you down here for a little visit ? I have thought that perhaps some time in the Spring the School might be taking holiday, and Harry might be striding off on a week or 10 days' country "breathe,"—and perhaps you would come to me ? Or if he were inclined for fresh fields and pastures new, that you would come together, and he might make his head-quarters here, and go over to Glastonbury, etc., etc., etc., whilst we took matters more quietly at home ?

I feel it is a long way to come, but it would be so very pleasant to me to welcome you under my own roof !

If you cannot get away in Spring, I *must* persuade you when London gets hotter and less pleasant !

You *must* miss your country home—and yet I envy you a few things ! London has cords of charm to attract in many ways ! I wish I could *fly over*, and see the Sir Joshuas and one or two things.

(I am stubbornly indifferent to the *Spectator's* dictum that we like " Sir Joshuas" because we are a nation of snobs ! ! !)
Ever affectionately yours,
JULIANA HORATIA EWING.

Do tell me what hope there is of seeing you—and showing you your own bramble on my own wall !

To MRS. GOING.

March 11, 1884.

MY DEAR MRS. GOING,
I do not think you will ever let me have my Head Gardener here again !
I CAN'T take care of him !
I really could have sat down on the door-step and cried—when our old cabby—"the family coachman" as we call him, arrived and had missed Mr. Going. How *he* did not miss his train, I cannot conceive ! He must have run—he must have flown—he *must* be a bit uncanny—and the flap-ends of the comforter must have spread into wings—or our clocks must have been beforehand—or the trains were behindhand—
Obviously luck favours him ! !
But where was his great-coat ?—
He got very damp—and there was no time to hang him out to dry !
Tell him with my love—I have been nailing up the children in the way they should go—and have made a real hedge of cuttings !
I wish the Weeding Woman could see my old Yorkshire "rack." It and its china always lend themselves to flowers, I think. The old English coffee-cups are full of primroses. In a madder-crimson Valery pot are Lent lilies—and the same in a peacock-blue fellow of a pinched and selfish shape. The white violets are in a pale grey-green jar (a miniature household jar) of Marseilles pottery. The polyanthuses singularly become a

XVIII. 19

pet *Jap* pot of mine of pale yellow with white and black design on it—and a gold dragon—and a turquoise-coloured lower rim.

I am VERY flowery. I must catch the post. I do hope my Head Gardener is not in bed with rheumatic fever ! ! ! ! I trust your poor back is rather easier?

Please most gratefully thank the girls for me.

Yours gratefully and affectionately,

J. H. E.

To the Rev. J. Going.

All Fools, 1884.

My Dear Head Gardener,

You are too good, and—as to the confusion of one's principles is sometimes the case—your virtues encourage my vices. You make me greedy when I ought only to be grateful.

I've been too busy to write at once, and also somewhat of set purpose abstained—for those bitter winds and hard-caked soil were not suited for transplantation, and still less fit for you to be playing the part of Honest Root-gatherer without your Cardigan Waistcoat ! ! ! !

To-day

"a balmy south wind blows."

I feel convinced some poet says so. If not I do, and it's a fact.

Moreover by a superhuman—or anyhow a super-frail-feminine —effort last Saturday as ever was I took up all that remained of the cabbage garden—spread the heap of ashes, marked out another path by rule of line (not of thumb, as I planted those things you took up and *set straight !*), made my new walk, and edged it with the broken tiles that came off our roof when "the stormy winds did blow"—an economy which pleased me much. Thus I am now entirely flower-garden—and with room for more flowers ! !

Now to your kind offer. I think it will take rather more than 50 bunches of primroses to complete the bank according to

your plan—though not 100. Say 70 : but if there are a few
bunches to spare I shall put them down that border where the
laurels are, against the wall under the ivy. They flower there,
and other things don't.

Now about the wild daffodils—indeed I *would* like some ! ! !
I fear I should like enough to do this : [*Sketch.*]

These be the Poets' narcissus along the edge of the grass
above the strawberry bank, and I don't deny I think it would be
nice to have a row of wild Daffys (where the red marks are) to
precede the same narcissus next spring if we're spared! The
Daffys to be planted *in the grass* of the grass-plat.

I doubt if less than two dozen clumps would ' do it handsome ' ! ! ! ! ! ! ! !

Now I want your good counsel. This is my back garden :
[*Sketch.*]

Next to Slugs and Snails (to which I have recently added a
specimen of)

Puppy Dog's Tails—

my worst enemy is—WIND !

The laurels are growing—for that matter, Xmas is coming !
—but still we are very shelterless. I think I would like to plant
in Bed A, *inter alia*—some shrubby things. Now I know your
views about moving shrubs are somewhat wider than those of the
every-day gardener's—but do you think I dare plant a bush of
lauristinus now ? It would have to travel a little way, I fancy.
There is no man actually in Taunton, I fear, with good shrubs.
I mean also to get some Japanese maples. I think I would like
a copper-coloured-leaved *nut tree*. Are nuts hardy ? I fear
Gum Cistus is coming into flower—and unfit to move ! How
about rhododendrons ? The soil here is said to suit them wonderfully. I could not pretend to buy peat for them—but I know
hardy sorts will do in a firm fair soil, and I should like to plant a
lilac one—a crimson—a blush—and a white. I think they
would do fairly and shelter small fry.

Can I risk it now ? and how about hardy azaleas—things I

love! If you say—we are too near summer sun for them to get established—I must wait till Autumn.

How has Mrs. Going stood the biting winds? Very unfavourable for one's aches and pains?

Tell her I have got one of those rather queer yellow flowers you condescended to notice!—to bring to her after Easter.

Is it not terrible about Prince Leopold? That poor young wife—and the Queen! What bitter sorrow she has known ; also I do regard the loss as a great one for the country, he was so enlightened and so desirous of use in his generation.

Yours, J. H. E.

To Mrs. Jelf.

My Dearest Marny,

Thank you, dear, with much love for your Easter card. It is LOVELY (and Easter cards are not very beautiful as a rule). It is on a little stand on my knick-knack table—and looks so well!

I send you a few bits from my garden as an Easter Greeting. They are not much—but we are in a "nip" of bitter N.E. winds—and nothing will "come out."

Also I rather denuded my patch to send a large box to Undine to make the Easter wreaths for my Mother's grave. I was really rather proud of what I managed to scrape together— every bit out of my very own patch—and consequently of my very own planting!

I've got neuralgia to-day with the wind and a fourteen-miles drive for luncheon and two sets of callers since I got back!— so I can't write a letter—but I want you to tell me when you think there's a chance of your taking a run to see me! I seem to have such lots to say! I have found another charm (besides red pots) of our market. If one goes *very early* on Saturday— one gets such nice old-fashioned flowers, "roots," and big ones too—very cheap! It's a most fascinating *ruination by penny-worths!*

Good luck to you, dear, in your fresh settling down in the Heimath Land.

Mrs. M—— (where we were *lunching*) asked tenderly after my large young family—as strangers usually do. Then she said, "But you write so sympathetically of children, and 'A Soldier's Children' is so real—I thought they MUST be yours." On which I explained the Dear Queers to her. To whom be love! and to Richard.

Ever, dear, yours lovingly,
J. H. E.

To Mrs. Going.

Midsummer Day, 1884.

My Dear Mrs. Going,

Not a moment till now have I found—to tell you I got home safe and sound, and that your delicious cream was duly and truly appreciated !

The last of it was merged in an admirable Gooseberry Fool !

The roses suffered by the hot journey—but even the least flourishing of them received great admiration—from their size— as the skeletons of saurians make a smaller world stand aghast ! !!

This last sentence smacks of Jules Verne! I don't care much for him—after all. It is rather *bookmaking*.

But I have had a lot of hearty laughs over "the Heroine"! It is very funny—if not *very* refined. Some of the situations admirable. There is something in the girl's calling her father "Wilkinson" all the way through—quite as comic as anything in *Vice Versâ*—a book which I never managed to get to the end of.

I hope your wedding went well to-day. My sister's—is postponed till the 28th—for the convenience of the best man. If *by Thursday* (you must be a full two days' post from a Yorkshire country place) the Master had *one or two* Bouquet D'Or or other white or yellow roses not very fully blown—and your handy Meta would wind wet rags about their stalks and put them in an empty coffee-tin and despatch them by parcels post to Miss Gatty, Ecclesfield Vicarage, Sheffield, Yorks, they would be greatly welcomed to eke out the white decorations of my Mother's grave for the wedding-day. I am wildly watering my Paris Daisies—and hope to get some wild Ox-eye daisies also—as her name was Margaret (and her pet name Meta!). I am applying prayers and slopwater in equal proportions—like any Kelt!—to my Bouquet D'Or and other white and yellow roses! I shall have some double white Canterbury Bells, etc.—but there is coming a *lull* in the flowers, and they won't re-bloom much till we have rain.

Please give my love to all your party, not forgetting the house dove and the dog—

I reproach my Rufus with his tricks and talents!

I have had great benefit in a fit of neuralgia from your chili paste.

Yours, dear Mrs. Going,
Sincerely and affectionately,
JULIANA HORATIA EWING.

TO MRS. JELF.

November 3, 1884.

DEAREST MARNY,

Enclosed is "Daddy Darwin"—for Richard!—and two of the Verse Books for the two dear Queers I had so many luncheons with!

You know I risked printing 20,000 D.D.D. on my own book to cheapen printing—so you'll be glad to hear that after ordering 10,000 at the beginning of last week—S.P.C.K. have ordered another 10,000 at the end of it!! But I've been having *such* "times" with the printers' and publishers' dæmons!!

I must not write, however, for I have been ill also!! A throat attack. We were afraid of diphtheria—but if it were that I should not be writing to you as you'll guess. There has been another outbreak of it just round us, and a good many throats of sorts in its train, but Dr. L—— does not seem to think mine due to much more than exhaustion—and he seemed to think nursing the dog had not been very good for me. He says distemper is typhoid fever!

We had a very jolly little visit from Colonel C——. He

was at his *very* funniest.   Mimicked us both to our faces till we
yelled again !   As Rex said—"Not a bit altered !   The old
man !   *Would any other play the bones about his bedroom in his
night-shirt ?*"

He went off waving farewells and shouting—"We'll *both*
come next time—and rouse ye well."

Your loving, J. H. E.

Saturday.
DEAREST MARNY,

You have indeed the sympathy of my whole heart !

God bless and prosper "Old Father" on the war-path and
bring him home to his Queers and to you full of honour and
glory and interesting experiences !

I know Mr. Anstruther—he is charming.   I cannot say how
I think it softens one's fears if Richard's strength were still a bit
unequal to the strain—to know that he has such a subaltern—
adjutant—and C.R.E.   He could not have gone arm-in-arm
with better comrades—unless the Giant had been ready as
sick-nurse in case of need !

But I do feel for you, dear—you are very gallant.

I am not fit to write yet—my head *goes* so—but I will write
you next week about Gordon Browne (a thousand thanks !) and
see if *I* possibly could.   Thank you so much.

The drummer's letter is charming.   I must copy the bit
about tip-toe for Sir Evelyn Wood !   I got the enclosed from
him—also from Wady Halfa—and I wanted you and R—— to
hear the weird drum-band drunkard tale ! and see how he likes
"Soldier's Children."

Can you kindly return it, dear?

Your most loving, J. H. E.

[*In pencil.*]

Where does R—— sail from ?

I see by to-day's *Times* the others have sailed from Dart-

mouth.   My dear Marny—can't you and R—— come here *en
route* if only for a night? It *would* be so nice! It would be
such a pleasure to Rex and me to Godspeed him—and he would
feel *quite like Gladstone* if he had an ovation at every stopping
point on the Flying Dutchman !

To COLONEL JELF.
                                           November 18, 1884.
   DEAR RICHARD,
            I wish you *could* have paused here—I wish that you
were even likely to run through Taunton station in the Flying
Dutchman, and that we could have run down to head a cheer
for you !—But Gravesend is handier for Marny.
   She's a real Briton—and it is that "undaunted mettle" that
does "compose" the sinews of "peace with honour" for a
country as well as war !
   Indeed I'm glad you have your chance—or make a very
respectable assumption of that *virtus!* and I take leave to be
doubly glad that it is in a fine climate and with good shoulder
to shoulder comrades.
   Tell Marny, Colonel Y. B—— in a letter about "Daddy
Darwin" is very sympathetic.   Another "old standard"—Jelf,
he says—is going, and "Mrs. J—— puts a good face on it."
   What will the theatricals and the Institute do?—
   "Do without," I suppose ! I am a lot better the last two
days—and struggled off to the town to-day to a missionary
meeting ! It was a most unusually interesting one about the
South American Missions.   I must tell Marny about it.—
However—at some tea afterwards, I was "interviewed" by one
or two people—and one lady asked to introduce a "Major"
—whose name I did not catch—as being so devoted to "Soldier's
Children."   I created quite a sensation by saying that "Old
Father" was ordered to Bechuanaland—"Oh, how old are
the Queers?   Are they really losing Old Father again so
soon?"
   I feel, by the bye, that it is part of that fatality which besets

you and me, that I should have stereotyped you in printers' ink as *Old* Father !!!

Good-bye.—Godspeed and Good luck to you.

Your affectionate old friend,

J. H. E.

To the Rev. J. Going.

December 3, 1884.

Dear " Head Gardener,"

I think there is a blessing on all your benevolences to me which defies ill luck !

After I wrote to Mrs. Going we'd a frost of ten degrees—and I got neuralgia back—and made a dismal picture in my own mind of your good things coming to an iron-bound border—and an Under Gardener deeply *died down* under eider down and blankets—(even my old labourer being laid up with sore throat and scroomaticks !—but lo and behold, on Monday the air became like new milk—I became like a new Under Gardener—and leave was given to go out. (I am bound to confess that I don't think rose-planting was medically contemplated !) Fortunately the border was ready and well-manured—I only had to dig holes in very soft stuff—but I am very weak, and my stamping powers are never on at all a Nasmyth Hammer sort of scale— but—good luck again !—Major Ewing's orderly arrived with papers to sign—a magnificent individual over six foot—with larger boots than mine and a coal-black melodramatic moustache ! Had the Major been present—I should not have dared to ask an orderly in full dress and on duty to defile his boots among Zomerset red-earth, but as I caught him alone I begged his assistance. He looked down very superbly upon me (swathed in fur and woollen shawls, and staggering under a full-sized garden fork) with a twinkle in his eye that prepared me for the least taste of brogue which kept breaking through his studied fine language—and consented most affably. I wish you'd seen him—balancing his figure with a consciousness of maids at the kitchen window, his cane held out, *toeing* and *heeling* your roses into their places!! He assured me he understood all about it, and he trode them in very nicely!

How good of you to have sent me such a stock,—and the pansies I wanted. The flower of that lovely mauve and purple one is on the table by me now. *One* (only one) of your other roses died—the second Gloire near the front door—so when I saw it was hopeless I had that border "picked" up—a very rockery of rubbish came out—good stuff was put in, and one of the Souvenirs de Malmaison is now comfortably established there I hope. This wet weather keeps me a prisoner now— but it is good luck for the roses to settle in. I have had some nice scraps and remains of flowers to cheer me indoors—there are one or two late rosebuds yet!

They are such a pleasure to me—and I am indeed grateful to you for all you have done for my garden! Some of those roses I bought have thrown up hugely long shoots. They were all small plants as you know—so I cut none of them in the autumn. I suppose in the spring I had better cut off these long shoots from the bushes in the open border away from the hedge?

I must not write more—only my thanks afresh. With our best regards.

I am very gratefully yours,
J. H. E.

[Written with a typewriter.]

To Mrs. Jelf.

Taunton. December 23, 1884.

Dearest Marny,

My right arm is disabled with neuralgia, and Rex is working one of his most delightful toys for me. He says I brought my afflictions on myself by writing too prolix letters several hours a day. I've got very much behindhand, or you'd have heard from me before. I must try and be highly condensed.

Gordon Browne has done some wonderful drawings for "Lætus." Rex was wild over a "Death or Glory" Lancer, and I think he (the Lancer) and a Highlander would touch even Aunty's heart. They will rank among her largest exceptions. I can't do *any* Xmas cards this year; I can neither go out nor write. I hoped to have sent you a little Xmas box, of a pair of old brass candle-sticks such as your soul desireth. D. and I made an expedition to the very broker's ten days ago, but when I saw the dingy shop choke-full of newly-arrived dirty furniture, and remembered that these streets are reeking with small-pox—as it refuses to "leave us at present"—I thought I should be foolish to go in. D. knows of a pair in Ecclesfield, and I have commissioned her to annex them if possible; but they can't quite arrive in time. In case I don't manage to write Xmas greetings to Aunty and Madre, give them my dear love; and the same to yourself and the Queers. I am proud to tell you that I have persuaded my Admiral to put the Soldiers' Institute on his collecting book of Army and Navy Charities; and when I started it with a small subscription he immediately added the same.

Dear Xmas wishes to you all, and a Happy New Year to Richard also from us both.

Your loving, J. H. E.

[In typewriting.]

To Miss K. Farrant.

Taunton. January 4, 1885.

Dearest Kitty,

I should indeed not have been silent at this season if I had not been ill, and I should have got Rex to print me a note before now, but I kept hoping to be able to write myself, and I rather thought that you would hear that I was laid up, either from D. or M. I have not been very well for some time more than yourself, and I am afraid the root of this breakdown has been overwork. But the weather has been very sunless and wretched, and I have had a fortnight in bed with bad, periodic neuralgia, which has particularly disabled my right arm and head—two important matters in letter-writing. It put an entire stop to my Christmas greetings. I made a little effort for the nephews one day, and had a terrible night afterwards. The lovely blue (china) Dog, who reminds me of an old but incomprehensible Yorkshire saying, "to blush like a blue dog in a dark entry,"—which is what *I* do when I think that I have not yet said "thank you" for him—is most delightful. You know how I love a bit of colour, and a quaint shape. He arrived with one foot off, but I can easily stick it on. Thank you so much. I must not say more to-day, except to hope you'll feel a little stronger when we see more of the sun ; and, thanking you and Francie for your cards—(I was greatly delighted to see my friends the queer fungi again)—and with love to your Mother—who I hope is getting fairly through the winter.

Yours gratefully and affectionately,
J. H. EWING.

To MRS. JELF.

January 22, 1885.

DEAREST M.,

I am *so* pleased you like the brazen candlesticks.

I have long wanted to tell you how *lovely* I thought all your Xmas cards. Auntie's snow scene was exquisite—and your Angels have adorned my sick-room for nearly a month ! Most beautiful.

I know you'll be glad I had my first "decent" night last night —since December 18 !—No very lengthy vigils and no pain to *speak* of. No pain to growl about to-day. A great advance.

Indeed, dear—I should not only be glad but *grateful* to go to you by and by for a short *fillip*. Dr. L—— would have sent me away now if weather, etc. were fit—or I could move.

After desperate struggles—made very hard by illness—I hope to see "Lætus" in May at *one shilling*. Gordon Browne doing well. Do you object to the ending of "Lætus"—to Lady Jane having another son, etc.? Do the Farrants? My dear love to them. This bitter—sunless, lifeless weather must have tried Kitty very much.

   *   *   *   *   *   *

Your loving,
J. H. E.

[*In typewriting.*]
Taunton. February 16, 1885.

My Dearest Marny,
Rex is "typing" for me, but my own mouth must thank you for your goodness, for being so ready to take me in. By and by I shall indeed be grateful to go to you. But this is not likely to be for some weeks to come. You can't imagine what a Greenwich pensioner I am. I told my doctor this morn-ing that he'd better send me up a wood square with four wheels, like those beggars in London who have no limbs ; for both my legs and my right arm were *hors de combat,* and to-day he has found an inflamed vein in my left, so *that* has gone into fomentations too.

But in spite of all this I feel better, and do hope I shall soon be up and about. But he says the risk of these veins would be likely to come if I over-exerted myself, so—anxious as I am to get to purer air, I don't think it would do to move until my legs are more fit. May I write again and tell you when I am fit for Aldershot? Dr. L—— highly approves of the air of it, but at present he thinks lying in bed the only safe course. Do thank dear Aunty next time you write to her for her goodness, and tell her that in my present state I should make her seem quite spry and active. A thousand thanks for the *Pall Mall.* I do *not* neglect one word of what you say ; but I need hardly say that I can't work at present.

The illustrations for "Lætus" are going on very well. I hope to send Richard a copy for perusal on the homeward voyage.

I daren't write about Gordon. Certainly not the least strange part of his wondrous career is this mystery which persists in clouding his close. I feel as if he would be like Enoch or Moses—that we shall never be permitted to know more than that—having walked with GOD—he "was not—for GOD took him," and that his sepulchre no man shall know.

Your loving,

J. H. E.